£16·50

GW00721802

Nutrition
and
Behaviour
in
Dogs and Cats

Other Pergamon publications of related interest

ANDERSON, R.S.
Nutrition of the Dog and Cat

EDNEY, A. T. B.
Dog and Cat Nutrition

LANE, D. R.
Jones's Animal Nursing, 3rd Edition

ROBINSON, R.
Genetics for Cat Breeders, 2nd Edition
Genetics for Dog Breeders

Nutrition
and
Behaviour
in
Dogs and Cats

Proceedings of the First Nordic Symposium on
Small Animal Veterinary Medicine, Oslo,
September 15-18, 1982

Editor

R. S. ANDERSON

Animal Studies Centre, Waltham-on-the-Wolds, Melton Mowbray, England

PERGAMON PRESS

OXFORD · NEW YORK · TORONTO · SYDNEY · PARIS · FRANKFURT

U.K.	Pergamon Press Ltd., Headington Hill Hall, Oxford OX3 0BW, England
U.S.A.	Pergamon Press Inc., Maxwell House, Fairview Park, Elmsford, New York 10523, U.S.A.
CANADA	Pergamon Press Canada Ltd., Suite 104, 150 Consumers Road, Willowdale, Ontario M2J 1P9, Canada
AUSTRALIA	Pergamon Press (Aust.) Pty. Ltd., P.O. Box 544, Potts Point, N.S.W. 2011, Australia
FRANCE	Pergamon Press SARL, 24 rue des Ecoles, 75240 Paris, Cedex 05, France
FEDERAL REPUBLIC OF GERMANY	Pergamon Press GmbH, Hammerweg 6, D-6242 Kronberg-Taunus, Federal Republic of Germany

First edition 1984

Library of Congress Cataloging in Publication Data
Nordic Symposium on Small Animal Veterinary Medicine
(1st : 1982 : Oslo, Norway)
Nutrition and behaviour in dogs and cats
Includes index.
1. Dogs — Food — Congresses. 2. Cats — Food — Congresses.
3. Dogs — Behavior — Congresses. 4. Cats —
Behavior — Congresses. 5. Dogs — Diseases — Congresses.
6. Cats — Diseases — Congresses. 7. Nutritionally
induced diseases in animals — Congresses.
I. Anderson, R. S. II. Title.
SF427.4.N67   1982   636.7   83-17281

British Library Cataloguing in Publication Data
First Nordic Symposium on Small Animal Veterinary
Medicine (1980: Oslo)
Nutrition and behaviour in dogs and cats
1. Dogs—Food—Congresses
I. Title   II. Anderson, R S
636.7'0852   SF427.4
ISBN 0-08-029778-1

In order to make this volume available as economically and as rapidly as possible the authors' typescripts have been reproduced in their original forms. This method unfortunately has its typographical limitations but it is hoped that they in no way distract the reader.

Printed in Great Britain by William Clowes, Beccles and London

Foreword

R. S. Anderson

Animal Studies Centre, Waltham, UK

Dogs and, to lesser extent, cats are dependent on their owners for providing food which will support their health, reproduction, growth, work and maintenance throughout their natural life span. They also depend on their owners to modify their natural behaviour to be acceptable, or even useful, in a variety of environmental conditions - indeed if their owners fail in this responsibility the consequences may be more immediately life-threatening than failure to provide the right diet!

Control of feeding and behaviour are, therefore, the two most important every day influences that owners have over their companion animals and, although veterinary curricula still devote relatively little time to their teaching, the status of small animal nutrition and behaviour has advanced considerably in recent years. That this is so is thanks to a relatively small number of individuals scattered round the world, a substantial proportion of whom were assembled for the First Nordic Symposium on Small Animal Veterinary Medicine in Oslo on 15-18 September 1982.

The seed of the Nordic Symposium was sown at the WSAVA Congress in Barcelona in 1980 and grew to fruition under the enthusiastic cultivation of Britta Öhlen and her organising committee of Nordic veterinarians, with the practical support of Masterfoods, Scandinavia and the Animal Studies Centre, Waltham, England. Those who attended the symposium were able to share the distillation of current developments from speakers at the forefront of the disciplines of small animal nutrition and behaviour at veterinary schools and other institutes in 5 European countries and the United States. Much that was presented had an immediate and practical application to improving the standards of veterinary practice and strengthening the triangular relationship - veterinarian, owner and companion animal - and so we hope that these proceedings will help to achieve that end for a wider audience.

I am most grateful to all those contributors who provided their papers in good time and order, particularly to those whose first language is not English. My special thanks are due to Chris Loxley whose high secretarial standards and cheerful commitment greatly lightened the editorial task.

Contents

PART 1 NUTRITION

Introduction

Nutrition of the dog and cat – an overview   3
R. S. ANDERSON

Feeding for Reproduction and Growth

Mineral metabolism and requirements in bitches and
suckling pups   13
H. MEYER

Care and feeding of the puppy in the postnatal and
weaning period   25
G. BJÖRCK

Feeding and care of kittens   35
S. E. BLAZA and G. G. LOVERIDGE

Foods and their Digestibility

Optimal regimens based on recipes for cooking in home
or hospital or on proprietary pet foods   43
D. S. KRONFELD

Nutrient digestibility and its relationship to
alimentary disorders in dogs   55
H. MEYER

Fibre in the dog's diet   71
J. LEIBETSEDER

Nutrition and Disease

Nutrition of the rapidly growing dog with special
reference to skeletal diseases   81
J. GRØNDALEN and Å. HEDHAMMAR

Common clinical and nutritional problems in racing
sled dogs   89
D. S. KRONFELD and H. L. DUNLAP

Food induced allergies   97
G. S. WALTON

Nutrition as it relates to dermatoses in dogs   103
A. HEDHAMMAR

Nutritional management in heart diseases and
diabetes mellitus   111
J. LEIBETSEDER

Nutrition and kidney function with reference to
old age and kidney disease   119
D. S. KRONFELD

PART 2   BEHAVIOUR

Introduction

Methods used to describe the normal and abnormal
behaviour of the dog and cat   131
R. A. MUGFORD

Physiological and Social

Neurophysiology of behaviour   139
H. URSIN

Human-animal relationships   147
V. L. VOITH

Scandinavian pet environment   157
B. KLAMMING

Behavioural Development

Behaviour development of the puppy in the home
environment   165
P. L. BORCHELT

Social behaviour in free-ranging domestic and
feral cats   175
O. LIBERG

Inheritance of behaviour in the dog   183
L. FÄLT

Development of behaviour in the dog during maturity   189
P. L. BORCHELT

Modification of Behaviour

Communication with the dog when training   201
T. OWREN

Behaviour problems in the dog   207
R. A. MUGFORD

Cat behaviour problems   217
V. L. VOITH

Possible pharmacological approaches to treating
behavioural problems in animals   227
V. L. VOITH

Index   235

Part 1 — Nutrition

INTRODUCTION

Nutrition of the Dog and Cat — An Overview

R. S. Anderson

Animal Studies Centre, Waltham-on-the-Wolds, Leicestershire, UK

ABSTRACT

An understanding of the feeding and behavioural needs of companion animals is
essential to their well-being and integration to modern society. The disciplines of nutrition and behaviour do not, however, rank highly in veterinary
teaching and specialisation. Some nutritional objectives for dogs and cats
are proposed and the status of our present knowledge relating to their
attainment is examined.

KEYWORDS

Nutrition; dogs; cats; growth; conformation; reproduction; old age; enjoyment; foods.

INTRODUCTION

There are well over 150 million dogs and cats in the 16 countries in which
figures are presented (Table 1) or about 12.5 dogs and 10.5 cats per 100
people on average. There are substantial national differences even within
Europe – varying from about 5 dogs per 100 people in Switzerland and Germany
to about 10 per 100 in the United Kingdom and about 17 per 100 in France.
The range is even wider outside Europe between, say, Japan (4 dogs per 100
people) and the United States (20 dogs per 100 people). The reasons for
these differences provide an interesting subject for speculation which is,
fortunately, beyond the scope of this paper.

On the basis of rather scanty data from some of the above countries I have
calculated that there are about one thousand dogs for every veterinarian in
general practice or two and a half thousand dogs for every small animal practitioner. Again there are large national differences with about 450 dogs per
general practitioner in Austria to about 1600 per general practitioner in
France.

Specialisation in small animal practice is continuing to grow at a healthy
pace, with, in the UK, about 2,300 members of the British Small Animal Veter-

3

inary Association and in Japan (with fewer dogs than Britain) about 2,800 members of the Japan Small Animal Veterinary Association. We have, therefore, as nations and as veterinarians a considerable investment in and responsibility for these companion animals which share our environment.

TABLE 1   Dog and Cat Populations (millions) in 16 Countries

Country	Dogs	Cats
European		
1. Austria	0.449	1.005
2. Belgium	1.150	1.016
3. Denmark	0.575	0.400
4. Finland	0.400	0.600
5. France	9.192	6.662
6. Germany	3.370	3.190
7. Italy	4.390	4.535
8. Netherlands	1.260	1.396
9. Norway	0.300	0.450
10. Sweden	0.835	0.835
11. Switzerland	0.335	0.565
12. United Kingdom	5.823	5.157
Sub-Total	28.079	25.811
Non-European		
13. Australia	2.339	2.033
14. Canada	4.085	4.870
15. Japan	4.470	2.320
16. United States	44.363	34.256
Sub-Total	55.257	43.479
Grand Total	83.336	69.290
	152.626	

This symposium is about two fundamental aspects of keeping dogs and cats – their feeding and their behaviour. It is indeed difficult to identify any other aspects which, on a day to day basis, are of more importance to the pet owner. And yet concern with feeding and behaviour does not figure prominently in a ranking of veterinary consultations (Evans, Lane and Hendy, 1974). It is interesting to speculate why ... could it be that the veterinarian is somewhat diffident of offering help in two areas in which he does not feel particularly well informed? It is noteworthy that we have apparently an abundance of veterinary expertise (and experts) in orthopaedics, cardiology, infectious and metabolic medicine, dermatology, immunology and ophthalmology, but the number of veterinarians who would list 'nutrition' or 'behaviour' among their specialities is small.

Why such a scarcity of veterinary experts in nutrition and behaviour? It would be easy to blame the veterinary schools for devoting too little teaching time to these subjects – or perhaps not presenting them in a way which emphasises their practical importance. In my view this is indeed part of the reason. Another possibility, however, is that there really are no

clinical problems in these disciplines which justify the better education of
the veterinarian or will drive the pet owner to consult him.

I would like to examine this proposition for nutrition, which is my brief.

Is nutrition of the companion animal a neglected discipline because there are
few nutritional problems? Do we know the incidence or range of disease in
dogs and cats which is of primary nutritional origin - or the result of bad
nutritional management?

It is most difficult to obtain reliable information on the spectrum of small
animal disease, whether it is based on cases in general practice, referred
cases, or other sources. In addition, there must be a significant component
of disease in companion animals which is never presented to the veterinarian;
these animals either make a complete or partial recovery - or die - with or
without 'home treatment'.

Obesity is an example of such disease. The incidence of obesity in dogs
attending veterinary clinics in Britain is estimated to be about 30% (see
Anderson, 1974) and about the same in Austria (Steininger, 1981). Unarguably
of nutritional origin, such a level must give obesity first place in the
ranking not only of nutritional disease, but of any disease affecting dogs.
Obesity is a simple disease - readily acquired and easily diagnosed, but
difficult to treat successfully. Possibly that is why it often goes
untreated, even though it may be a primary factor in the development of skin,
joint and cardio-respiratory disease.

The high incidence of obesity in the dog and the relatively much lower
incidence in the cat (see Anderson, 1974) exemplifies two interesting aspects
of the companion animal nutritional scene which have emerged in recent years:

1.   the similarity between dogs and man with respect to certain nutrition-
      related diseases;

2.   the difference between dogs and cats with respect to their nutritional
      needs and metabolism.

Other than the companion animals (including the horse), man is the only
domestic species in which obesity is recognised as a problem. (In most wild
animals obesity, other than as a physiological response to aid survival, is
probably rare and presumably self-limiting.) Obesity is not usually recognised or treated as a problem - indeed rather the reverse - in cattle, sheep
and pigs. A degree of obesity is often an objective of feeding these animals
and, once attained, life expectancy is very short! In dogs and man, however,
life is not usually terminated abruptly once a certain degree of fatness is
attained and the state of obesity in both species may be a factor in the
early onset of degenerative and other diseases such as diabetes mellitus.
In environment and life style, dogs are much closer to man than any other
domestic animals - with the result that disease patterns in the dog are
closer to those of man than they are to the other animals in his care.

The cat, however, '... walked by himself' (Kipling, 1908) and, though sharing
much the same environment as man and his dog, has characteristically retained
its metabolic individuality. There is a growing list of metabolic differences
between the dog and cat (Morris and Rogers, 1982) which have practical
relevance to the feeding of cats and dogs both on an individual basis and in
the formulation of commercially prepared foods. The main concept which
characterises these metabolic differences is that of the cat's stricter

adherence to and dependence on a carnivorous life style in contrast to the dog's characteristically more adaptable and labile metabolic armamentarium. It is an indication of the healthy interest and progress in our understanding of these differences that there is only a four-year gap between this meeting and the last significant international Symposium on the Nutrition of the Dog and Cat (Hannover, 1978), whereas there was a fourteen-year gap between the Hannover Symposium and its predecessor in London (1964). In the four years since the Hannover Symposium there has been a significant number of contributions from several individuals and institutes, many of whom are represented at this Symposium.

One of the consequences of the different life styles of the small, companion or pet animal and those of other domestic species is the difference in nutritional objectives. While the feeding of farm animals has well defined and measurable nutritional objectives such as weight gain, carcase quality or milk or egg production achieved at the lowest possible cost, there are few such measurable objectives in feeding dogs and cats.

There are, nevertheless, other objectives which can be applied to the feeding of dogs and cats and these have much in common with those we apply to ourselves and our families.

NUTRITIONAL OBJECTIVES FOR COMPANION ANIMALS

1. To support normal growth

2. To fulfil genetical potential in conformation

3. To sustain physical and mental health and activity

4. To provide for optimum reproductive performance

5. To achieve healthy old age

6. To give enjoyment

It is easier to state these objectives than to measure their achievement, and they beg many questions, some of which one can refine, though few of which can be fully answered.

1.   Normal Growth

What is normal growth? Is it the same as maximum growth? Most nutritionists working with dogs or laboratory animals are aware of the published work which seriously questions whether maximal growth is compatible with optimal skeletal development (see Hedhammar and others, 1974). The Cornell workers drew attention to the detrimental effects of a high plane of nutrition on skeletal development of Great Dane puppies compared to litter-mates fed a restricted level of the same food. There is also evidence that rapid growth and weight gain caused by increased calorie intake are factors in the earlier occurrence and increased severity of hip dysplasia in susceptible dogs (Kasstrøm, 1975).

At the other end of the life cycle it is generally accepted that chronic overfeeding, or other dietary excesses or imbalances, curtail the life-span of laboratory rodents (see Ross, Lustbader and Bras, 1976) relative to those on a lower plane of nutrition. The problems of testing this relationship in

dogs are great in that one would require to maintain a large number over a
10 to 20 year period under stable conditions - and so far as I know no one
has made such a commitment. There is, however, some evidence that large or
giant breeds have a lower life expectancy than small breeds (Comfort, 1956)
which may be due to a higher incidence of tumours in the large breeds
(Cotchin, 1954) and the increased vulnerability of large individuals to
cardiac or respiratory disease. It also seems not unlikely that the owners
of large breeds contribute to their short life expectancy by feeding and
supplementing for maximum growth and size. Domestic cats, on the other hand,
appear to have not only longer life expectancy but are physically better
preserved than dogs in old age (Comfort, 1956) - a difference which may be
related not only to their relative uniformity in body size but also the
relative infrequency with which they indulge or are indulged in 'over-
nutrition'.

2.   Conformation

No species has such a wide range of conformation as the dog - some breeds
having attained the bizarre state of being dependent on surgical interference
for their health or survival. Because of this wide range of phenotypes, a
new fashion in conformation can be attained within a few generations and one
can see quite marked differences between current specimens of a breed and
those of previous decades. The Bull Terrier is an example. All veterinarians
are aware of the anatomical problems which can accompany the development of
fashionable conformation features and it is not surprising that there is
growing evidence of inherited metabolic disease which becomes patent through
selective breeding for physical characteristics (Foley, Lasley and Osweiler,
1979) - not to mention the behavioural abnormalities which will be described
later in this symposium.

Do we have evidence of different nutritional requirements for breeds of
different conformation? Do heavy-boned dogs need more calcium and phosphorus
than light-boned breeds? In general, there is no such evidence. Little dogs
can thrive on the same nutritional package as large ones provided the size of
the package is right. There is, however, well documented evidence of breed
sensitivity to particular nutrients such as the Bedlington Terrier's susceptibility to copper toxicosis (Twedt and others, 1979) and it seems more than
likely that with the improvement of diagnostic techniques, more breed related
metabolic idiosyncracies will be recognised.

3.   Physical and Mental Health and Activity

Health is not simply the absence of disease. One is conscious of the
difference between a dog with a bright alert eye, glossy coat, healthy
appetite and acute responsiveness to its surroundings - and the dog in which
all these characteristics are somehow muted, and yet has no clinical sign of
disease. How does one quantify and evaluate the difference, how does one
treat the dog which is not blooming with health, but not suffering from
disease? It is often a shot-gun of multi-vitamins and a hope for the best.
The difference may, however, be due to an identifiable environmental factor.
Hurni (1981) describes an experience in which two keepers were in charge of
a colony of cats. When one of the keepers was on duty, the cats consumed a
measured 30% more food than when the other was on duty. One of the differences
between the keepers was that the first always talked to himself while working
and the cats always knew when he was coming and were never startled by his
appearance. Regardless of whether this was the specific reason, there seemed

to be a management factor related to the two keepers which affected food
intake and (presumably) health. The question remains, however, how one
identifies and quantifies degrees of health in the absence of clinical disease.

4.   Reproductive Performance

Both Professor Björck and Dr Blaza will be discussing nutritional management
during reproduction in dogs and cats. This is obviously the most nutritionally
demanding phase in the life-cycle of dogs or cats, and yet, unless something
goes seriously wrong, the veterinarian may have little opportunity to influence
nutritional management.

There is still insufficient appreciation among breeders of the increase in the
nutritional needs of the bitch or queen with a large litter, coming into peak
lactation. There is a lack of common sense in ensuring that the 3- or even
4-fold increase in nutritional requirement is met not only by an increase in
the amount provided, but by an increase in meal frequency.

The effect of a rising plane of nutrition at mating on increasing the number
of foetuses conceived has been demonstrated in sheep and pigs under certain
conditions. Whether the same effect can be obtained in the bitch or queen
does not seem to have been recorded.

There are few quantitative studies on digestibility and metabolism during
pregnancy and lactation. Is there enhanced mineral and vitamin absorption
during lactation? Do energy, vitamin and mineral requirements increase in
proportion, or is there a real need to provide a protein/mineral/vitamin
enriched diet at this time? What is the practical importance of carbohydrate
in the diet of the lactating bitch? Pregnant bitches on a carbohydrate-free
diet developed hypoglycaemia and ketosis in late pregnancy, had fewer pups
alive at birth and a lower percentage surviving 3 days than did bitches
receiving a diet containing carbohydrate (Romsos and others, 1981). If
dietary carbohydrate is needed during late pregnancy, how much? Does the
pregnant queen need dietary carbohydrate?

5.   Old Age

The degenerative diseases of old age in dogs and cats are familiar to all
veterinarians and we have already touched on the possibility that nutrition
and rate of growth in the young animal may advance or delay their onset.
But there are other questions ... does the old dog or cat have different
requirements because of its age alone, or are its special needs the algebraic
sum of the problems of degenerating absorptive, metabolic and excretory
organs? If so, can any single food or dietary regime be suitable to the
majority of old dogs?

6.   Enjoyment

Enjoyment is an essential feature of man's dietary habits, whereas it is
given little consideration in the feeding of farm livestock. How important
is it and can it be quantified in dogs and cats?

If we accept that palatability is an important factor in influencing an
animal's enjoyment of its food, there are several aspects in which palatability
and enjoyment are important in the nutrition of dogs and cats.

The animal. There is a measurable degree of boredom attendant on the feeding of a single food for a prolonged period to dogs or cats (Mugford, 1977), and this can be shown by a relative increase in the liking for an alternative food in a choice situation. There is also some evidence that feeding of a rota of different foods can improve the reproductive performance of breeding queens (Hurni, 1981), though whether this is due to the effect of variety on palatability or to a more balanced diet is unclear. Also, improving palatability can be a critical factor in maintaining the increased food intake necessary to support peak lactation in the bitch. Palatability of the food may, therefore, be a critical factor in the management and husbandry of both dogs and cats.

The owner. Feeding is one of the most important occasions of the day for both the owner and the animal - and our own data provide evidence that most owners are concerned about how well, in their view, a particular food is liked by their animal, and there is some evidence that the owner's attitude may influence the animal's response. Thus, no matter how sound the nutritional advice of the veterinarian or with what nutritional expertise a prepared food is formulated, if the owner thinks the animal won't or doesn't like it, then the animal is unlikely to get it more than once or twice!

These are some of the questions which the veterinarian and the nutritionist must ask himself or the food manufacturer. As a veterinarian who is closely involved with food manufacture, I often find that I am asking myself these questions.

The research and manufacture of foods for dogs and cats has come a long way in the last decade or so. Research on the nutrition of dogs and cats in academic institutes such as those in Hannover, Vienna and Davis, California and in research establishments such as the Animal Studies Centre have extended and deepened our understanding of their nutritional needs and posed the challenge of incorporating this new knowledge into the practical formulation of prepared foods for companion animals.

Meetings such as these provide an important opportunity for the exchange and updating of this new knowledge, ideas and even criticism between the practising veterinary surgeon, the academic expert and the nutritional adviser to food manufacturers. They are all looking at the same animals and the same problems from different angles and perhaps by putting their views together we can obtain a 3-dimensional image. If we also include the owner or the breeder, we complete the picture.

As we said earlier, the daily feeding and daily behavioural interaction with his or her companion animal are the most important points of contact and influence an owner can have on its (and perhaps his own) well-being. I have touched on a few areas in which there is still much to be found out about the optimum conditions of nutrition for different circumstances and, like the rest of us, I look forward to having my knowledge extended in these and other areas by the speakers who follow.

REFERENCES

Anderson, R. S. (1974). In C. S. G. Grunsell and F. W. G. Hill (Eds.), The Veterinary Annual. John Wright, Bristol. pp. 182-186.

Burger, I. H., R. S. Anderson, and D. W. Holme (1980). In R. S. Anderson
    (Ed.), Nutrition of the Dog and Cat. Pergamon, Oxford.
Comfort, A. (1956). Proc. Zool. Soc. Lond., 127, 27-34.
Comfort, A. (1956). J. Mammal., 37, 118-119.
Cotchin, E. (1954). Vet. Rec., 66, 879-885.
Evans, J. M., D. R. Lane, and P. G. Hendy (1974). J. small Anim. Pract.,
    15, 595-607.
Foley, C. W., J. F. Lasley, and G. D. Osweiler (1979). Abnormalities of
    Companion Animals. Iowa State University Press, Ames.
Hedhammar, A., F-M. Wu, L. Krook, H. F. Schryver, A. de Lahunta, J. P. Whalen,
    F. A. Kallfelz, E. A. Nunex, J. F. Hitz, B. E. Sheffy, and G. D. Ryan
    (1974). Cornell Vet. Suppl., 5, 64, 1-160.
Hurni, H. (1981). Z. Versuchstierk., 23, 102-121.
Kasström, H. (1975). Acta Radiol. Suppl., 344, 135-179.
Kipling, R. (1908). Just So Stories - for little children. McMillan,
    London. pp. 175-197.
Morris, J. G., and Q. R. Rogers (1982). In A. T. B. Edney (Ed.), Recent
    Advances in Feline Nutrition, Waltham Symposium No. 4. J. small Anim.
    Pract., 23, 599-613.
Mugford, R. A. (1977). In The Chemical Senses and Nutrition. Academic Press,
    New York.
Romsos, D. R., J. H. Palmer, K. L. Muiruri, and M. R. Bennink (1981).
    J. Nutr., 111, 678-689.
Ross, M. H., E. Lustbader, and G. Bras (1976). Nature, 262, 548-553.
Steininger, E. (1981). Wien. tierarztl. Mschr., 68 Jahrgang, Heft 3/4,
    122-130.
Twedt, D. C., I. Sternlieb, and S. R. Gitbertson (1979). J. Am. vet. med.
    Ass., 175, 269-275.

FEEDING FOR REPRODUCTION AND GROWTH

Mineral Metabolism and Requirements in Bitches and Suckling Pups

H. Meyer

Institut für Tierernährung, Tierärztliche Hochschule, Hannover, Federal Republic of Germany

ABSTRACT

The mineral requirements of pregnant and lactating bitches (calculated by the factorial method) can be given as follows (in mg/kg BW/d):

	pregnant* bitches	lactating bitches
Ca	160	270
P	140	210
Mg	15	23
Na	105	125
K	95	140
Fe	2.5	2.1
Cu	0.16	0.55
Zn	1.40	2.80
Mn	0.14	

* last 3 weeks of pregnancy

The highest losses of Ca and P take place in the 3rd and 4th week of lactation. The Ca and P content of pups (at birth 6.4 and 4.7 g/kg BW respectively) increases during the first month of life only to a small extent, although the Ca and P taken up with the milk is utilised to a high degree (80 to 90%). The intake of Na and K with milk seems to be higher than necessary for retention in the newly built tissues. The intake and absorption of iron with the milk in the suckling pup is less than necessary for keeping the Fe concentration at a normal level (risk of anaemia), while the uptake of copper and zinc seems to be suitable.

KEYWORDS

Breeding bitch; suckling pup; mineral and trace element metabolism.

13

INTRODUCTION

In the past the mineral metabolism of breeding bitches and suckling pups has
received only minor attention. The requirement figures of the NRC (1974) are
based on estimations only. Calculations by the factorial method could not be
made because base figures were lacking. In the following contribution quantitative data about the mineral metabolism in the bitch and suckling pup are
given and recommendations for the mineral supply to these classes of dogs are
outlined.

BASE FIGURES FOR CALCULATING THE MINERAL REQUIREMENT IN
BITCHES AND PUPS

In the dog the litter weight at birth represents about 12% of the bitch's live
weight (Table 1).

TABLE 1   Litterweight in Bitches of Different Breeds*
          (Sierts-Roth, 1953; Kaiser, 1971)

Breed	n*	Bodyweight kg	Litterweight kg	% BW
Miniature	11	4	0.5	12.5
Small	14	9	1.1	12.2
Medium	13	20	2.2	11.0
Large	7	32	3.8	11.9
Giant	6	60	4.3	7.2

* number of breeds

There seems to be no wide variation between breeds because with increasing
number of pups per litter the birth weight goes down and vice versa. Representative figures are lacking for giant breeds. Whether or to what extent an
extrauterine mineral retention takes place in the bitch during gestation is
unknown. In the following calculation no such retention has been taken into
account.

The main growth of the foetus takes place in the last 3 weeks of gestation
(Fig. 1). Only at this time can a pronounced increase in the mineral requirement of the bitch be expected. Therefore, an additional mineral requirement
has been calculated for this period only. For simplification a linear growth
of the foetus during this time has been assumed. For mineral retention in
the placenta and foetal fluids only Na and K were taken into account.

TABLE 2   Daily Milk Production in Bitches*
          (Mean and range, n = 19)

Week of lactation	Milk production % BW
1	2.5 (1.6-4.7)
2	3.0 (2.3-5.7)
3	4.0 (2.4-7.5)
4	4.3 (2.2-6.2)
5	4.0 (1.4-6.4)

* from Meyer, 1981; Dammers and Meyer, 1982.

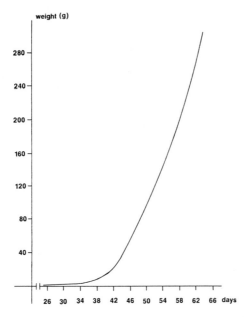

Fig. 1.   Growth of the foetus in dogs (Beagle) (calculated
          from data of Evans, 1974)

There are only a few investigations about the bitch's milk production.   Our
own results from 19 bitches are given in Table 2.   In general, production
increases from the 1st to the 4th week of lactation.   A relationship to the
number of pups in a litter is possible but has not been quantified.

TABLE 3   Weight Gains in Suckling Pups (Mean ± S.D., n = 16)

Weeks of age	Gain (% of BW)
1	6.2 ± 2.0
2	6.2 ± 1.8
3	4.4 ± 1.0
4	3.1 ± 0.9

* milk intake only;   from Dammers and Meyer, 1982

The daily gain of suckling pups during the 1st month is about 5% of the body
weight (Table 3).   However the relative weight gain in the 3rd and 4th week
is much less than in the first 2 weeks.

METABOLISM AND REQUIREMENTS OF THE MAJOR ELEMENTS IN THE
BITCH

During pregnancy the bitches need additional minerals mainly for mineral
retention in the foetus.   The mineral content in new born pups is given in
Table 4.

There is a much larger variation in Ca and P content than in that of Na and K.
Because Ca and P are mainly deposited in the bones, the relative size of the
skeleton seems to vary to a large extent. However, between breeds of different
size we did not see systematic effects.

The mineral requirements of the lactating bitch depend on the mineral excretion
with milk. The existing figures on the mineral content of the milk (summarised
by Thomee, 1978) show a wide variation; for example Ca values range between
66 and 280 mg/dl. Our own results (fig. 2) demonstrate that the time of
lactation may be an important factor of variation. Both Ca and P content
increase, while the Na content decreases and Mg and K concentrations remain
constant during the course of lactation.

TABLE 4   Mineral Content (mg/100g) in Newborn and Adult
          Dogs (Mean ± S.D.)*

	Newborn (n=22)		Adult (n=53)	
	Wet wt.	Fat free wt.	Wet wt.	Fat free wt.
Ca	635±139	640	1070±390	1390
P	472± 68	476	590±170	770
Mg	26± 3	26	26± 5	33
Na	184± 17	185	121± 18	153
K	211± 19	213	172± 29	214

* from Stadtfield, 1978; Meyer and others, 1981.

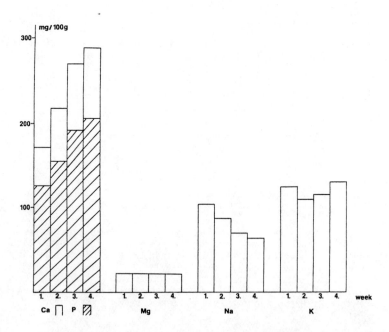

Fig. 2.   Mineral content in dogs milk during lactation (n=50;
          from Meyer and others, 1981; Dammers and Meyer, 1982)

TABLE 5   Mineral Requirements in Pregnant and Lactating Bitches

		Pregnancy*					Lactation				
		Ca	P	Mg	Na	K	Ca	P	Mg	Na	K
Retention in foetal mass foetal fluids (20% of foetal	mg/kg BW/d	30	25	1.3	10	11	-	-	-	-	-
mass)	mg/kg BW/d			0.1	9	1	-	-	-	-	-
Excretion by milk (4% BW)	mg/kg BW/d			-	-	-	100	75	4	32	45
Endogenous losses, maintenance level	mg/kg BW/d	35	30	3	60	65	35	30	3	60	65
Utilisation of food minerals	%	40	40	30	75	80	50	50	30	75	80
Total requirement	mg/kg BW/d	160	140	15	105	95	270	210	23	125	140

* last 3 weeks (from Meyer, 1978; Meyer and others, 1981)

Based on the figures given above the mineral requirement of pregnant and lactating bitches have been calculated (Table 5). For reasons of safety, the rate of utilisation of the minerals fed is set at the lower range.

During the last 3 weeks of pregnancy the total requirement of most minerals increases by about 50% of the maintenance requirement while during lactation a 2.5 to 3 fold increase seems to be necessary. In this connection it should be mentioned that undercutting these figures by 10 to 20% will not necessarily lead to disturbances in the mineral metabolism because the animals are able to compensate, mainly by increasing the absorption rate.

In relation to disturbances of the Ca metabolism in the bitch, the Ca retention as well as Ca excretion during the last 3 weeks of pregnancy and the first 4 weeks of lactation are important. In Fig. 3, average data are presented. The additional Ca requirement of the bitch during this time continuously increases. In contrast to the cow, there is no abrupt increase from the end of pregnancy to the beginning of lactation.

This may explain why regulatory problems of Ca homeostasis in this phase are not common in the bitch. On the other hand Ca losses reach a peak in the 3rd and 4th week of lactation. In breeding bitches with a continuously low Ca intake (meat, offals, oats, rice) a hypocalcaemic crisis can be expected during the peak of lactation. In fact, hypocalcaemic tetany in lactating bitches most often occurs at this time (Austad and Bjerkas, 1976).

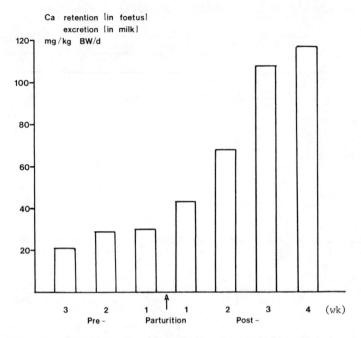

Fig. 3. Foetal Ca retention during the last 3 weeks of
         pregnancy and Ca excretion in the milk in the
         first 4 weeks of lactation (calculated from Figs.
         1 and 2, and Tables 1, 2 and 4).

METABOLISM AND REQUIREMENTS OF TRACE ELEMENTS IN THE BITCH

Only the elements Fe, Cu, Zn and Mn will be discussed under this topic because
data for the other elements are lacking.

TABLE 6   Iron, Copper, Zinc and Manganese Content (mg/100g)
          in Newborn and Adult Dogs (Mean ± S.D.)

	Newborn (n=22)			Adult	
		Fat free wt.	Wet wt.	Fat free wt.	n
Fe	7.6 ±2.41	7.7	10.0	12.7	8
Cu	0.38±0.09	0.39	0.73	12.7	38
Zn	2.31±0.41	2.34	8.2	0.95	38
Mn	0.07±0.03	0.07	0.16	0.20	8

The trace element concentrations in newborn dogs are less than in the adult
dogs (Table 6) particularly Cu and Mn. The variation at birth is large.

Regarding the Fe content, there was a tendency to find lower figures in pups
from larger breeds which, in general, are born in a stage of lower maturation
(higher body water content) than pups of small breeds. From earlier investigations (Widdowson, 1974; and others) it is known that the main Fe retention
in the foetus takes place just before birth. A systematic effect on the Fe
reserve, therefore seems possible in larger breeds with, in general, a relatively
shorter pregnancy.

TABLE 7   Iron, Copper, Zinc and Manganese Content of Bitches Milk
(μg/100g) (n = 44, mean $\pm$ S.D.)

Fe	687 ± 343
Cu	334 ± 81
Zn	1147 ± 482
Mn	40

(from Meyer and others, 1979; Dammers and Meyer, 1982)

The trace element content of bitches' milk (Table 7) is relatively high
compared to other species (Underwood, 1971), particularly the Cu and Zn
content. There seems to be no relationship to the stage of lactation.
Recommendations for the trace element supply for bitches are given in Table 8.
The figures are preliminary, particularly because data on endogenous losses
and absorption rates are based on estimates. Nevertheless the data demonstrate
that the Fe requirement in the last weeks of pregnancy is as high as during
lactation, while the requirements for Cu and Zn during lactation may reach
3 to 5 times the maintenance requirement.

MINERAL METABOLISM IN SUCKLING PUPS

The new born pup is a 'nestling' with little ability for movement. The Ca
and P content of the body is remarkably less than in adult dogs (Table 4).
When compared to newborn animals of other species (Fig. 4) too, the low
concentrations of Ca and P in the body of newborn dogs (and cats) are evident.
Since 99% of the Ca is deposited in the skeleton, at birth the mineralisation
of the skeleton or its relative weight must be low.

TABLE 8   Recommendations for Trace Element Supply to Bitches

		Fe	Cu	Zn	Mn
Endogenous losses*	ug/kg BW	360	30	240	10
Retention in foetus**	ug/kg BW	380	19	115	4
Excretion by milk***	ug/kg BW	275	135	460	
Utilisation of food minerals	%	30	30	25	10
Total requirement: pregnancy	mg/kg BW	2.5	0.16	1.40	0.14
lactation	mg/kg BW	2.1	0.55	2.80	

    * estimates: from Meyer, 1983;   (from Meyer and others, 1979)
   ** last 3 weeks of pregnancy;
 *** milk production: 4% BW

Ca. g/kg fat free BW

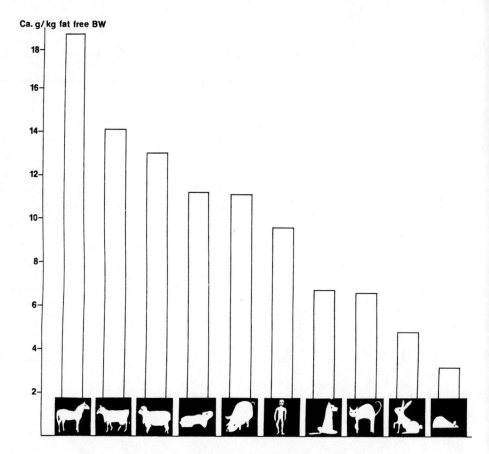

Fig. 4 Ca content at birth (fat free BW) in different
species (from Widdowson, 1950; Ellenberger and
others, 1950; Becker, 1976; Meyer and Ahlswede,
1976; Sykes and Field, 1972)

The ash, Ca and P content of different bones (Table 9) in the newborn dog
reaches about 60% of that of adults. On the other hand the Ca content in the
fat free body of the pups comes up to only 46% of that for adults.

Therefore the low Ca and P content in newborn pups can be explained both by
a lower relative size of the skeleton and a lower mineralisation of the bone
as compared to adult dogs.

The retention of minerals by pups taking up milk during the first 4 weeks of
life is presented in Table 10. The calculation is based on balance experiments
and analysis of body composition at birth and 4 weeks of age in relation to
intake.

Regarding Ca and P, both methods lead to nearly the same results. The Ca and
P taken up with milk is retained to 80 to 90%. In the 1st and 2nd week,
however, the Ca and P concentrations in the gain are less than in the whole
body at birth. In the 3rd and 4th week the retention increases.

TABLE 9   Ash, Ca and P Content in Bones of Dogs of Different Ages

	Ash	Ca	P
Long bones			
newborn %	38.8	14.3	7.1
8-11 months old %	57.8	22.4	10.6
% newborn to adult	67	64	67
Mandibula			
newborn %	35.7	13.3	6.9
8-11 months old %	63.5	24.6	12.4
% newborn to adult	56	54	56
Ca content whole body			
(fat free BW)			
% new born to adult		46	
(Table 4)			

(from Morgan, 1939;   Rauchfuss, 1978)

Nevertheless at 4 weeks of age the Ca concentration in the body (as shown also by Orgler, 1910; Drüge, 1913; Eckert, 1913) is elevated only to a small degree (Table 4). The work of Burns and Henderson (1936) confirms that the mineral content of the bones at this time has increased only to a small extent. Furthermore Andersen and Floyd (1963) demonstrated that ossification in the long bones of pups starts just at 21 days of age.

TABLE 10   Retention of Minerals in Pups during Suckling Time

	Retention % of intake		Retention (mg) per 100g gain		Content at 4 weeks of age
	Balance period	calculated*	1st+2nd (Weeks)	3rd+4th	mg/100g
Ca	90 ± 8.4	99	542	1024	710
P	82 ± 12.4	79	380	588	460
Mg	74 ± 21.3		20	24	23
Na	69 ± 20.6	45	143	212	158
K	56 ± 30.1	32	235	202	147

* by difference between body composition at birth and 4 weeks of age and milk intake.

(after Meyer and others, 1981;   Dammers and Meyer, 1982.)

It seems worth while to test whether stress to the very sensitive skeleton of the growing pup (for example overfeeding) can lead to damage which manifests in later stages of growth.

Regarding Na and K, from both methods the retention is less than for Ca and P, but in the results between the two methods there are large differences. This may be explained by some losses of Na and K from the skin and the saliva which during the balance period could not be collected. Furthermore there may be some uncontrolled losses of urine. Therefore the figures estimated by analysis of body composition seem to be more realistic.

Nevertheless the intake of Na and K with milk seems higher than necessary for
retention in the newly built tissue. The suckling pups eliminated (via the
kidney) about 25% of Na and K taken up. During the 3rd and 4th weeks this
figure increases for K to more than 50%. The surplus of these minerals in
the milk may be important for the function of the kidney during early life.
McCance and Widdowson (1958) demonstrated that one day old pups were only
able to eliminate water given by stomach tube after adding sodium chloride.
The requirements of suckling pups for Na and K, therefore, cannot be calculated only from the retention of these minerals in the newly built tissues.

TABLE 11   Iron, Copper and Zinc Retention in Suckling Pups (n = 6)

	% intake	Retention* mg/100g gain
Fe	51	1.17
Cu	91	1.06
Zn	72	3.94

* losses by urine neglected.

(from Meyer and others, 1979.)

Regarding the requirement of suckling pups for trace elements, only preliminary
figures can be given. Looking at Fe metabolism, the concentration per 100g
of weight gained (1.17 mg/100g; Table 11) was lower than in the whole body at
birth (7.6 mg/100g; Table 6). In fact, body analysis of 4 week old pups
demonstrates that the Fe content decreases to 2.2 and 4.3 mg/100g (Fontes and
Thivolle, 1925; Lintzel and Radeff, 1931; Meyer and Dammers, 1982).

The reduction in the Fe content of the body may lead to anaemia in suckling
pups. This is confirmed by several investigations of their blood status
(Lintzel and Radeff, 1931; Ederstrom and Debuer, 1946; Müller, 1968; Crabo
and others, 1970; Rüsse, 1971; see Fig. 5). Particularly disposed seem to
be pups with low Fe reserves in the liver (prematures, large breeds), with
high milk intake and late supplemental feeding, and pups reared in a low Fe
environment.

There seems to be no problem regarding the Cu and Zn supply as demonstrated
in Table 11. The calculated concentration in the gain for these elements is
remarkably higher than that of the whole body at birth. Therefore, an increase
in the concentration of the body during suckling time can be expected.

Looking to the Cu metabolism it should be mentioned that pups, in contrast to
some other species but in accordance with rabbits and rats (Fig. 6) have low
Cu reserves in the liver at birth. But this is compensated by high concentrations of Cu in the milk.

The mineral requirement of the suckling pup can easily be derived from the
intake with milk (Table 12). From the results discussed above, the mineral
intake with milk (except for iron) should be enough for health and normal
development of the young. Only for the 4th week in which pups normally take
up additional feed an increase of 10 to 20% seems to be necessary. With milk
the pup gets up to only 1 mg (1st week) to 0.7 mg Fe (4th week) per kg bodyweight per day. Assuming an Fe utilisation of 50% (a value, which was observed
by Lintzel and Radeff (1931) by feeding iron citrate), the Fe intake of rapidly
growing pups (Table 3) should be about 8 mg/kg BW/d to keep the Fe content of
the body constant.

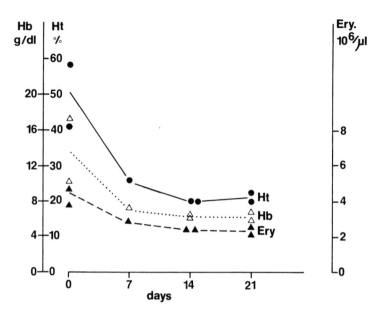

Fig. 5 Haematocrit, haemoglobin and number of red cells
        in suckling pups during the first 3 weeks after
        birth (from Crabo and others, 1970)

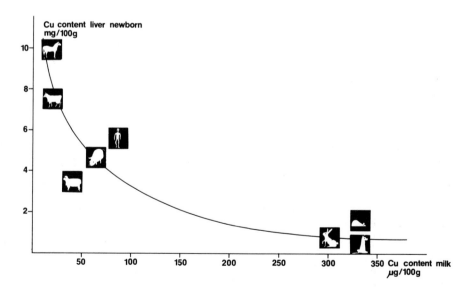

Fig. 6 Cu content in the liver of newborn and the milk in different species
        (from Widdowson, 1950; Meyer and Ahlswede, 1976; Kamphues, 1982)

REFERENCES

Andersen, A.C., and M. Floyd (1963). Am. J. vet. Res., 24, 348-351.
Austad, S., and E. Bjerkas (1976). J. small Anim. Pract., 17, 793-798.
Becker, K. (1976). Übers. Tierernährg., 4, 167-195.
Burns, C. M., and N. Henderson (1936). Biochem. J., 30, 1207-1214.
Crabo, B., E. Kjellgren, and A. W. Bäckgren (1970). Svensk Vet. Tidn., 22, 857-861.
Dammers, C., and H. Meyer (1982). Unpublished.
Dröge, K. (1913). Pflügers Arch. Physiol., 152, 437-475.
Eckert, E. (1913). Ursache und Wesen angeborener Diathesen. zit. after Radeff (1930).
Ederstrom, H. E., and B. Debuer (1946). Anat. Rec., 94, 663-670.
Ellenberger, H. B., J. A. Newlander, and C. H. Hones (1950). Univ. Vermont Agric. Exp. Stat. Bull., No. 558, 1-66.
Evans, H. E. (1974). Prenatal development of the dog. Gaines Vet. Symp., 18-28.
Fontes, G., and L. Thivolle (1925). C. r. Séanc. Soc. Biol., 93, 681-683.
Kaiser, G. (1970). Z. Tierzücht. Züchtbiol., 88, 316-340.
Kamphues, J. (1982). Unpublished.
Lintzel, W., and T. Radeff (1931). Arch. Tierernährg. und Tierzucht, 6, 316-352.
McCance, R. A., and E. M. Widdowson (1951). J. Physiol., 112, 450-458.
McCance, R. A., and E. M. Widdowson (1958). J. Physiol., 141, 81-87.
Meyer, H. (1975). Prakt. Tierarzt 56 coll. vet. 1975, 42-45.
Meyer, H. (1978). Übers. Tierernährg., 6, 31-54.
Meyer, H. (1983). Ernährung des Hundes. Eugen Ulmer, Stuttgart. Accepted for publication.
Meyer, H., and L. Ahlswede (1976). Übers. Tierernährg., 4, 263-292.
Meyer, H., A. Thomee, and R. Rauchfuss (1979). Kleintier-Praxis, 24, 135-140.
Meyer, H., H.-C. Mundt, A. Thomée, and R. Rauchfuss (1981). Kleintier-Praxis, 26, 115-120.
Meyer, H., and C. Dammers (1982). Unpublished.
Morgan, A. F. (1939). Univ. Calif. Publ. Physiol, 8, 61-106.
Müller, U. (1968). Blutuntersuchungen von Hundewelpen im Zeitraum vom 1. bis 75. Lebenstag. Vet. Diss., Leipzig.
National Research Council (1974). Nutrient Requirements of Dogs. National Academy of Sciences, Washington, D.C.
Orgler, A. (1910). Biochem. Z., 28, 359-373.
Rauchfuss, R. (1978). Untersuchingen uber die Körperzusammensetzung neugeborener Hundewelpen unterschiedlich grosser Rassen. Staatsexamensarbeit Hannover.
Russe, J. (1971). Berl. Münch. Tierärztl. Wschr., 74, 249-252.
Sierts-Roth, U. (1953). Geburts- und Aufzuchtgewichte von Rassehunden. Paul Schöps Verlag, Frankfurt a. Main.
Stadtfeld, G. (1978). Untersuchungen über die Körperzusammensetzung des Hundes. Vet. Diss. Hannover.
Sykes, A. R., and A. C. Field (1972). J. agric. Sci. Camb., 78, 119-125.
Thomee, A. (1978). Zusammensetzung, Verdaulich-und Verträglichkeit von Hunde-milch und Mischfutter bei Welpen unter besonderer Berücksichtigung der Fettkomponente. Vet. Diss. Hannover.
Thomee, A. (1980). Dtsch. tierärztl. Wschr., 87, 88-90
Underwood, E. J. (1971). Trace Elements in Human and Animal Nutrition. 3rd edn. Academic Press, New York/London.
Widdowson, E. M. (1950). Nature, 166, 626-628.
Widdowson, E. M. (1974). Proc. Nutr. Soc., 33, 275-284.

Care and Feeding of the Puppy in the Postnatal and Weaning Period

G. Björck

Animal Hospital, Veterinary Institute at Skara, S-532 00 Skara, Sweden

ABSTRACT

The paper discusses the three different periods in the life of a puppy from birth to weaning, including a table for normal physiological values for neonatal puppies and statistics concerning puppy mortality. In the neonatal period, artificial raising is discussed in detail.

KEYWORDS

Puppy management; artificial raising of puppies.

INTRODUCTION

The purpose is to present problems and questions a small animal practitioner will meet in the daily work.

Keeping a litter of puppies alive from birth to weaning means, for the breeder, a bringing together and balancing of many factors. Four important areas influencing puppies are: genetical, physiological, nutritional, and psychological. For the breeder there is also the question of how environmental conditions influence the final results.

To discuss each factor separately is of little value as they are so intimately connected with each other. It is better to consider different easily distinguished periods in the life of the puppy and growing dog, and to discuss the different factors within each single period.

The following periods can be readily identified:

Whelping.

The neonatal period. Extending from whelping to the opening of the puppies' eyes.

The transition period. The time from the opening of the eyes to 3 weeks of age.

The socialisation period. The time from 3 weeks of age to weaning (7 to 10 weeks).

WHELPING

It is important to stress to breeders the value of checking the preparturient temperature of the bitch. The normal lowering of body temperature about one day before parturition predicts the time of whelping. It is also important to stress the necessity of preparing in advance a special whelping place for the bitch. The majority of bitches follow the same whelping pattern. Freak (1968) has made a vivid description of this.

The bitch should be allowed to take care of a normal whelping by herself. The breeder must, however, make sure that the whelping is progressing normally.

NEONATAL PERIOD

During this period it is of vital importance for the puppy to eat and to keep warm. The puppy should train itself to find nourishment - from the teats of the bitch. If everything progresses normally, the bitch should be allowed to care for the puppies without external involvement.

During this period an adjustment to inherited systems, e.g. intake of food, is going on, despite inactivity in the central nervous system. The puppies quickly learn to find the teats of the bitch when the bitch lies down for nursing. Artificially raised puppies will not develop this natural way of finding food. The opinion has been raised that these will have a life-long handicap in using their nose. I am not of this opinion after having followed some of the puppies I have raised artificially.

One can check the puppies' health condition during this period of life by studying them at sleep. A normal puppy never sleeps deep and quiet, but with involuntary muscle contractions, not to be compared with shivering. A puppy sleeping without any movements may be sick and should be kept under observation.

Normal physiological values for neonate puppies are given in Table 1.

TABLE 1   Normal Physiological Values for Neonate Puppies
(Cornell Res. Lab., 1974; Mosier, 1981)

Body temperature	Weeks 1-2: $34.5^{o}C$ to $37.2^{o}C$; Weeks 2-4: $36.1^{o}C$ to $37.8^{o}C$; Week 4+ : $37.8^{o}C$ to $38.3^{o}C$.
Heart rate	220 per minute. Abrupt decline starts at two weeks of age as vagal development occurs.
Respiratory rate	15 to 35 per minute.
Weight gain	Double weight in 8 to 10 days. Increase about 2 g per day per kg expected adult weight.

Eyes open	10 to 14 days.
Visual perception (owner recognition)	Absent less than 3 weeks, present at 4 weeks.
Differention of the retina	Not complete until 6 weeks.
Reaction to auditory and visual stimuli	3 to 4 weeks
Ears open	13 to 17 days.
Eruption of teeth	3 to 4 weeks, first in the mandibula and the canine teeth.
Attitude	Activated sleep 90% of time. Flexor dominance for 3 days, then extensor dominance from 5 to 21 days.
Muscle tone	Firm, pups stand upright at 3 weeks with normal tone and postural reflexes. Walking and running by 4 weeks.
Shivering reflex	Develops 6 to 8 days after birth.
Caloric requirement	130 to 220 kcal per kg body weight per day.
Water requirement	125 to 190 ml per kg body weight per day.
Urine specific gravity	Generally 1.006 to 1.017.

An extensive list of neonatal diseases is published by Cornell Laboratory for Diseases of Dogs (1974), Suter (1977), and by Mosier (1978, 1981).

ARTIFICIAL REARING

Most puppies have all their nutritional requirements met by the bitch during the neonatal period. Nevertheless there are cases when the bitch is unable to care for her puppies, and they must be fed artificially in order to save their lives.

Some of the indications for artificial rearing are:

Death of the bitch;
The bitch disowns one or more of the puppies;
A larger litter is born than the bitch can care for adequately;
Partial or complete lactation failure of the bitch;
Mammary gland or uterine infections of the bitch;
The puppies are weak or sick so they cannot suck normally.

Whatever the reason is for choosing to rear the puppies artificially, they must be nourished and nursed in such a way so they can survive and develop normally. The easiest and often best way is to let another bitch with puppies of about the same age and size take care of them. A possibility also worth trying is to use a pseudolactating bitch as a fostermother. If she gives enough milk and takes good care of the puppies, she can nurse them up to weaning age. A continuous follow-up is very important.

If none of these suggestions can be followed, other ways have to be tried, for instance complete artificial rearing or supplementary feeding while the puppies are still with the dam.

In artificial rearing as in the case of a fostermother, it is an advantage if the puppies have had colostrum during the first day of life. However, the development of the canine placenta permits some exchange of immunoglobulins between maternal and foetal blood, and the puppies are to some extent covered by the bitch's antibodies. Puppies can therefore be artificially reared with success without colostrum, which is not always the case in other species, for instance in artificial rearing of foals.

Complete Artificial Rearing

Successful hand rearing of puppies requires:

An environment adapted to the special requirements of puppies;
A milk substitute that supports normal growth, given in a manner accepted by the puppies;
Scrupulous management;
Patience by the breeder.

Environmental Requirements

It is of the utmost importance for a newborn puppy to maintain correct body temperature. If a normal newborn puppy, unable to regulate the body temperature, is kept at too low a temperature, it will quickly pass into a state of hypothermia. The first three days of life are the most critical (Crighton, 1968). The critical body temperature of a newborn puppy is $32^{\circ}C$. Below this point, the bowel movements stop, and digestion cannot function. Immediate artificial rearing of such a puppy is as a rule unsuccessful. It must first be warmed up and given fluids and glucose injections parenterally.

In order that the puppies maintain a normal, constant body temperature, they must be kept in the right environment, with a constant, satisfactory temperature. The following data are guidelines for the temperature in an incubator:

from birth to 5 days of age: $28-32^{\circ}C$
from 5 to 20 days: $26^{\circ}C$
from 20 to 34 days: $23^{\circ}C$

Composition of Milk Substitute

A complete table of the milk composition from different species is given by Kendall (1978) and summary of literature data on dog's milk by Baines (1981). A comparison of the milk from <u>cow</u> and <u>dog</u> demonstrates that dog's milk has almost twice as much solids as cow's milk. The content of fat and protein in dog's milk is more than two times higher. This demonstrates that if cow's milk is used for puppies, fat and protein must be added as well as vitamins and minerals.

Different commercial milk substitutes are available and can be used with success. But it is cheaper to prepare ones own mixture with cow's milk as the main component. Baines (1981) has compared different compositions, and recommends among others a composition developed in Sweden as early as 1957 (Björck and others).

The composition is as follows:

Cow's milk (3% fat)	800	ml
Half-cream (12% fat)	200	ml
Bone meal	6	g
Citric acid	4	g
1 egg yolk	15	g
Vitamin A	2000	IU
Vitamin D	500	IU

The recommended milk substitute is given as follows:

Age in weeks	kJ/kcal per kg body weight	g of milk substitute per 100g body weight
1	820/195	22
2	920/220	25
3	1030/245	28
4	1110/265	30

At the beginning, the puppies are fed 6 times per day, not at night. Published results indicate that a lower frequency of feeding will also give acceptable results (Strasser and Schumacher, 1968; Sheffy, 1978).

Puppies from heavier breeds can be fed using an ordinary nursing bottle for babies. For puppies of smaller breeds a special small animal nurser can be used. Those small puppies can also be fed from a syringe with a small piece of rubber tubing on the nozzle of the syringe. With the syringe the puppies are given the milk mixture drip by drip directly into the mouth.

It is very important to keep records of the amount given, and also of the body weight of the puppies.

At an age of 18 to 21 days, the puppies can start to drink from a bowl and the time-consuming bottle feeding can be discontinued. Ordinary dog food is gradually mixed with the milk, and it is therefore no problem to feed these puppies in the same manner as normal puppies, nursed by a bitch.

Tube Feeding

There is always a potential risk of aspiration of milk when bottle feeding puppies, especially weak ones. Instead of bottle feeding, the puppies can be given the milk by a tube. A complete instruction in tube feeding is given in English by Collins (1973) and Sheffy (1978) and in Swedish by Björck and Hedhammar (1981).

Supplementary Feeding

Supplementary feeding may be a reality when the bitch has so many puppies that she cannot give milk to all of them. If the breeder wants to keep them all, the bitch must be given some help. Normally she can take care of an oversized litter in the first postparturient days, but the supplementary feeding must start before the end of the first week. Split the litter in two halves, try to keep puppies of the same size in each half. One group is allowed to stay with the bitch, the other one is taken away and is given a milk replacer. The groups are exchanged three to four times a day. It is important to feed the group that has been away from the bitch before they are returned. If so, they will be full and will not suck the bitch as hard as when they are hungry.

TRANSITION PERIOD

During the transition period the bitch is still responsible for the feeding and caring of the puppies.

In a large litter some extra food can be given to individual puppies, especially the small ones. As soon as they are 10 to 12 days old, they can be hand-fed with small quantities of ground beef. At an age of 18 to 21 days, they can eat from a bowl.

SOCIALISATION PERIOD

Developmentally, three weeks of age is a very important and critical age for the growing puppy.

As to caring, the puppies are now able to accept external stimuli. During the period of socialisation, the ability of a puppy to socialise with other puppies or humans gradually diminishes. The earlier within the period of socialisation the puppy is introduced to the environment in which it will remain, the more well adapted to that environment it is when it reaches adulthood (Breazile, 1978).

The puppy is able to establish a voluntary control of urination and defaecation during this period. If a special toilet area can be kept for the puppies to take care of these elementary functions, a good start for further housetraining is established (Campbell, 1975).

The puppies are fed during this period with a smooth change-over to the definite weaning at an age of 8 to 10 weeks. The milk production of the bitch reaches a peak when the puppies are 2.5 to 4 weeks of age, and her great nutritional requirement must be met. If she is given a commercial dog food, preferably a food designed for growth should be used. It will meet the requirements both for the bitch and also for the puppies. Canned dog food is given as it is. Dry dog food can be given dry to puppies of larger breeds, and soaked with warm water or milk to smaller puppies. These feedings should be offered at the same time the bitch is fed. It is a mistake to introduce too many different kinds of food over the short weaning period, as this can result in digestive upsets.

When the milk production of the bitch begins to decline, the nutritional need of the puppies continues to increase. They can in the beginning be fed 4 to 5 times a day. At the time of complete weaning, it is enough to feed

3 to 4 times daily. A detailed feeding instruction is given by Sheffy (1978).
Good success with self feeders for dry dog food is reported by Nelson (1982).

It is important during this period to keep a record of the growth of the
puppies. If some individuals are growing too fast, the amount of food given
can be reduced. In an overfed, growing dog, bone problems can start at this
time (Hedhammar and others, 1974).

For the inexperienced breeder, it would be of value to compare the growth
rate of the puppies with a normal growth curve for the actual breed. Such
curves exist (Kirk and Bistner, 1969; 1981). According to Swedish experience,
these curves demonstrate too fast a growth. It is very important to get new
growth curves for normal dogs fed restricted levels of food from weaning up
to 6 months of age.

Worming

The first worming of the puppies can be done at an age of 18 to 21 days.
Thereafter, they are wormed every two weeks.

Vaccination

The first distemper and hepatitis vaccination should be done one week before
the puppy leaves the breeder. The second one is given 4 to 5 weeks later.
The vaccination is repeated every second year. If the puppies are living in
an area with little risk for distemper and hepatitis, they can be vaccinated
at 10 to 12 weeks of age with a new vaccination every second year.

Canine parvovirus infection is a new disease about which we are still learning. This is also true in our knowledge of active and passive immunity. A
number of research projects are going on all over the world in these fields.
The recommendations for vaccination may be changed with improved knowledge.
Today the breeders are advised to vaccinate their puppies one week before
transfer to their new owner, and to repeat the vaccination 4 to 5 weeks later.
The vaccinations can be done simultaneously with the distemper and hepatitis
vaccinations. Some failures with manifest disease in spite of vaccination
may be due to the individual variation in immunity after the vaccination
(Winters, 1981).

MORTALITY

A realistic parameter of success in dog breeding is the registration of the
neonate puppy mortality. Table 2 demonstrates statistics available (Mosier,
1981) and may be of guidance for veterinarians and breeders.

The registered pup mortality variation among breeders is great, depending on
breed, time of the year, and litter size. With good management, it is
possible to keep such causes of mortality as stillbirth, dystocia, trauma,
and exposure low.

It is of definite interest to discuss mortality of true or suspected genetic
background. With improved knowledge in the heredity of different conditions,
special breeding programmes can be established. If they are followed, the
frequency of conditions which influence mortality from birth up to weaning
age will decrease (Sandefeldt, 1972; Kock, 1974).

TABLE 2   Statistics Concerning Mortality
(Mosier, 1981)

Mortality of puppies born alive to weaning age
Anderson	29.4%
McCay	33.0%
Purina	11.9%
Pfizer (to 4 mo.)	33.0%
Rowland (to 2 mo.)	34.0%
Morris	16.0%

Percent of deaths by age from birth to 6 weeks
Birth	37.0%
First week	28.1%
Second week	10.0%
Third week	6.1%
Fourth week	4.7%
Fifth week	14.1%

Cause of death
Stillbirth	15.0%
Dystocia	11.0%
Trauma or crushing	13.0%
Exposure	16.0%
Disease	10.0%
Undetermined	9.0%
Accidents	6.0%
Weak puppies	5.0%
Cannibalism	3.0%
Lactation failure	4.0%
Parasites	3.0%
Excessive licking	3.0%
Deformity	2.0%

REFERENCES

Baines, F. M. (1981). J. small Anim. Pract., 22, 555-578.
Björck, G., B. Olsson and S. Dyrendahl (1957). Nord. Vet. Med., 9, 285-304.
Björck, G., and A. Hedhammar (1981). Rapport, Information from Doggy-Foder,
    5, 4-5.
Breazile, J. E. (1978). In J. E. Mosier (Ed.) Veterinary Clinics of North
    America, 8, 31-45.
Campbell, W. E. (1975). Behaviour Problems in Dogs. Am. Vet. Publ. Inc.,
    Santa Barbara, California. pp. 133-178.
Collins, D. R. (1973). The Collins Guide to Dog Nutrition. Howell Book House,
    Inc., New York, N.Y. pp. 199-222.
Cornell Research Laboratory for Diseases of Dogs (1974). Neonatal Puppy
    Mortality. Lab. Report Series 2, No. 4.
Crighton, G. W. (1968). J. small Anim. Pract., 9, 463-472.
Freak, M. J. (1968). In M. W. Fox (Ed.) Abnormal Behavior in Animals. W. B.
    Saunders, Philadelphia, Penn. pp. 464-475.
Hedhammar, A., F. M. Wu, L. Krook, H. F. Schryver, A. de Lahunta, J. P. Whalen,
    F. A. Kallfelz, E. A. Nunez, H. F. Hintz, B. E. Sheffy, and G. D. Ryan
    (1974). Cornell Vet., 64, Suppl. 5.
Kendall, P. T. (1978). Pedigree Digest, 5, No. 4, 6-7.

Kirk, R. W., and S. J. Bistner (1969). Handbook of Veterinary Procedures and Emergency Treatment. W. B. Saunders, Philadelphia, Penn.

Kock, E. (1974). Retinal Dysplasia. Thesis, Stockholm.

Mapletoft, R. J., A. P. Schutte, R. I. Coubrough, and R. J. Kühne (1974). J. South Afr. Vet. Ass., 45, 183–189.

Mosier, J. E. (1978). Veterinary Clinics of North America, 8, 79–100.

Mosier, J. E. (1981). Proc. Am. Anim. Hosp. Ass. Ann. Meeting, Atlanta, Georgia. pp. 339–347.

Nelson, W. (1982). Personal communication.

Sandefeldt, E., J. F. Cummings, A. de Lahunta, G. Björck, and L. Krook (1973). Cornell Vet., 63, Suppl. 3.

Sheffy, B. E. (1957). Gaines Vet. Symp., 9–11.

Sheffy, B. E. (1978). In J. E. Mosier (Ed.) Veterinary Clinics of North America, 8, 7–29.

Strasser, H., and W. Schumacher (1968). J. small Anim. Pract., 9, 603–612.

Suter, M. (1977). Time dependent decreases of maternal canine virus antibodies in newborn pups. Thesis, Zürich.

Winters, W. D. (1981). Vet. Rec., 108, 295–299.

Feeding and Care of Kittens

S. E. Blaza and G. G. Loveridge

Animal Studies Centre, Freeby Lane, Waltham-on-the-Wolds, Melton
Mowbray, Leics., UK

ABSTRACT

This paper considers the factors which limit normal growth and development
in kittens. Particular emphasis is given to nutrition and feeding, and to
the management of disease in both large colonies and one cat households.

KEYWORDS

Kittens; nutrition; feeding; vaccination; husbandry; disease.

INTRODUCTION

The purpose of this paper is to review the factors which interfere with the
successful rearing of kittens and to indicate the areas in which careful
husbandry, in its most general sense, can eliminate or reduce these risks.
Although our experience is largely of cats living in colonies, the problems
are those which apply to individual litters, greatly multiplied. The average
cat breeder or boarding cattery owner, with one or two litters at a time,
falls between the extremes of large colonies and individual cat households.

There are many factors which influence the health and growth of kittens.
These include nutrition, disease, general care, congenital abnormality and
degree of maternal care. The two latter will not be considered here as we
will assume that careful selection has eliminated genetic abnormality and
that observation has identified those queens which make poor mothers.
Similarly, the rearing of orphan kittens will not be covered as this is a
specialist topic requiring more detail than is possible in this paper.

NUTRITION

Some thought should be given to the nutrition of kittens even before weaning
begins. The milk of the domestic cat is apparently more concentrated than
that of the cow, and is particularly high in protein (Widdowson, 1964). The
ability of the queen to produce a sufficient quantity of milk of a suitable

composition depends in part on her own nutritional status; it is important
that she is in good condition when mated and that a palatable, balanced diet
is offered through pregnancy and lactation. Most cats regulate intake well
and can be allowed to determine their own level by ad libitum feeding.
Kittens which are adequately fed by the queen are likely to be warm and quiet,
whereas those receiving insufficient milk may be noisy and cold with individuals isolated from the rest of the litter. It is important to determine at
an early stage whether this is the result of an inadequate dietary regime for
the mother, or some other cause which may require veterinary attention.

At three to four weeks of age the kittens should be starting to show interest
in soft and palatable solid food and weaning can begin. The most simple
method is to offer food in a very shallow dish which the kittens can reach
and to encourage the kittens to lap at it. Gradually they will take more
solid food and demand less from the queen, allowing her to decrease milk
production to match demand. Weaning should be completed by eight weeks.

The ideal situation is one in which the kittens are weaned on to the food
which will form their diet until fully grown. Any food intended for kittens
must meet certain criteria. Not only must nutrients be present in the food
in the appropriate proportions, but the food must be sufficiently energy and
nutrient dense to allow the nutrient requirements to be satisfied without
the consumption of excessive bulk. Queens' milk has an energy density of
142 kcal/100g which is very high compared with cows' milk at 65 kcal/100g
(Widdowson, 1974; McCance and Widdowson, 1978). An ideal weaning food would
be of a similar energy density. At weaning the kitten requires approximately
250 kcal/kg bodyweight, compared with 60-85 kcal/kg bodyweight required by a
fully grown cat (Miller and Allison, 1958); therefore its energy intake, in
relation to bodyweight is three to four times that of an adult cat. In
addition to being concentrated, food for kittens must have high digestibility
and availability of nutrients to allow maximum benefit to be gained from a
reasonable level of intake. Further, it needs to have a smell and taste
which encourages the kitten to eat and a texture which makes this possible.
'Poor nutrition' of kittens can therefore be the result of either inadequate
provision of nutrients, or inadequate intake of a food which may be
nutritionally satisfactory but which is indigestible, insufficiently palatable
or too dilute. Unfortunately, the initial symptoms of a single nutrient
imbalance (inappetance, poor growth) are also those associated with an
inadequate level of intake for these other reasons.

The cat requires the nutrients needed by other monogastric mammals including
protein (for amino acids and as glucose precursors), fat (for essential fatty
acids and as an energy source), minerals and vitamins. Although it probably
has no absolute requirement for carbohydrate, the cat is able to make good
use of it. In addition to these general requirements, the cat has some
further unique needs. For example, it requires the aminosulphonic acid,
taurine (Rabin, Hayes and Berson, 1973; Hayes, Carey and Schmidt, 1975).
The cat is also thought to need a preformed source of arachidonic acid
(Rivers, Sinclair and Crawford, 1975) and preformed sources
of vitamin A (Gershoff, Andrus, Hegsted and Lentini, 1957) and niacin
(Da Silva, Fried and de Angelis, 1952), all of which other mammals can
synthesise in part from other components of the diet. It is also thought
that the cat has an unusually high protein requirement, probably because of
limited ability to regulate the activity of transaminases and urea cycle
enzymes (Rogers, Morris and Freedland, 1977). These special requirements,
which are covered in detail in the National Research Council's 'Nutrient
requirements of cats' (1978), mean that any practical diet for cats must
contain material of animal origin.

Specialist kitten foods are designed to meet all these criteria but these foods are not available in every country. Some canned cat foods are formulated to meet the requirements of cats at all stages of the life cycle and these are also suitable. Other cat foods may be appropriate if they meet the above criteria, with or without supplementation. If there is any doubt, the manufacturers should be able to provide information on the nutrient content of their foods to allow some assessment of their suitability. If home-made diets are used, careful attention should be paid to the nutritional content. It is a common misapprehension that since the cat is an obligatory carnivore it will thrive on a diet composed entirely of muscle meat. This takes no note of the wild cat's habit of eating the whole of its prey, including gut and bone. Although fresh meat is useful as part of a diet, alone it provides little except protein of a high quality, and some minerals and vitamins.

Careful thought should be given to the vitamin content of the diet if materials are used which have been preserved by cooking. This is because many vitamins are heat labile and cooking will therefore reduce the vitamin content considerably. However, indiscriminate vitamin supplementation should be avoided, particularly of fat soluble vitamins, as these accumulate in the fatty tissues and may reach toxic levels. For example, hypervitaminosis A is still seen in cats (de Vries, Aalfs, Goedegeburre, 1974; Gialamas, 1977), often as a direct result of excessive feeding of liver which is a very concentrated source of vitamin A. Ideally, the liver content of the diet should be restricted to 10-20% (de Vries and others, 1974). Similarly milk is an excellent source of most nutrients, but some kittens (particularly Siamese) lose the ability to digest the milk sugar, lactose, and experience severe diarrhoea when milk is fed; and even cats which tolerate milk may not be able to handle large quantities effectively.

Some consideration should be given to the 'anti-nutritional factors' present in some foods, which may interfere with the digestion, absorption or utilisation of nutrients. For example, some raw fish contains the enzyme thiaminase which destroys vitamin B1 (Smith and Proutt, 1944). Fortunately thiaminase is heat labile, therefore any fish which is cooked while still fresh should not be affected. Similarly, avidin (found in raw egg white) forms a stable, inactive complex with the vitamin biotin, making it unavailable to the body and eventually resulting in biotin deficiency (Carey and Morris, 1975). Again cooking alleviates the problem.

There are many pitfalls associated with feeding home-made diets. Cooking of the food will on the one hand aid preservation and eliminate the problems of thiaminase, avidin and the availability of carbohydrate from starch - but on the other hand will substantially reduce the content of the heat-labile vitamins. Thus, although some vitamin and mineral supplementation may be required, great care should be taken to ensure that oversupplementation does not result. The use of a wide variety of materials, including meat, liver, milk, fish (fresh and canned), fat or oil, eggs, cheese, and some cereal reduces the possibility of specific deficiencies, but particular attention should be given to the high protein and energy levels required by growing kittens.

For most cats, but particularly young kittens, feeding to appetite in several small meals a day is the optimum regime. Domestic cats tend not to be meal feeders, but return frequently to their food throughout a 24-hour period (Mugford and Thorne, 1980). If unlimited access is not convenient, the food should be made available for as long periods as possible. With difficult feeders, intake may be improved if the food is offered at body temperature, and in any case refrigerated food should not be given until it has been

allowed to reach room temperature. Kittens suffering from respiratory disease
will usually respond better to a food which has a very strong smell, such as
fish. Finally, fresh water should be available at all times: this is
essential, particularly when food of a low moisture content is fed, but is
easily overlooked.

HUSBANDRY

The Concise Oxford Dictionary gives a definition of husbandry as 'careful
management'. This covers the many different aspects of husbandry, from
feeding and general care to the eradication of parasites and disease. Although
in terms of care, kittens have very simple needs for warmth and shelter, the
management of disease and parasites can be rather difficult, particularly
where groups of kittens are concerned.

A recent article in the British Veterinary Journal, entitled 'Neonatal
diseases of dogs and cats' concluded that 'in general the neonatal kitten is
subjected to similar hazards as the neonatal puppy' although conceding that
very little was known of the causes of mortality in kittens (Fisher, 1982).
For example, although hypothermia appears to be a problem in very young
puppies there is little reported of this condition in unweaned kittens. Both
puppies and kittens can be regarded as facultative homeotherms in that they
will move along a thermal gradient towards a heat source (Crighton, 1968;
Olmsteade, 1979). Thermoregulation is not fully developed in the kitten until
approximately 45 days after birth, and is particularly poor until 14 days, so
this behavioural regulation is important in keeping the kittens close to the
ideal heat source, their mother. In general, an ambient temperature of $18-25^{o}$C
should be quite satisfactory for kittens before weaning, and even lower
temperatures are acceptable as the kitten matures.

Other aspects of general care which should be considered after weaning include
provision of a sleeping area (bed or box) and somewhere, away from the feeding
area, where the kitten can defaecate and urinate. Some stimulation, in the
form of toys, is desirable especially if kittens are housed alone. In family
accommodation attention should be paid to areas where the kitten might suffer
physical trauma through falling, being trapped, etc.

Although these aspects of care are important, they are secondary to the problems
of disease control. Table 1 shows the striking improvements in kitten survival
and growth in a cat colony which was kept free of respiratory virus and other
diseases when compared with a conventional colony on the same site where various
diseases (feline calicivirus, feline rhinotracheitis, feline infectious
peritonitis) were endemic. All other husbandry practices (feeding, cleaning,
etc.) were common to both colonies.

The control of disease is crucial. Where large colonies are involved, the
contagious nature of the diseases mentioned above makes it difficult to rear
a satisfactory proportion of the kittens unless disease-free cats are kept in
a barriered colony. While this is unlikely to be a reasonable proposition
for most cat breeders, there are several simple precautions which can be
taken to reduce the spread of disease. These fall into the two categories
of immunisation and hygiene.

Immunisation includes both a vaccination programme and also the transfer of
immunoglobins through colostrum. Failure to take in sufficient colostrum
increases the susceptibility to a variety of organisms, such as feline
panleucopaenia and feline respiratory diseases. It is useful to observe

kittening and ensure that each kitten suckles within the first few hours, reducing the possibility that individual kittens are deprived of colostrum. Feline leukaemia virus may limit the development of the immune system by causing thymic atrophy, and since infected cats remain carriers for the rest of their lives (Jarrett, 1976), it is essential to remove cats which have been exposed to the disease from any breeding colony and to screen thoroughly any newcomers. Vaccination programmes vary from country to country, according to availability; some programme should be evaluated and decided upon for each colony. The following programme using 'live' vaccines has been adopted at the Animal Studies Centre in a respiratory virus free colony.

Age	Route	Vaccination against
12 weeks	intra-nasal	FCV/FVR combined
12 weeks	intra-muscular	FIE (FP)
14 weeks	intra-muscular	FIE (FP)
16 weeks	intra-nasal	FCV/FVR combined

Key: FCV - feline calicivirus
      FVR - feline rhinotracheitis
      FIE - feline infectious enteritis (feline
            panleucopaenia)

The spread of disease and parasites can also be limited by various hygiene measures. For example, the changing of outer clothing such as overalls and boots is important when cats are housed in colonies, to avoid taking in parasites or disease from the outside world. In multi-cat households where kittens are at risk, the kittens should be housed separately from the other cats and handled first, after hands have been washed. Feeding utensils should be well washed and rinsed, or preferably disposable dishes can be used. Good ventilation is also important, particularly in colonies, where 12 air changes per hour is a reasonable target.

For cats housed in colonies or in homes, it is important that their accommodation is easily cleaned. There are many virucidal disinfectants available, but as Scott (1980) points out, these may not be effective against all viruses. He observed that sodium hypochlorite (household bleach) 'appeared to be the best overall virucidal product for routine disinfection or decontamination of cages, floors and food dishes in animal facilities'. At his recommended dilution of 1/32 (0.175% sodium hypochlorite), there should be no unpleasant odour, no ill effects on the cats (unlike phenolic disinfectants) and the major feline viruses (feline calicivirus, feline viral rhinotracheitis, feline panleucopaenia) are destroyed. Bleach can also be used to clean out litter trays after the removal and disposal of soiled litter. There are several commercial cat litters; if these are not available, sawdust can be used, provided this is dust-free and has been heat treated to drive off contaminants used in the wood treatment (e.g. cresols and phenols). Grass meal or corn cob pellets can also be used.

These are some of the steps which can be taken to keep kittens free from disease. Combined with suitable treatment (anthelmintics and ectoparasiticides) these hygiene measures should also control parasites which may weaken or debilitate a growing kitten.

Careful observation of the kitten's rate of growth and coat condition should give an early warning of any nutritional problem; early attention to symptoms

of disease and isolation of affected kittens together with hygiene practices
listed above, should reduce disease to a minimum.

TABLE 1   A Comparison of Kitten Survival and Growth in
Two Colonies

		Colony A[1]	Colony B[2]
1.	Birth to weaning		
	Survival (%)	65	98
	Mean weight (g)	502	770
2.	Birth to 6 months		
	Survival (%)	43	93
	Mean weight (g)	2030	2760

[1] conventional colony (n = 67)

[2] barriered, respiratory virus-free colony (n = 197)

REFERENCES

Carey, C. J. and J. G. Morris (1975). J. Anim. Sci., 41, 309.
Carvalho da Silva, A., R. Fried, and R. C. de Angelis (1952). J. Nutr., 46,
399-409.
Crighton, G. W. (1968). J. small Anim. Pract., 9, 463-472.
Fisher, E. W. (1982). Br. Vet. J., 138, 277-284.
Gershoff, S. N., S. B. Andrus, D. M. Hegsted and E. A. Lentini (1957).
Lab. Invest., 6, 227-240.
Gialamas, J. (1977). Zentralblatt für Veterinärmedizin, 24, 160-176.
Hayes, K. C., R. E. Carey and S. Y. Schmidt (1975). Science, 188, 949-951.
Jarrett, O. (1975). J. small Anim. Pract., 16, 409-413.
Jarrett, O. (1976). Pedigree Digest, 3, 11-12.
Miller, S. A. and I. B. Allison (1958). J. Nutr., 64, 493-501.
Mugford, R. A and C. J. Thorne (1980). Comparative studies of meal patterns
in pet and laboratory housed dogs and cats. In R. S. Anderson (Ed.),
Nutrition of the Dog and Cat, Pergamon Press, Oxford. pp. 3-14.
National Research Council (1978). Nutrient requirements of cats. No. 13 in
series 'Nutrient requirements of domestic animals'. National Academy of
Sciences, Washington, D.C.
Olmstead, C. E., J. R. Villablanca, M. Torbiner and D. Rhodes (1979).
Physiology and Behaviour, 23, 489-495.
Paul, A. A. and D. A. T. Southgate (1978). The Composition of Foods. H.M.S.O.,
London.
Rabin, A. R., K. C. Hayes and E. L. Berson (1973). Invest. Ophthalmol., 12,
694-704.
Rivers, J. P. W., A. J. Sinclair and M. A. Crawford (1975). Nature, 258,
171-173.
Rogers, Q. R., J. G. Morris and R. A. Freedland (1977). Enzyme, 22, 348-356.
Scott, F. W. (1980). Am. J. Vet. Res., 41, 410-414.
Smith, D. C. and L. N. Proutt (1944). Proc. Soc. Exp. Biol. Med., 56, 1.
de Vries, H. W., R. H. G. Aalfs and S. A. Goedegebuure (1974). Tijdschrift
voor Diergeneeskunde, 99, 315-322.
Widdowson, E. M. (1974). In O. Graham-Jones (Ed.), Canine and Feline
Nutritional Requirements. pp 9-17.

FOODS AND THEIR DIGESTIBILITY

Optimal Regimens Based on Recipes for Cooking in Home or Hospital or on Proprietary Pet Foods

D. S. Kronfeld

School of Veterinary Medicine, University of Pennsylvania, Kennett Square, Philadelphia, PA, USA

ABSTRACT

An optimal regimen consists of a balanced diet and suitable feeding management. A balanced diet should contain optimal ranges of proportions of energy and nutrients. These ranges are broad for undemanding situations, e.g. maintenance but becomes narrower for more demanding situations, e.g. growth or stress. Thus, dietary systems are needed that allow variation of concentrations of energy and nutrients. Any such system should be flexible, safe, convenient, and cost effective relevant to the performance desired of the animal. Two systems are described. One system involves cooking. It is equally effective in home, commercial kennel or animal hospital. It employs volume measurements of common feedstuffs (meat, rice, bran) and a basal supplement (liver, bone meal, corn oil, iodised salt). The Basic Recipe is for maintenance of dogs. The Meaty Recipe is for maintenance of cats and above-maintenance conditions of dogs. Basic is easily modified for high fibre, low salt, low phosphorus, low protein, low fat, and low purine diets. The other system uses proprietary pet foods. It involves mixing dry food - predominantly grain, with canned food - predominantly meat and meat by-products. The less expensive food predominates in the less demanding situations, the more expensive food in more demanding situations. Both of these feeding systems are described in relation to breeding and growing.

KEYWORDS

Diet; ration; nutrient requirements; minimal requirements; optimal requirements; petfoods; meat; grain; rice; bran; feeding management; breeding; gestation; lactation; weaning; growing.

INTRODUCTION

An optimal regimen consists of a balanced diet and appropriate management. The feeding routine should integrate with all aspects of husbandry. Most good diets (composition of food) are too palatable to be offered free choice, so the ration (daily intake of food by animal) should be decided by the manager. Tables are available that recommend daily intakes of energy and the main types

(dry, semi-moist and canned) of proprietary pet foods (Anon., 1974; Anon.,
1978). These figures relate to average energy requirements for maintenance.
Variation in maintenance requirements among pets is probably more like that
of humans (coefficient of variation about 15%) than farm animals (about 5%).
So the manager should adjust the ration to suit individuals and the desired
level of performance.

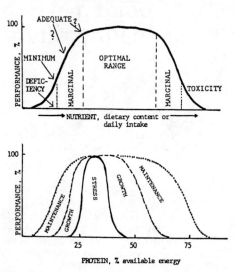

Fig. 1

Figure 1. The optimal range of nutrient intake is usually thought of as broad
because of an animal's ability to adapt, homeostasis. The upper figure is
re-drawn from Mertz (1981), with added indications of the <u>minimum</u> nutrient
requirement and the indeterminate word <u>adequate</u> used by the NRC (Anon., 1953,
1974, 1978). The lower figure concerned the protein requirements of dogs,
comparing optimal ranges for maintenance of adults, growth of pups, and stress.
The range is broad for the undemanding situation, but becomes more narrow as
nutritional demands increase. Ranges covering about 85% of maximal performance
are 15 to 65% for maintenance, 25 to 50% for growth, and 30 to 40% for the
stress of repeated exhaustive exercise. (These ranges are the best estimates
from available data; lower limits are better determined than upper.)

A balanced diet is one that is utilised with maximal energetic efficiency for
a particular purpose (Kleiber, 1961). Theoretically, only one set of proportions of nutrients may achieve the peak of efficiency. In practice, however,
nutritional methods determine ranges of proportions of nutrients. These ranges
depend not only on imperfections in methods but also on variability and
homeostasis in animals. It follows that the ranges tend to be broad in
undemanding situations and to become more narrow as demands increase.

An optimal range is illustrated in Figure 1. As the daily intake or dietary
content of a nutrient increases, beginning at a very low level, the index of
performance rises to a plateau, then falls. The plateau represents the
optimal range. The shoulders of the curve represent marginal zones that abut
on deficiency or toxicity. Given the shape of this curve, clearly determined
points of inflection are needed to determine minimal and maximal requirements,
otherwise these determinations would be arbitrary and best left to authoritative
committees.

NUTRITIONAL STANDARDS

Dietary standards have an interesting history of use and abuse (Truswell, 1981). The first standard was the least cost per head per week for food to avert starvation of unemployed during the English cotton famine of 1862. An American standard for food energy was devised to feed the army and the nation in World War 1. The British and the League of Nations developed minimal standards during the 1930s. Then the tone changed with the U.S. National Research Council's first recommendations in 1941 that aimed for "buoyant health ... the building up of our people to a level of health and vigor never before attained or dreamed of ...".

Less ambitious and more realistic was the NRC's first attempt to determine the nutrient requirements of dogs (Anon., 1953). It differentiated between maintenance and growth, recommending minima of 15 and 20% protein on a dry matter basis, respectively, and maxima of 84 and 77% carbohydrate. Thus it recognised the need for two diets. The word adequate was applied to its recommendations with the implication that an adequate requirement approaches the minimum; "additional information is needed if values closer to the minimum are to be established" (Anon., 1953).

The 1962 revision again recommended adequate requirements, but these were embodied in a single diet, with a 22% minimum for protein and an 80% maximum for carbohydrate. The 1974 revision retained the 22% protein minimum but deleted the carbohydrate maximum. The single set of nutrient requirements were claimed to provide "adequate nutrition of both growing puppies and adult dogs ... the nutrients required for the entire life cycle of all breeds" (Anon., 1974). One diet (composition of food on a dry matter basis) suffices, in this view, only the ration (daily intake of the diet by the animal) needs to be varied according to demands, e.g. for maintenance, breeding, growing or hard work.

Similarly, a single diet on a dry matter basis has been proposed for cats. It is 'presumed adequate to support maintenance and growth" (Anon., 1978). This adequate cat diet appears to be based mainly on studies of growth, so it may be more generally useful than the adequate diet for the dog.

The NRC recommendations for dogs and cats pay little attention to energy density and less to interactions among ingredients. The first traditional step in formulating a least-cost diet is to decide on the minimum protein content on an energy basis, the nutritive ratio. Let us assume that 30% is for hard work and stress in dogs or all conditions in cats (Table 1). The next step is to decide upon the energy density (energy/mass) which depends largely on the fat content by weight. Ironically, the optimal fat content of the diet is not well established for cats or dogs, except for hard work in dogs (Downey and others, 1980). Nevertheless, the decision about fat content also determines the protein content on a weight basis (Table 2).

Interactions among ingredients largely concern the adverse effects of starch, vegetable fibre, phytin and calcium on the efficiency of digestion and absorption. The mineral requirements for dogs (Anon., 1974), for example, relate well to meat-based diets but may be too low for diets based on cereal grains and soy beans heavily supplemented with calcium.

An unresolved dilemma about standards for dogs is the conflict between the broad ranges of nutrients found under experimental conditions and the narrower ranges preferred by competitive breeders of show dogs and racers. In one study, nine diets were rated equal and satisfactory even though protein ranged

from 20 to 48% of metabolisable energy, fat from 13 to 76%, and carbohydrate
from 0 to 62% (Romsos and others, 1976). Such broad ranges have little
utility when advising clients who seek high performance. Practical experience
of feeding dogs runs contrary to the scientific literature and suggests much
narrower optimal ranges, like those in Table 1.

TABLE 1 Tentative Guidelines for Optimal Ranges of Protein,
         Fat and Carbohydrate

	Metabolisable energy %		
Dogs	Protein	Fat	Carbohydrate
Maintenance	15-65	5-65	5-65
Growth, breeding	25-50	25-60	5-45
Stress*	30-40	45-55	5-25
Cats			
All conditions	30-40	45-55	5-25

* Stress is the general response of the body to any extra
  demand, physical or emotional. The degree of stress
  addressed here would be sufficient to induce anaemia
  (Adkins and Kronfeld, 1982).

TABLE 2 The Effect of Dietary Fat Content on a Weight Basis
         on Energy Density and Dietary Protein Content on a
         Weight Basis in order to maintain Constant Dietary
         Protein at 30% of Metabolisable Energy

Fat content % dry matter	Energy density kcal/gram	Protein content % dry matter
5	3.4	25
10	3.7	28
15	4.0	30
20	4.4	33
30	5.0	37
40	5.6	42

The discrepancy between laboratory data on dogs and widespread experience in
the field may arise from housing and social conditions and from the kinds and
sensitivity of observations. Laboratory studies usually have concerned body
weight and analysis of blood, occasionally other tissue or the whole body.
Dog fanciers look for body conformation and feel (saturation of subcutaneous
fat?), coat sheen and pliability, spontaneous activity, responsiveness to
training, and attitude to tasks such as guarding, herding, showing and racing.
It is wrong for the scientific investigator to dismiss subtle attributes as
intangibles, and to point to the absurd extreme of show-judging as evidence.
It is equally wrong for the dog fancier to scorn research on dogs as if they
are little pigs. The fact is that little pigs and other livestock and poultry
are fed various diets geared to performance according to recommendations of
the NRC and other authorities, but little dogs and cats are fed a single

'adequate' diet as if science does not know how to recognise and measure whatever constitutes performance in the eyes of pet fanciers.

In our studies of racing sled dogs, responses to diets have been compared in laboratory and field. The value of adapting the dog to a high fat diet during training has been demonstrated in both situations (Hammel and others, 1977; Downey and others, 1980). The red blood cell depression, presumably due to stress, that is prevented by a high protein diet, has been found only in the field (Kronfeld and others, 1977; Adkins and Kronfeld, 1982). The impression that a little carbohydrate in the diet improves 'feedability' or resistance to gastrointestinal upsets during introduction of the diet and during periods of severe stress (Dunlap, Adkins, and Downey, personal communication) has not been confirmed by comparative trials in the field or on the treadmill (Downey and Kronfeld, unpublished data). Our drivers remain convinced about the gastrointestinal benefit of a little carbohydrate despite the data. The non-significant results were obtained under conditions of insufficient stress, according to the drivers who are experts in judging stress. Overall these studies indicate that optimal diet for dogs subjected to hard work and stress should contain as much fat as possible contingent with the minimum protein needed to prevent anaemia and the minimum carbohydrate to confirm 'feedability'; the proportions are 51, 32 and 17% of metabolisable energy as fat, protein and carbohydrate, respectively (Kronfeld, 1982a).

Perhaps the only other optimal diets known for dogs and cats are their milks. Proportions are about 60, 30 and 10% of metabolisable energy for fat, protein and carbohydrate in the milk of the bitch, and respectively 40, 40 and 20% in that of the queen (calculated from data reviewed by Jenness and Sloan, 1970). The similarity between our optimal diet for hard work and stress and the analysis of bitches' milk is striking, especially when one considers that the protein quality of milk is probably slightly higher than that of chicken and pork lungs, and that the carbohydrate content of our diet is not determined well and could easily be lower.

RECIPES FOR HOME OR HOSPITAL

The traditional approach to diet formulation is to decide first upon the main energy source(s) or staple(s), for reasons of supply and economy, then to assemble a least-cost supplement that will make good any deficiencies for the particular purpose of the diet or desired performance of the animal. The main staples for dogs and cats, however, have similar deficiencies, so that a single supplement has been designed that is suitable for any combination of staples that includes at least one-third medium-fatty meat to ensure enough protein and fat (Kronfeld, 1978).

The second step in simplifying the system of recipes was the adventitious finding that equal volumes of dry rice and medium-fatty meat contained equal amounts of food energy, e.g. about 700 kcal or 3000 kJ in a standard breakfast cup that holds 8 fl. oz. or 240 ml. This amount of food energy is the average maintenance requirement of a dog that weighs 10 kg.

If rice or other similar grain for home use, such as pearl barley, is used, then cooking becomes very simple. The mixture is boiled. After cooling, it may be fed directly or refrigerated for a few days or frozen for longer periods.

The Basic Recipe consists of 2/3rds rice and 1/3rd meat (Table 3). Including the supplement (Table 4), it provides 750 to 800 kcal in proportions of 18%

protein, 27% fat and 55% carbohydrate on a metabolisable energy basis, and 1.4% calcium, 1.3% phosphorus and 0.5% sodium on a dry matter basis. It is suitable for the maintenance of adult dogs that are relatively inactive in comfortable surroundings.

The Meaty Recipe has the basic proportions of rice and meat reversed (Table 3). It provides 33% protein and 40% fat. It is suitable for cats in all conditions, for maintenance of small dogs, and for all dogs under demanding conditions, such as growth, breeding, hard work, stress and convalescence.

TABLE 3   A Basic Recipe of Meat and Rice for Maintenance
          of Dogs together with three Modifications for
          more Demanding Conditions in Dogs or all
          Conditions in Cats, for Body Weight Reduction in
          Dogs, and for Older Dogs

	Basic	Meaty	Reducing	Geriatric
Rice, dry	2/3*	1/3	1/3	1/3
Meat, medium fat	1/3	2/3	1/3	1/2
Wheat bran	-	-	2/3	1/2

* Measures are by volume; the numbers refer to standard breakfast cups (8 fl. oz. or 240 ml.) and are suitable for a 10 kg
  dog at maintenance.

TABLE 4   A Supplement for Mixtures of Rice, Meat and Bran (Table 3)
          that Combine to Provide 650 to 700 kcal or 2600 to 3000 kJ

Ingredient	Measures		Supplies
	grams	teaspoonful	
Liver	30*	6	Vitamins and trace elements
Bone meal, steamed	8	2	Calcium
Corn oil	5*	1	Linoleic acid, vitamin E
Iodized salt	3	1/2	Iodine

* Liver and corn oil each provide about 45 kcal or 190
  kJ, so this supplement provides 90 kcal or 380 kJ.
  the energy supplied by the staples and supplement
  approximates the daily average maintenance requirement of a 10 kg dog. It is enough for three days
  for most cats.

The Reducing Recipe substitutes wheat bran for half of the rice in the Basic Recipe (Table 3). The meat is lean instead of medium-fat. About four volumes of wheat bran are needed to match the energy of one volume of dry rice, so the replacement of 1/3rd cupful of rice with 2/3rd cupfuls of bran reduces the energy of the recipe by 15%. It provides 20% protein, 25% fat and 55% protein (energy basis).

The Geriatric Recipe exchanges wheat bran for some rice and some meat in the Meaty Recipe. It provides about 10% less energy than the Basic Recipe in proportions of 23% protein, 37% fat and 40% carbohydrate. Older dogs require more protein than young adults at maintenance (Kronfeld, 1982b). The bran promotes regularity which may not be necessary for the dog but comforts most clients.

The supplement comprises liver, bone meal, corn oil and iodized salt (Table 4). Liver accounts for 2 to 6% of the weight of animals, with little animals having relatively larger livers. Dogs and cats probably evolved on diets that probably included about 6% liver. This would supply enough of all the vitamins with the exception of vitamin E and possibly vitamin D for dogs and kittens. Similarly, liver is a good source of trace elements except iodine. The supplement supplies vitamin E in corn oil and iodine in iodized salt (Table 4).

Cooking is simple. The rice and twice its volume of water are placed in an uncovered pot with the bone meal, salt and corn oil and brought to the boil. The heat is reduced, the pot covered, and the mixture simmered for 20 minutes. The meat and liver are added, and the complete mixture is simmered for another 10 minutes. Cool before feeding.

Exchanges may be made in the staples to obtain many other diets that are occasionally desired in veterinary practice. Diets with reduced contents of protein, phosphorus and salt are discussed in the companion article on 'Nutrition and Kidney Function'.

A low-fat diet is obtained by replacing the 1/3rd cupful (about 90 g) of medium-fat meat in the Basic Recipe with 120 g lean meat, heart, or lean fish, with about three medium sized (50 g each) eggs, or with 300 g of cottage cheese. The 5 g of corn oil may be replaced by 3 g of safflower or sunflower oil. If it is necessary to leave out all fat and oil for a few days, remember that deficiencies of essential fatty acids are insidious and that some fat is needed for the absorption of fat-soluble vitamins.

All triglycerides are digested and absorbed well in normal cats and dogs. They enter the splanchnic lymph in the form of chylomicrons. Fatty acids of 12 or less carbons, on the other hand, are absorbed directly into the portal blood. The 'medium chain triglycerides' (carbons 8, 10 and 12) may be utilised in some conditions involving malabsorption of lymphatic abnormality.

A Bland Diet is obtained by using one cupful of rice dry, i.e. about two cupfuls of cooked rice. Cottage cheese, about one half-cupful, is stirred into the rice. This yields about 20% protein on both a dry matter and an energy basis. This mixture may be useful as an elimination diet for testing food allergies. It is deficient in fat and most micronutrients, however, and its use is not recommended for more than a few days. So the supplement (Table 4) should be tested in a few days. If the supplement proves allergenic, liver is the most likely allergen and should be replaced by a vitamin-mineral preparation that contains vitamins B_2 and B_{12} (which are often omitted). Most dermatologists will test foods that are likely to be allergenic in order to make a definitive diagnosis before seeking an allergen-free food. Alternatively, one may leave out the diagnostic testing and immediately seek non-allergenic foods. These are usually foods that are new to the animal, e.g. if it has eaten beef and maize, it is tested with turkey and rice.

Gluten is present in wheat, oats, barley and maize but not rice. Syndromes
in dogs that resemble gluten enteropathy, characterised by intractable
diarrhoea and multiple deficiencies, should respond well to mixtures of rice
and meat.

Low-purine diets are obtained by deleting meat and liver. Foods with a low
purine content include eggs, cheese and cereal grains. High purine contents
are found in liver, other organ meats, many fish, shellfish, and brewers'
yeast. In the medium range of purines are many vegetables: peas, beans,
asparagus, spinach and most greens. The meat in the Basic Recipe is readily
replaced by eggs and cheese. The replacement of liver is much more difficult;
it requires a vitamin-mineral preparation that contains vitamins B_2 and B_{12}.

PROPRIETARY PET FOODS

The three main forms are dry, semi-moist and canned. They differ primarily
according to means of processing and preservation. They also differ in
composition, i.e. ingredients and chemical analysis (Kronfeld, 1975), especially
the proportions of protein, fat and carbohydrate (Table 5).

TABLE 5   Representative Values of Available Energy and
          Proportions of Protein, Fat and Carbohydrate in
          the Main Types of Commercial Petfoods in the USA

	As fed kcal/g	Dry matter kcal/g	Available energy % Protein	Fat	Carbohydrate
Dog Foods					
Dry, general	3.4	3.7	25	25	50
Dry, puppy	3.5	3.8	29	27	44
Semi-moist	3.0	4.1	26	31	43
Canned mixed	1.0	4.1	35	35	30
Canned meat	1.3	5.0	41	52	7
Cat Foods					
Dry	3.7	4.0	32	42	26
Semi-moist	3.0	4.0	31	36	52
Cans, large	1.3	4.9	40	47	13
Cans, small	1.2	4.4	62	31	7

Some pet foods are formulated to supply sufficient of all essential nutrients,
i.e. to constitute the whole ration. Others are intended to form only part of
the ration, i.e. to be used as supplements or treats.

Petfoods also vary greatly in expense. Cereal grains are by far the least
expensive source of good food energy for dogs and cats, at least in the USA.
In this country, food energy costs about 5 times more in canned than in dry
dog food. The meat-based canned products, however, are the least expensive
source of supplementary protein (Kronfeld, 1982c). For the combined purposes
of economy, safety, convenience and flexibility in relation to the desired
level of performance of the animal, a system of mixing dry petfoods with canned
petfoods is recommended. Safety is ensured if each product is formulated so
that it could be used alone. Economy is achieved by using relatively more dry

food in undemanding situations. A higher level of performance is facilitated
by relatively more canned meat. The effect of using various ratios of dry to
canned foods is shown in Table 6.

Most cats and dogs fare fairly well on dry petfoods when at maintenance.
Nevertheless, cats should not be restricted to dry cat foods unless there is
no need to reduce the risk of urethral obstruction (Reif and others, 1978).
Also, dogs that retain potential for breeding or competition may benefit from
a small mixture of canned food into dry. This establishes a routine in feeding
management and a better adjusted starting point for improving the diet when
higher demands arise.

Comparison of Tables 1 and 6 suggests that even a small amount of canned meat
and meat by-products mixed with dry dog food (mixtures of 10:1 to 3:1 of dry:
canned, Table 6) should suffice for gestation, lactation and growth. More
protein and fat (mixtures of 1:1 to 1:3 of dry:canned, Table 6) may be better
for hard work and stress.

FEEDING FOR BREEDING

A bitch or queen who is a candidate for breeding should not be overweight.
If necessary, she should be reduced to medium condition well before mating.
She should also be up-to-date in health programmes for worming and vaccinations.
Both species have a gestation period of 9 weeks. The pregnant cat starts to
gain weight appreciably in 1 or 2 weeks, but the pregnant dog gains little
until about 6 or 7 weeks. The average bitch may increase her body weight by
35%, the average cat by 25%.

TABLE 6   Volumes (e.g. canfuls) of Dry Dog Foods and Canned
          Meat Dinner in Proportions Suitable for Various
          Levels of Performance or Nutritional Demand

| Proportions* | | Available energy % | | |
Dry	Canned	Protein	Fat	Carbohydrate
10	1	27	31	42
3	1	30	37	33
1	1	33	43	24
1	3	35	47	18

* One standard US can contains 140 to 180 g of
  dry dog food and 410 to 420 g of canned meat
  dinner.

A queen that is fed at least a 1:1 mixture of dry and canned food before mating
needs no change in her diet during gestation, only a progressive increase in
daily intake. As an initial guide, her ration should increase about 5% per
week, starting in the second week. In contrast, a bitch should be held to her
maintenance level of intake until 5 or 6 weeks of gestation, then the daily
itake increased about 10% per week.

The real metabolic challenge lies in lactation, so part of the feeding programme
during the last third of pregnancy is concerned with preparation for lactation.
In both species, the daily intake is divided into 2 meals from 6 weeks onwards.

Queens and small bitches have the proportion of protein and fat increased, changing to a 1:3 ratio of dry:canned by volume (equal parts on an energy basis) or to the Meaty Recipe. Large breeds of dogs may change to about 1:1, dry:canned. In this way the digestive and metabolic systems of the animals are completely adjusted to the diet before lactation commences, then the ration is increased only by increasing the daily intake of the diet without further change in the diet.

Appetite may be lost during parturition, perhaps 12 hours before. Any unconsumed food is removed. The animal is tempted from time to time with a little fresh food.

After she starts eating again she may need 2 to 3 times her maintenance intake. The peak should be reached gradually. She is allowed about one-half more than maintenance during the last 10 days of pregnancy, in two meals, and returned to the same regimen immediately after parturition for two or three days. She is then offered increasing amounts of food until given all she wants by the seventh or eighth day. This amount may be so large that three or four meals are easier on her than two. Overwhelmed digestive processes may be manifested as sloppy stools or diarrhoea. These signs suggest division of the daily intake into more meals or reduction of the intake. If the quantity of food must be reduced, the food quality should be improved at the same time, so that her intake of fat and protein do not decrease, i.e. less dry food is used with the same amount of a little more canned food.

Classical studies in bitches showed that milk production is greatly influenced by dietary protein (Daggs, 1931). The milk of a bitch or queen also contains much fat, so they should achieve their best genetic capabilities of milk production when fed a diet that contains abundant protein and fat.

FEEDING DURING GROWTH

Pups and kittens are often weaned at 6 weeks of age. Pups may benefit from another week or two with the bitch. Creep-feeding is recommended from 3 or 5 weeks onwards, offering a little canned food to the little ones beyond the reach of their mother. Creep-feeding reduces nutritional demands on the mother and helps the digestive system of the pup or kitten gradually adapt from the composition of milk to the post-weaning diet. This approaches 1:3 mixture of moistened dry food and canned food by 10 weeks. The ratio changes to 1:1 by the time the growing animal is about 20% of its intended mature weight.

For home-cooking, kittens and cats all receive the Meaty Recipe (Table 3), i.e. a 1:2 ratio by volume of dry rice to meat. Pups are creep-fed small amounts of meat then introduced to the meaty mixture about the time of weaning. They continue on this until nearly fully grown then change gradually to the basic formula (2:1, rice:meat) for maintenance.

No exact amounts of feed are prescribed. Instead, the client is told about adverse effects of underfeeding (poor growth, less activity) and overfeeding (diarrhoea, less activity, perhaps bone abnormalities in large breeds). Emphasis is placed on adjusting the ration every week to obtain the desired rate of growth, coat, bodily conformation and spontaneous activity.

At weaning, a pup of a large breed may weigh 5 kg and require a daily intake like that of a mature dog of 15 kg. By 4 months, it may be half-grown at 20 kg and require daily intake like that of its own expected mature weight, 40 kg.

When it is three-quarters grown, i.e. about 30 kg, its daily intake may be
like that of an adult which is 45 kg. So the level of intake is about 3 times
maintenance at first and gradually decreases towards maintenance. This
recommendation differs from the NRC (Anon., 1974), which is 2 times maintenance
throughout growth.

Daily intakes for kittens from weaning to 5 months follow a similar progression.
At 10 weeks, for example, a kitten should be fed about 30 g of dry food and
60 g of canned, or 120 g of canned alone.

The systems of feeding described in the article have operated smoothly in
several kennels that have been successful in showing or racing. They are not
claimed, however, to be exclusively superior or to be thoroughly reconciled
with nutritional science. As discussed above under 'Nutritional Standards',
more latitude is allowed by science than by the spur of competition.

REFERENCES

Adkins, T. O., and D. S. Kronfeld (1982). Can. vet. J., 23, 260-263.
Anonymous (1953). Nutrient Requirements for Dogs. National Academy of Sciences,
   National Research Council, Washington, D.C.
Anonymous (1974). Nutrient Requirements of Dogs. National Academy of Sciences,
   National Research Council, Washington, D.C.
Anonymous (1978). Nutrient Requirements of Cats. National Academy of Sciences,
   National Research Council, Washington, D.C.
Daggs, R. G. (1931). J. Nutr., 4, 443-467.
Downey, R. L., D. S. Kronfeld, and C. A. Banta (1980). J. Am. Anim. Hosp.
   Ass., 16, 273-277.
Hammel, E. P., D. S. Kronfeld, V. K. Ganjam, and H. L. Dunlap (1977). Am. J.
   clin. Nutr., 30, 409-418.
Jenness, R. and R. E. Sloan (1970). Dairy Sci. Abstr., 32, 599-612.
Kleiber, M. (1961). The Fire of Life. John Wiley & Sons. pp 1-455.
Kronfeld, D. S. (1975). J. Am. vet. med. Ass., 166, 487-493.
Kronfeld, D. S. (1982a). Feeding dogs for hard work and stress, in Dog and
   Cat Nutrition, ed. A. T. B. Edney. Pergamon Press, Oxford.
Kronfeld, D. S. (1982b). Compendium on Continuing Education for the Practicing
   Veterinarian (in press).
Kronfeld, D. S. (1982c). J. Am. Anim. Hosp. Ass., 18, 679-683.
Kronfeld, D. S., E. P. Hammel, C. F. Ramberg, and H. L. Dunlap (1977). Am. J.
   clin. Nutr., 30, 419-430.
Mertz, W. (1981). Science, 213, 1332-1338.
Reif, J. S., K. C. Bovee, C. J. Gaskell, R. M. Batt, and T. G. Maquire (1977).
   J. Am. vet. med. Ass., 170, 1320-1324.
Romsos, D. R., P. S. Belo, M. R. Bennink, W. C. Bergen, and G. A. Leveille
   (1976). J. Nutr., 106, 1452-1464.
Truswell, A. S. (1981). Proc. Nutr. Soc. Austr., 6, 9-20.

Nutrient Digestibility and Its Relationship to Alimentary Disorders in Dogs

H. Meyer

Institut für Tierernährung, Tierärztliche Hochschule, Hannover, Federal Republic of Germany

ABSTRACT

In healthy dogs mixed fats are highly digestible ($<$ 95%). High concentrations of calcium reduce fat digestion in high fat rations. Isolated fatty acids have specific effects on the alimentary tract (C4 - C12 fatty acids: reduced acceptability, laxative and sometimes emetic effects; long-chain saturated fatty acids: constipation). The faecal fat excretion in healthy adult dogs is - even during high fat intake - less than 0.3 g/kg BW/d.

Protein digestibility in dogs shows a wide range, depending mainly on source and processing of the protein fed. Proteins of plant origin are in general less digestible than proteins of animal origin, but with note-worthy exceptions: overheated animal proteins, fresh egg white, keratins, fresh bones fed in high amounts. Low digestibility proteins seem to be digested partly by enzymes of the intestinal flora, with increasing risks of intestinal dysfunction (loose stools, gas production, diarrhoea) particularly at high intakes.

The daily faecal crude protein output varies from 0.2 - 2 g/kg BW, depending on the kind and amount of protein fed. Unlike fats, this parameter does not give information about protein digestive capacity unless the amount and kind of dietary protein is known. For testing the protein digestive capacity of dogs, a meal of muscle protein is recommended. Independent of the amount fed, faecal crude protein output should not be higher than 0.25 g/kg BW/d.

KEYWORDS

Dog; fat; protein; digestibility; faecal excretion; compatibility to gut function.

INTRODUCTION

The digestibility of a dog food is important in two ways. Firstly, it gives information about the real value of the food with respect to its main components (energy, protein) and secondly, it is an indication of its compatibility with normal gut function. In the dog there is an increased risk of uncontrolled

bacterial activity in the alimentary tract after the intake of foods which
are resistant to breakdown by digestive enzymes. In the following survey
both aspects will be discussed in relation to fats and proteins.

DEFINITIONS: APPARENT AND TRUE DIGESTIBILITY

The apparent digestibility of a food is very easily estimated by measuring
food intake, sampling faeces and calculating the percentage of the food (or
its parts) which have not been excreted in the faeces (Table 1). Faeces
however contain not only undigested food material, but also the unabsorbed
parts of the secretions which are mixed with the chyme on the way through
the alimentary tract. For calculating the true digestibility we need figures
for the endogenous faecal excretion 'e' (see Table 1).

TABLE 1   Apparent and True Digestibility

Apparent digestibility % = $\dfrac{\text{food} - \text{faeces}}{\text{food}}$ x 100

True digestibility %   = $\dfrac{\text{food} - (\text{faeces} - e)}{\text{food}}$ x 100

In the above equation food and faeces represent weight
of dry matter, organic matter, protein, fat, etc. in food
or faeces. e = endogenous faecal excretion: amount of
endogenously secreted nutrient, which is excreted in the
faeces.

Calculated* difference between true and apparent digestibility

| | Digestibility % | | | |
| % fat or | Fat | | Protein | |
protein in diet	True	Apparent	True	Apparent
2	95	80	–	–
5	95	89	90	80
10	95	93	90	82
15	–	–	90	85
20	95	93.5	90	86
25	–	–	90	87

* assuming faecal endogenous fat excretion 50 mg,
  protein excretion 150 mg/kg BW/d, food intake
  20 g DM/kg BW/d

The amount of endogenous excreted fat or protein can be determined in different ways: for example by feeding fat- or protein-free rations, or by
regression analysis after feeding different amounts of the substance being
tested and extrapolating to zero intake. Both methods have their limits,
but in relation to the topic discussed below, we need only approximate figures
for the endogenous faecal excretion.

The endogenous faecal excretion of fat using fat-free rations was determined
by Sperry and Bloor (1924) to be 54 mg/kg BW/d. A similar figure (56 mg/kg BW)

was calculated by regression analysis (Fig. 1) using digestion trials in adult dogs with varying fat intake.

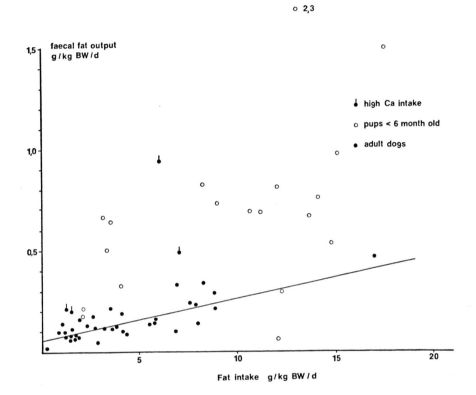

Fig. 1.   Relationship between fat intake and faecal fat output and
          the effect of high dietary Ca in dogs (For adults n = 65.
          r = 0.50***).   (From Göcke, 1970; Riklin, 1973; Drochner,
          1975; Meyer and others, 1978; Thomee, 1978; Meyer and
          others, 1979; Meyer and Mundt, 1982)

According to Allison and Wannemacher (1965), the faecal crude protein excretion in dogs fed protein-free diets is about 150 mg/kg BW/d.   By evaluation of older experiments with meat feeding, the faecal crude protein excretion during zero protein intake is only 75 mg/kg BW/d (Fig. 2).

As seen in experiments in other species, the endogenous faecal N excretion may vary in relation to bacterial activity in the hind gut.   Feeding a food with a low pre-caecal digestion of protein or carbohydrates may also lead to an increase of the endogenous faecal N excretion in dogs.

Assuming, under average conditions, an endogenous faecal excretion of fat and protein of 50 and 150 mg/kg BW/d respectively, we can estimate the difference between apparent and true digestibility (Table 1).   When testing foods or rations with low fat or protein content we get large differences between true

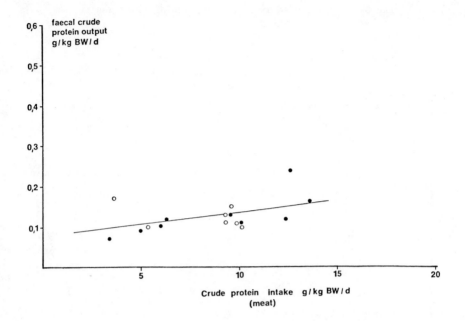

Fig. 2.   Relationship between crude protein intake (meat)
          and crude faecal protein output (n=16, r=0.48*)
          o - from Pettenkofer and Voit (1873)
          ● - from Muller (1884)

and apparent digestibility. Low digestibility figures under such conditions
are artefacts. In food with more than 10% fat or more than 20% crude protein
the difference is small and can be neglected.

Food is digested not only by enzymes produced by the animal, but also by
enzymes from bacteria. The compatibility of the food with normal gut function
is dependent on the extent to which it is broken down by these digestive or
bacterial enzymes. To differentiate these processes requires quite sophisticated methods and so results in this field are lacking.

            DIGESTION OF FATS

In adult dogs the apparent digestibility of mixed fats in general is very high.
In most experiments with fats of animal or plant origin the digestibility is
95% or more, independent of chain length and saturation of the fats (Table 2).
In healthy dogs the true digestibility of fats will be near 100%.

Over a wide range, the amount of fat intake does not influence fat digestibility.
In an experiment with adult dogs in which the fat intake per meal was increased
from 8.5 to 17 g fat/kg BW, the fat digestion decreased only from 94.4 to 92.1%
(Meyer and others, 1979).

Pups, too, have a high capacity for digesting fats. Suckling pups take up
about 12 g fat/kg BW/d, and digest the fat to about 99% (Thomee, 1978).

TABLE 2   Apparent Digestibility of Different Fats (%)

Tallow, cattle	94	Soybean oil, fresh	96
Tallow, sheep	93	Soybean oil,	
Lard	96	deep fried	93
Goose fat	98	Peanut oil	97
Fish oil	97	Linseed oil	97
Butter fat	95-97	Cotton seed oil	97-99
		Corn oil	97
		Olive oil	98
		Cocoa fat	97

See Meyer and others (1981)

Fats other than milk fat will also be digested to a high degree by pups 2 to 3 weeks old (Lloyd and Crampton, 1957).   There seems to be no influence of the length of the carbon chain or the saturation of the fatty acids on digestibility (Table 3).

TABLE 3   Apparent Digestibility of Fat in Pups
(about 2-3 weeks old)

Molecular weight of fatty acids	Apparent digestibility %	Iodine number of fat	Apparent digestibility %
260	98.2 ± 1.2	95	96.6 ± 5.9
260-285	95.8 ± 6.9	95-135	97.1 ± 1.9
285	96.5 ± 2.5	135	97.5 ± 1.3

In most investigations no interaction has been observed between fat digestion and degradation of other components in the diet (Schmitt, 1978).   The experiments of Heersma and Annegers (1948) demonstrated that a high protein and crude fibre content in the diet did not reduce fat digestion.   Magee and others (1954) reported that a substitution of starch for protein in a protein-free diet decreased fat digestibility.   They assumed that the protein intake led to higher pancreatic lipase activity.

TABLE 4   Digestibility and Faecal Fat Excretion in Dogs
Fed Different Amounts of Bone Meal

	Fat intake g/kg BW	Ca intake mg/kg BW	App. digest. of fat (%)	Faecal fat excretion g/kg BW
Low fat intake	1.25	160	81.5 ± 1.9	0.23
	1.22	672	83.9 ± 1.9	0.20
	1.08	1650	79.4 ± 1.7	0.22
High fat intake	8.22	169	95.7 ± 0.7	0.35
	6.97	675	92.7 ± 3.9	0.51
	5.92	2064	84.0 ± 2.5	0.95

Whilst most practical rations have a wide variety of fatty acids and in healthy dogs no difficulties arise in digesting the fat, some fats with a predominance of one fatty acid may lead to problems. According to Wikoff and others (1943 and 1947), small amounts of short chain fatty acids, such as butyric or caproic acid, reduce the acceptance of a diet and have laxative effects. Feeding less than 1 g/kg BW/d reduced faecal dry matter (Fig. 3). However, Lloyd and Crampton (1957) did not observe any adverse effects in pups fed rations containing butter fat. Their animals consumed nearly 0.35 g fatty acids/kg BW/d with a chain length of 10 or less.

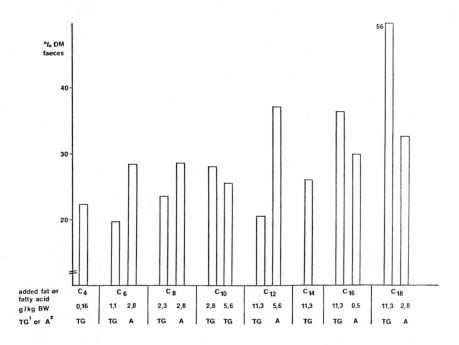

Fig. 3.   Influence of fatty acid chain length on faecal
          dry matter in dogs (from Wikoff and others,
          1943; 1947)

Fatty acids of the type C 8 to C 12 fed in moderate amounts have laxative and sometimes emetic effects (Wikoff and others, 1943; 1947). Because such fats are employed in rations for dogs with a pancreatic insufficiency, this observation is of practical importance. Mundt (1982) also reported that feeding more than 3 g fat per kg BW, containing up to 90% lauric and myristic acids, to healthy dogs or dogs with pancreatic insufficiency reduced feed intake and had laxative or emetic effects. Possibly these fatty acids retard emptying of the stomach. From the experience of Quigley and Meschan (1941) it is known that Na-myristic acid, for example, decreased the flow of chyme from the stomach to the duodenum.

Feeding only long chain saturated fatty acids presents other problems. Stearic acid or tristearin is poorly digested (Table 5). Wikoff and others (1943) cause constipation by feeding a diet with 20% stearic or tripalmatic acid. Furthermore, the faecal dry matter increased (Fig. 3).

TABLE 5   Apparent Digestibility of Different Fats and Fatty Acids

	%
Tristearin	11.3
Stearic acid	44.0
Na stearate or palmitate	88.5
Palmitic acid	75.2
Oleic acid	88.5
Na oleate	100.0

From Levites (1900); Lyman (1917);
Coffey and others (1940).

From the veterinary medical point of view, the question arises whether high
fat diets favour the incidence of pancreatitis. Some authors (Lindsay and
others, 1948; Haig, 1970; Goodhead, 1971) claim such a connection based on
their experiences with experimental diets. However, they used some rations
with extreme compositions, for example with a low protein content. On the
other hand, there are in practice no negative experiences from feeding rations
with 20-30% fat (Kronfeld, 1980).

In a feeding experiment lasting 3 months with 3 to 5 month old pups and a
daily intake of 8 to 14g fat/kg BW, we did not see any negative effects on
pancreatic activity, although in our animals the faecal fat excretion in
general was higher than that in adult dogs (Meyer and others, 1979).

In general, digestive disturbances due to high fat intakes in dogs are not to
be expected because wild carnivorous animals also take up high amounts of fat.
Pancreatic function may be disturbed primarily by other components in the
food, but the first sign of pancreatic insufficiency is a low fat digestion,
particularly during high fat intake.   Thomee (1978) recently investigated the
fat digestion in pups which had ingested large amounts of fat (more than 10g/
kg BW/d) from different sources (Fig. 4). With a commercial diet for pups,
the animals had chronic diarrhoea and the digestion of the fat, which had a
balanced composition of fatty acids, was relatively low. After a 4 week
feeding period one animal had a chronic pancreatitis, another an oedematous
pancreas. On the other hand, pups fed a self-mixed ration with wheat meal,
meat scraps, casein, soybean meal, alfalfa meal, and soybean oil and/or beef
tallow, had a high fat digestion and no symptoms of pancreatic insufficiency.
After these observations we may assume that the fats were not the cause of
low pancreatic activity, but other components in the diet. It is possible
that the amount of low digestibility carbohydrates in the commercial food
could have favoured the growth of an atypical bacterial population in the
alimentary tract leading to damage to the pancreas.

For diagnosing normal fat digestion and absorption, the daily faecal fat
excretion can be used. In Fig. 1 the daily faecal fat excretion in relation
to fat intake and age of the animals is summarised. In health adult dogs the
faecal fat excretion is, in general, lower than 0.2 g/kg BW and increases
during high fat intake, up to 0.3 g. Only by ingesting high amounts of fat
and Ca will the output reach 0.5 g or, at very high Ca intake, 1 g fat/kg
BW (Table 4).

In growing pups we see in general a higher faecal fat excretion, particularly
when ingesting high amounts of fat. Only during the suckling period or feeding
rations with a mixture of different fats was the faecal fat output as low as

in adult dogs. In the litter mentioned above (Thomee, 1978) fed the commercial diet the faeces fat excretion reached amounts which are typical of adult dogs with pancreatic insufficiency (Burrow, 1981).

animals n ration:	suckling pups 6 dogs milk	4 commercial diet for pups	6	weaned pups		
				4 wheat meal (24 %) soybean meal (8 %) + soybean oil (39 %)	4 meat scraps (6 %) alfalfa meal (4 %) + tallow (39 %)	4 casein (17 %) tallow (12 %) soybean oil (27 %)
intake g/kg BW/d						
crude protein	11.2	14.2	19.0	6.8	6.9	7.6
NFE	6.3	3.8	5.1	8.1	8.6	9.3
fat	11.9	13.0	17.5	10.6	11.0	12.2

fatty acids

Sonstige C 12
C 14
C 14 : 1
C 16
C 16 : 1
C 18
C 18 : 1
C 18 : 2
C 18 : 3
% weight   10   30 | 10   30 | 10   30   50 | 10   30 | 10   30

| fat digestion % | 99.0 | 82.7 | 90.6 | 93.8 ± 1.2 | 93.5 ± 1.4 | 97.7 ± 0.4 |
| faecal fat output g/kg BW/d | < 0.1 | 2.3 | 1.5 | 0.7 | 0.7 | 0.3 |

Fig. 4. Intake, digestibility and faecal output of fat in weaned pups fed different kinds of fat (from Thomee, 1978)

DIGESTIBILITY OF PROTEINS

As carnivorous animals dogs are assumed to have a high capacity for digesting proteins, but in fact the digestibility of proteins is quite variable, ranging from more than 95% for fresh meat to only 50% in treated feather meal. This large variation is related to the source and processing (cooking, heating) of the protein or the presence of other components in the food (low digestibility carbohydrates, fibre, trypsin inhibitors). The amount of protein fed seems to be less important, particularly in proteins of high digestibility (Table 6).

Of the proteins of animal origin, fresh muscle and casein reach a digestibility of more than 95% (Fig. 5). The next category of animal protein which includes liver, lung, milk, forestomach and egg yolk, has a digestibility of 90-95%, although the structures of the proteins are quite different. It is surprising that the proteins of milk and liver do not reach a higher digestibility than the protein of the stomach or lung with a high content of connective tissue. On the one hand carbohydrates such as glycogen or lactose, present in liver and milk, which stimulate bacterial growth in the chyme, and food nitrogen fixing may be responsible for this phenomenon. This could also be the reason why, for example, horse meat with the highest glycogen content has relatively the lowest digestibility of meat products. The high digestibility of connective tissue protein, on the other hand, may be partly due to additional degradation by bacterial enzymes. Unfortunately we have no figures about the pre-caecal digestion of this material in the dog, but there are some indirect indications

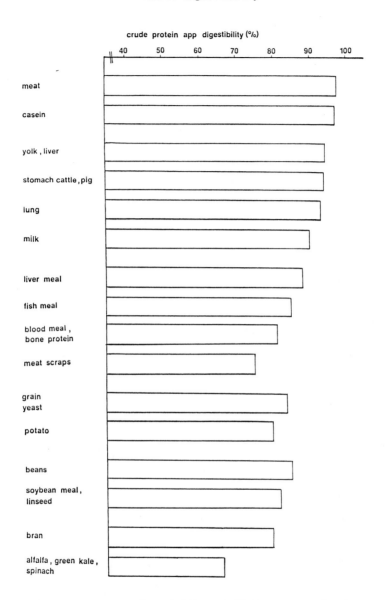

Fig. 5. Apparent digestibility of different proteins in the dog (from Schmitt, 1978)

TABLE 6   Protein Intake and Apparent Protein Digestibility

Protein intake g/kg BW/d	Protein source	Dogs	Apparent digestibility %
4.7	Canned food	Adult	86.5 ± 2.2
12.4			86.3 ± 0.5
4.7	Dry dog food	Adult	87.6 ± 1.2
7.6			87.6 ± 0.9
4.0	Slaughterhouse	Adult	90.8 ± 0.9
7.7	offals		93.3 ± 1.0
5.8	Casein	Adult	88.9 ± 8.2
17.0			94.5 ± 1.4
5.8	Slaughterhouse	Pups,	93.1 ± 1.6
7.5	offals	5-6 months	93.5 ± 2.7
14.4		old	93.1 ± 1.1
5.9	Fish & meat meals,	"	78.0 ± 0.8
6.5	milk powder,		75.9 ± 5.0
12.6	oats		82.7 ± 0.6

from Schmidt (1977); Meyer and others (1980).

that connective tissues will be degraded in part by bacterial activity.
Leibetseder and others (1982), for example, noted, after feeding high amounts
of connective tissue, an increase in ammonia and indican in the peripheral
blood (Fig. 6). In addition, we observed that feeding raw lung leads to a
soft, watery stool with low pH and gas production in the intestines. After
cooking, the protein digestibility increased and the unfavourable symptoms
diminished (Table 7). Cooking proteins of this kind (for example during
canning) increases their digestibility and reduces the risks of gastrointestinal disturbances.

TABLE 7   Effects of Cooking Lung on Faeces Parameters and
Apparent Protein Digestibility

	Uncooked	Cooked
Faeces		
dry matter %	18.2 ± 3.9	32.6 ± 8.8
pH	5.93 ± 0.28	6.40 ± 0.21
consistency	loose	firm
Apparent		
digestibility %	95.8 ± 1.5	98.5 ± 0.70
protein %	92.3 ± 1.1	

from Meyer and Thomee (1979)

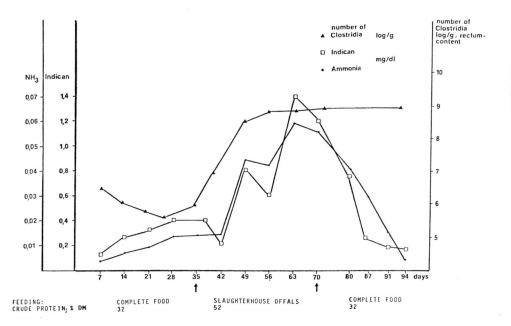

Fig. 6. Indican and ammonia content in the blood serum
and faecal concentration of Clostridium perfringens
after feeding rations with different amounts and
quality of protein (from Leibetseder and others,
1982)

Drying proteins of animal origin will in general reduce their digestibility
to 80-90%, sometimes even more (Fig. 5; Table 6) by formation of enzyme-
resistant compounds between the amino acids or, in milk products, reactions
between amino acids and sugars. The low digestibility of some fish meals or
dried meat scraps can be explained by such reactions, furthermore by their
composition (high percentage of indigestible keratins; see below).

In some proteins of animal origin specific situations arise. The trypsin
inhibitor in egg white, first observed by Steinitz (1898) and described in
more detail by Bateman (1916), may disturb the digestion of egg white and
induce diarrhoea. Because this factor is only partly inactivated by short
heat treatment (Morgan and others, 1951) large amounts of egg white, even as
heat dried material, has a limited value in dog rations.

The digestibility of the protein of whole or broken bones decreases with
increasing amounts fed, because the connective tissue protein is protected
by the mineral layer which is only partly dissolved under such conditions
(Meyer and Mundt, 1982).

Keratin cannot be digested either by the dog's own or microbial proteolytic
enzymes. Slaughterhouse offal may have high quantities of keratin from hair
or skin, which overestimate the protein values. The digestibility of keratin
can be improved by treatment with high temperature and pressure, but even

under these conditions only 50% of the protein was digestible (Drochner, 1977).
The use of such a low digestible protein does not, however, lead to digestive
disturbances, because keratin is also unavailable to bacteria. Protein of
plant origin has in general a lower digestibility than protein of animal
origin. Protein from grains or legumes is digested to 80-85%. Isolated
grain proteins such as glutelin or gluten have been reported to have a digestibility greater than 90%.

The reasons for the lower digestibility of plant proteins are less well known.
Doubtless the connection to plant fibre lowers their digestion (Fig. 7), but
the distribution of the values clearly shows that there are some other factors
which also influence plant protein digestion. In this connection the N fixing
by increased bacterial activity in the hind gut induced by fibre itself or
the presence of other carbohydrates with low degradation rates by the digestive
enzymes and a higher endogenous N excretion may play a role.

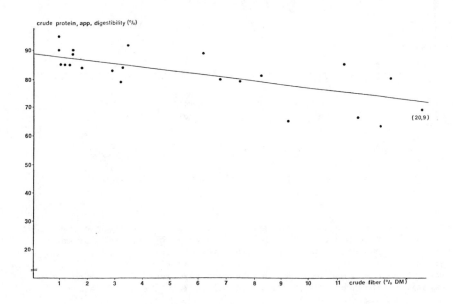

Fig. 7.   Relationship between crude fibre and protein
          digestibility in foods of plant origin in dogs
          (n = 19, r = 0.74**)(from Meyer and others, 1981)

Because of the relatively low digestibility of plant protein in dogs, the risk
of disturbances in the alimentary tract increases with higher plant protein
intakes. After feeding leguminous protein, a higher gas production or even
severe diarrhoea may occur. By feeding about 20 g soybean protein/kg BW/d,
Schmidt (1977) saw continuously loose stools or diarrhoea in dogs.

In the future it will be necessary to develop new methods to increase plant
protein digestion in dogs. Heating the proteins of plant origin seems to
increase their digestibility, but only to a small degree (Table 8).

TABLE 8   Apparent Digestibility of Plant Proteins (cooked
or uncooked, %)

Ration	CP %	% protein from *				Uncooked	Cooked	Diff.
		Rice	Oats	Corn	Soybean			
Rice	18.0	25		25	50	77.5	81.6	4.1*
Oats	22.8		30	30	40	78.8	82.1	3.3
Corn	22.5			60	40	77.0	78.6	1.6

* approximate, recalculated from Moore and others (1980)

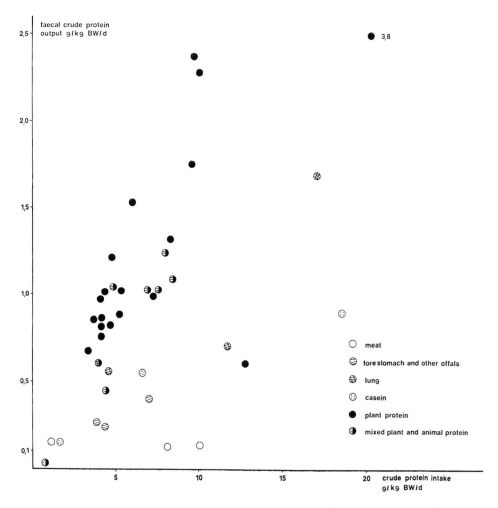

Fig. 8.   Faecal protein output in dogs fed different amounts
and kinds of protein (from Fig. 2 and from Mendel
and Fine, 1912; Morgan and others, 1951; Meyer and
Thomee, 1979; Kendall, 1980; Meyer and others, 1980;
Moore and others, 1980; Apel, 1981)

In contrast to fat, the faecal crude protein excretion cannot be used to
diagnose disturbances of protein digestion or absorption without knowledge of
the amount and kind of protein fed (Fig. 8). To test the protein digestion
capacity of a dog, therefore, a meat meal should be given. Independent of
the amount fed, the faecal crude protein excretion should be lower than
0.25 g/kg BW/d.

REFERENCES

Apel, U. (1980). Untersuchungen über Akzeptanz und Verträglighkeit protein-
    armer Rationen für Hunde. Vet. Diss., Hannover.
Allison, J. B., and R. W. Wannemacher (1965). Repletion of depleted protein
    reserves in animals. In W. H. Cole (Ed.), Amino Acid Malnutrition, 1-13.
    Rutgers University Press, New Brunswick/New Jersey.
Bateman, W. G. (1916). J. Biol. Chem., 26, 263-291.
Burrow, C. F. (1981). The assessment of canine gastrointestinal function:
    Recent advances and future needs. Proc. 31st Gaines Vet. Symp., 1-9. Gaines
    Dog Research Center, White Plains, N.Y.
Coffey, R. J., F. C. Mann, and J. L. Bollmann (1940). Am. J. Digest. Dis., 7,
    141-143.
Drochner, W. (1975). Kleintier-Praxis, 20, 218-221.
Drochner, W. (1977). Dtsch. tierarztl. Wschr., 84, 165-204.
Göcke, A. (1970). Uber die Zusammensetzung und Verdaulichkeit von Hundefertig-
    futtermitteln. Vet. Diss., Hannover.
Goodhead, G. (1971). Arch. Surg., 103, 724.
Haig, T. H. (1970). Surg. Gynecol. Obstet., 131, 914.
Heersma, J. R., and J. H. Annegers (1948). Am. J. Physiol., 153, 143-147.
Kendall, P. T. (1980). Unpublished.
Kronfeld, D. S. (1980). Feeding, nutrition, and gastrointestinal disorders.
    In N. V. Anderson (Ed.), Veterinary Gastroenterology. Lea & Febiger,
    Philadelphia. pp. 223-246.
Leibetseder, J., H.J. Flüsshoff, E. Forhnapfel, and B. Schärft (1982). Über
    den Einfluss hoher Bindegewebsgaben auf Verdaulichkeit und Kotflora beim
    Hund. Report, 14, 1-13. Effem Forschung für Kleintiernährung, Hannover.
Levites, S. (1900). Z. physiol. Chem., 3, 349.
Lindsay, S., C. Entenman, and I. L. Chaikoff (1948). Arch. Path., 45, 635-638.
Lloyd, L. E., and E. W. Crampton (1957). J. Anim. Sci., 16, 377-382.
Lyman, J. F. (1917). J. Biol. Chem., 32, 7-11.
Magee, D. F., K. S. Kim, and A. J. Ivy (1954). J. Physiol., 175, 310.
Mendel, L. B., and M. S. Fine (1912). J. Biol. Chem., 10, 439-455.
Meyer, H., W. Drochner, and C. Weidenhaupt (1978). Dtsch. tierärztl. Wschr.,
    85, 133-136.
Meyer, H., K. Daxl, and A. Thomee (1979). Dtsch. tierärztl. Wschr., 86, 215-220
Meyer, H., and A. Thomee (1979). Kleintier-Praxis, 24, 269-276.
Meyer, H., H.-C. Mundt, and A. Thomee (1980). Kleintier-Praxis, 25, 267-274.
Meyer, H., P. J. Schmitt, and E. Heckötter (1981). Ubers. Tierernahrg., 9,
    71-104.
Meyer, H., and H.-C. Mundt (1982). Unpublished.
Morgan, A. F., C. N. Hunt, L. Anrich, and U. F. Lewis (1951). J. Nutr., 43,
    63-75.
Moore, M. L., H. J. Fottler, G. C. Fahey, and J. E. Corbin (1980). J. Anim.
    Sci., 50, 892-896.
Müller, F. (1884). Z. Biol., 20, 327-377.
Mundt, H.-C. (1982). Unpublished.
Pettenkofer, M., and V. Voit (1873). Z. Biol., 9, 1-40.
Quigley, J. P., and I. Meschan (1941). Am. J. Physiol., 134, 803-807.

Riklin, M. (1973). Untersuchungen über den Einfluss von Strukturelementen im Futter auf Verdauung, Peristaltik und Kotkonsistenz beim Hund. Vet. Diss., Hannover.

Schmidt, M. (1977). Einfluss überhöhter Eiweissgaben auf die Verdauungsvorgänge sowie den intermediären Stoffwechsel beim Hund. Vet. Diss., Hannover.

Schmitt, P. J. (1978). Die Verdaulichkeit der für die Ernährung des Hundes einsetzbaren Futtermittel. Vet. Diss., Hannover.

Sperry, W. M., and W. Bloor (1924). J. Biol. Chem., 60, 261-287.

Steinitz, W. (1898). Arch. ges. Physiol., LXXVI, 75.

Thomee, A. (1978). Zusammensetzung, Verdaulich- und Verträglichkeit von Hundemilch und Mischfutter bein Welpen unter besonderer Berücksichtigung der Fettkomponente. Vet. Diss., Hannover.

Wikoff, H. L., J. F. Caul, and B. H. Marks (1943). Am. J. Digest. Dis., 10, 335-399.

Wikoff, H. L., B. H. Marks, J. F. Caul, and W. F. Hoffman (1947). Am. J. Digest. Dis., 14, 58-62.

Fibre in the Dog's Diet

J. Leibetseder

Institute of Nutrition, University of Veterinary Medicine, Vienna,
Austria

ABSTRACT

Because of anatomical and metabolic differences some of the diseases which
fibre apparently protects against in man are not generally recognised as
severe problems in the dog. Nevertheless dietary fibre influences digestion
in dogs as well as in man with physiological and pathological consequences.
Dietary fibre increases the rate of food passage and the amount of faeces,
reduces the number of bacteria in the faeces and improves faeces consistency.
The digestibility of some nutrients is changed by fibre either in a positive
or negative sense. Finally recommendations on fibre content in dog food are
given and the dietetic usefulness of higher intake of dietary fibre in some
diseases is shown.

KEYWORDS

Dietary fibre; digestibility; dog; recommended intake; dietetic effects.

INTRODUCTION

In recent years, a great deal of attention has focussed in the medical,
scientific and lay press on the role of fibre in the diet of humans. Much of
the interest in fibre for humans is derived from national and international
surveys where the frequency of numerous diseases has been related to intake
of food components including fibre. The functional action of fibre in the
gastro-intestinal tract is due to the physical properties of swelling,
adsorbing and ion exchange. The following diseases are stated to be a direct
consequence of a low fibre diet: constipation, appendicitis, varicose veins,
diverticulosis, large bowel cancer, diabetes mellitus, chole- and urolithiasis,
cardiac and circulatory diseases (Siebel, 1981). The range of mechanisms by
which dietary fibre can influence health is wide, and it is doubtful if any
one mechanism operates in isolation. The cancer protecting effect is probably
caused by the reduction of bioavailability of carcinogens taken in or
synthesised by the gut flora due to adsorption by the fibre and due to the
reduced gut transit time. Because of anatomical and metabolic differences
some of the diseases against which fibre apparently protects in man are not

generally recognised as severe problems in dogs. Nevertheless dietary fibre
influences digestion in general in dogs as well as in man with physiological
and pathological consequences.

TERMINOLOGY OF DIETARY FIBRE

The definition of the term dietary fibre is still a matter of continuing
discussion.

The term crude fibre was invented more than a hundred years ago as one of the
fractions of the proximate analysis and denotes the organic residue remaining
after plant material has been treated with dilute acids and alkali and
solvents. Hipsley (1953) used the term 'dietary fibre' first and stated that
it consisted of cellulose, lignin and hemicellulose. Trowell's definition
(1972) is the most widely used and accepted. He has defined dietary fibre as
remnants of plant cell walls which are not hydrolysed by enzymes of the human
alimentary tract. Today a more general classification is necessary because
some food additives must be included in the term fibre. Table 1 shows the
substances which are components of dietary fibre (Baker and others, 1979).

TABLE 1   Classification of Dietary Fibre Components

Source	Component
Plant cell wall	
1. Structural: Polysaccharides	Cellulose, hemicelluloses Pectic substances
Non-carbohydrate polymer	Lignin
2. Non-structural and food additives	Pectin, gums, mucilages, modified polysaccharides

Cellulose, hemicelluloses and lignin are the most important components in
dietary fibre. Most of the bound pectic substances are part of the fibre
fraction but free pectins are soluble and therefore not included in total
fibre. The inclusion of additives in the fibre fraction depends on their
solubility. The crude fibre method is unsatisfactory for this reason. The
demand for accurate estimates of dietary fibre has prompted investigations
of alternatives to the crude fibre method. The acid-detergent and neutral-
detergent fibre methods, and some enzymatic and fractionation procedures
were developed in the last twenty years. These methods produce more complete
data than the crude fibre method, but they are time-consuming and impractical
for routine analysis of large numbers of samples. Most of the published
fibre values are therefore crude fibre data.

The term dietary fibre is still not exactly defined and therefore confusing.
Trowell's definition is not entirely appropriate for dogs and appears
inappropriate for cats which consume much more roughage of animal origin than
humans. In this connection it should be pointed out that the type of dietary
fibre is characterised best by the method of its determination. In scientific
publications therefore the method used for determining fibre has to be
indicated always.

DIGESTIBILITY OF DIETARY FIBRE IN DOGS

The digestibility values of fibre in dogs show a great variation. In some investigations cellulose was completely indigestible (Knieriem, 1885; Scheunert and Löetsch, 1909; Thomas and Pringsheim, 1918), in other experiments 18% of cellulose of dried brewer's grains (Visek and Robertson, 1973), 25 to 30% of cellulose in wheat bran and paper (Rubner, 1916) and up to 80% of crude fibre in wheat, rice and boiled potatoes (Lössl, 1931) were digested by dogs.

Factors influencing the digestibility of crude fibre in dogs are:

   source of crude fibre (different content of cellulose, lignin, hemicelluloses, pectic substances, etc.);

   level of fibre in the diet;

   different grinding of the fibre-containing food components;

   methods of determining digestibility.

No mammal produces cellulase, but limited amounts of cellulose and some other fractions of dietary fibre can be digested by microbial fermentation in the large intestine. Van Soest and Robertson (1977) noted that the fibre fermenting bacteria were obligate anaerobes and were of a similar nature to ruminal or caecal microorganisms of herbivores. The main metabolites of the microbial fermentation are volatile fatty acids and gases, e.g. carbon dioxide. The volatile fatty acids produced by the microorganisms are probably not a significant source of the metabolisable energy in dogs.

BENEFICIAL EFFECTS OF DIETARY FIBRE IN DOGS

Some beneficial effects of dietary fibre in the digestive physiology of dogs are reported.

Gut Transit Time and Frequency of Defaecation

An increased intake of dietary fibre increases the rate of food passage through the gut. In an experiment to find out whether and in what quantity structural components are necessary in dog food, Riklin (1973) used increasing quantities (5, 10 and 15% resp.) of crude wood product containing 62.8% of crude fibre (28.6% lignin), given to a basic diet consisting of wheat flour, meat and bone meal, casein, soybean meal and oil. Three Beagles were fed all the different diets. The results are shown in Table 2.

In a collaborative study between the Animal Studies Centre and our Institute of Nutrition, adult Beagles and cats were given semi-purified diets containing 0, 5, 10 or 20% purified $\propto$-cellulose (solka floc) or the same diets with carrageenan, the extract of red seaweed consisting of linear galactans with a common backbone structure which is used as a gelling agent (Pedersen, 1974) (both purified $\propto$-cellulose and carrageenan provide 100% dietary fibre). In both species the amount of faeces was significantly increased with increasing intake of cellulose and carrageenan (Table 3).

TABLE 2 Influence of Crude Fibre on Defaecation and
Faecal Consistency (Riklin, 1973)

| | Diet | | | |
	A	B	C	D
Wood product (%)	0	5	10	15
Total crude fibre in diet				
(% in dry matter)	0.6	4.4	7.7	10.2
Beginning of excretion (hrs)	9-12	10-15	12-18	12-18
End of excretion (hrs)	60-69	44-48	34-38	48
Number of defaecations/day	1.7	2.9	3.7	4.3
Amount of faeces (g DM/day)	39.5	67.5	75.8	83.8
Water content of faeces (%)	75.5	74.1	71.5	70.9

The inclusion of 5% cellulose in dogs and 5 and 10% in cats had relatively
small effect on faeces outpout, whereas carrageenan was effective even at the
5% level.

The increased rate of food passage through the gut causes a lower number of
bacteria indicating much less microbial activity and undesirable metabolites.

TABLE 3 Effect of Dietary Fibre on Mean ($\pm$ Standard Error)
Daily Faecal Dry Matter Output (g) of 3 Dogs and
3 Cats (after Vock, 1982)

| | Dietary Fibre % | | | |
	0	5	10	20
Dogs				
Cellulose	$217^a\pm25$	$228^a\pm40$	$369^b\pm36$	$539^c\pm41$
Carrageenan	$195^a\pm19$	$337^b\pm29$	$410^b\pm6$	$789^c\pm40$
Cats				
Cellulose	$43^a\pm5$	$63^a\pm11$	$58^a\pm7$	$94^b\pm5$
Carrageenan	53 ± 5	109 ± 7	118 ± 30	112 ± 37

Means with shared superscripts (^{a,b,c}) were not
significantly different (p > 0.05)

Adsorbing Property of Dietary Fibre

The adsorbing feature of dietary fibre has two aspects: the adsorption of
microbial toxic metabolites and bile acids, substances which may be implicated
in the aetiology of some diseases, at least in man. These toxic substances
would otherwise have to be detoxified by the liver, thus promoting an overall
improvement in efficiency. Similar metabolic stress seems to be present in
dogs fed only with meat. The 'all meat syndrome' disappears if the diet is
more complex and contains dietary fibre. On the other hand dietary fibre
interacts considerably with various components of the diet and may inhibit
the absorption of essential nutrients like minerals which become less
metabolically available or it promotes excretion of nutrients, e.g. of lipids
(Furda, 1979).

INFLUENCE OF DIETARY FIBRE ON DIGESTIBILITY

The influence of crude fibre on apparent digestibility of nutrients is well
documented in domestic as well as in experimental animals. Riklin (1973)
and Vock (1982) studied this interaction in dogs and cats. Tables 4, 5 and
6 show the results.

TABLE 4   Effect of Dietary Fibre on Apparent Digestibility
          (%) (Riklin, 1973)

		Diet		
	A	B	C	D
Total Crude Fibre (% DM)	0.6	4.4	7.7	10.2
Apparent digestibility %				
Organic matter	90.6	82.2	78.3	75.2
Crude protein	79.0	79.2	84.0	85.2
Ether extract	92.8	94.9	95.9	95.7
Crude fibre	36.7	0.7	0.5	0.4
N-free extract	95.1	88.0	84.3	82.5
Energy	90.1	82.6	78.9	76.4

In Riklin's experiment, the correlation between crude fibre and digestibility
was significant for all nutrients (Tables 4, 5 and 6).

TABLE 5   Correlation between Crude Fibre and Apparent
          Digestibility (Riklin, 1973) (y = apparent
          digestibility, x = % crude fibre in the dry
          matter of the diet)

Nutrient	Equation	r	n
Organic matter	$y = 90.6 - 1.58 \ x$	-0.95	12
N-free extract	$y = 95.1 - 1.33 \ x$	-0.93	12
from basic diet only	$y = 95.1 - 0.88 \ x$	-0.81	12
Crude protein	$y = 77.7 + 0.72 \ x$	0.70	12
Ether extract	$y = 92.9 + 0.33 \ x$	0.82	12

In Vock's studies, the digestibility of all the nutrients for dogs and cats
was significantly reduced by carrageenan, whereas cellulose impaired the
digestibility of the N-free extract only in both species (Table 7).

TABLE 6   Apparent Digestibility of Minerals (%)(Riklin, 1973)

		Diet		
	A	B	C	D
Calcium	18.4	18.6	39.3	60.2
Phosphorus	37.0	37.6	59.4	79.0
Sodium	93.2	85.8	71.8	60.9
Potassium	92.2	90.6	91.7	93.2
Magnesium	25.8	17.6	38.6	65.2

TABLE 7   Effect of Dietary Fibre on Mean ($\pm$ Standard Error) Apparent Digestibility (%) Measured in 3 Dogs and 3 Cats (after Vock, 1982)

	Dietary Fibre %			
	0	5	10	20
Dogs				
Cellulose				
Organic matter	89.7^a ±1.1	$86.1^{ab}\pm1.3$	82.2^b ±1.4	73.5^c ±0.7
Crude protein	87.8 ±0.5	89.7 ±1.3	89.8 ±0.7	88.4 ±0.5
Ether extract	87.2 ±1.7	91.5_b ±2.5	88.7_b ±1.4	90.4 $\pm14.$
N-free extract	93.9^a ±0.8	77.5^b ±5.1	77.2^b ±7.9	44.3^c ±2.4
Ash	47.1 ±3.5	44.2 ±6.7	42.4_b ±5.0	45.3 ±9.3
Energy	89.1^a ±1.2	$87.5^{ab}\pm1.3$	84.7^b ±0.9	79.4^c ±1.2
Carrageenan				
Organic matter	91.0^a ±0.7	84.1^b ±1.5	$80.6^{bc}\pm0.9$	65.7^c ±4.1
Crude protein	89.3^a ±0.6	$86.8^{ab}\pm1.2$	84.6^b ±0.3	77.3^c ±1.0
Ether extract	88.8^a ±1.0	80.8^b ±0.7	77.9^b ±1.0	73.0^c ±1.6
N-free extract	94.7^a ±0.6	$84.0^{ab}\pm5.4$	80.9^b ±2.5	51.1^c ±4.3
Ash	51.9_a ±3.5	56.4_a ±4.3	49.9_a ±4.1	34.5_d ±9.6
Energy	90.4^a ±0.8	84.8^b ±0.6	81.8^c ±0.5	69.8^d ±4.3
Cats				
Cellulose				
Organic matter	86.3^a ±2.2	80.7^a ±2.9	$77.8^{ab}\pm3.1$	68.3^b ±2.7
Crude protein	84.7 ±3.2	86.5 ±3.3	86.4 ±2.0	87.6 ±0.1
Ether extract	80.3 ±3.1	80.1_b ±2.0	80.4_b ±4.2	82.3 ±3.6
N-free extract	94.9^a ±0.6	77.2^b ±4.0	68.6^b ±2.8	38.9^c ±8.4
Ash	42.1 ±5.1	35.0 ±5.9	39.3_a ±11.3	18.4_b ±9.9
Energy	84.2^a ±2.7	83.1^a ±1.7	$79.9^{ab}\pm3.3$	73.3^b ±1.5
Carrageenan				
Organic matter	86.2^a ±0.2	77.2^b ±2.7	70.6^b ±1.4	57.0^c ±1.0
Crude protein	85.6^a ±1.2	82.3^a ±0.7	$75.0^{ab}\pm5.9$	77.2^b ±1.1
Ether extract	78.2^a ±0.8	$68.2^{ab}\pm6.4$	$60.3^{ab}\pm11.3$	54.5^b ±4.0
N-free extract	96.1^a ±0.7	84.3^b ±1.1	63.2^c ±2.0	41.8^d ±4.4
Ash	46.1_a ±3.0	56.0_a ±3.6	52.2_a ±11.9	46.1_b ±6.8
Energy	83.7^a ±0.5	75.5^a ±4.1	$64.8^{ab}\pm9.4$	61.7^b ±2.3

Means with shared superscripts $(^{a,b,c})$ were not significantly different ($p > 0.05$)

DIETETIC EFFECTS OF DIETARY FIBRE

In contrast to man, fibre is largely irrelevant for dogs and cats with respect to protection against abdominal and colonic diseases. Fibre could, however, help prevent constipation in dogs. The main benefit of increased fibre intake is to protect dogs against, or be used in the treatment of metabolic diseases, such as obesity and diabetes mellitus. In obesity the significant reduction of the availability of food energy is essential. By analogy with studies in man, diabetes and increased dietary fibre intake would appear to exert a positive influence in the management of diabetes in dogs by reducing the rate of the post-prandial glucose absorption and consequently the plasma glucose concentration and animal's requirement for insulin.

CONCLUSION

The carnivores, the dog and the cat, need a certain amount of structural, bulky indigestible components in their food. Dietary fibre improves some of the digestive processes such as frequency of defaecation, consistency of faeces, digestibility of crude protein and ether extract. It is difficult to indicate the optimum concentration in the complete food, but about 5% dietary fibre in the dry matter seems to be adequate. Higher concentrations are well tolerated but increase the amount of faeces and the number of defaecations. For dietetic purposes 10 to 15% of dietary fibre can be used for obese or diabetic dogs, remembering that increased Na requirement due to the higher faecal Na losses. In summarising the possible nutritional implications of adding dietary fibre to dog and cat food, some points need to be taken into account. First of all it is important to differentiate between the types of dietary fibres. Improper definition of the fibre and insufficient consideration of the interactions of fibres with other nutrients has resulted in some contradictory results. Better chemical definition of dietary fibre would help in clarifying the nutritional effects of various fibre components. Generalisations cannot be made regarding the interactions of dietary fibre with other food ingredients. The effects of cellulose and carrageenan on the apparent digestibility of other nutrients cited in this paper demonstrate the differences of different types of fibrous components.

An important aim of future research should be to assess the nutritional significance of all types of dietary fibre by quantifying the metabolic response produced by each in order to utilise the benefits and to avoid the disadvantages of individual fibrous constituents.

REFERENCES

Baker, D., K. H. Nouris, and B. W. Li (1979). In G. E. Inglek and S. U. Falkhag (Eds.) Dietary Fibers: Chemistry and Nutrition. Academic Press, New York.
Furda, J. (1979). In G. E. Inglek and S. U. Falkhag (Eds.) Dietary Fibers: Chemistry and Nutrition. Academic Press, New York.
Hipsley, E. H. (1953). Br. Med. J., 2, 420.
Knieriem, W. von (1885). Z. Biol., 21, 67.
Lüssl, H. (1931). Z. Hundeforsch., 2, 69.
Pedersen, S. K. (1974). Cerea Science Today, 19, 8.
Riklin, M. (1973). Diss. Tierärztl. Hochschule Hannover.
Rubner, M. (1916). Arch. Anat. Physiol., Physiol. Abtlg., 93.
Scheunert, A., and J. Lütsch (1909). Berl. Tztl. Wschr., 47, 867.
Seibel, W. (1981). Ernährung - Nutrition, 5, 507.
Thomas, K., and H. Pringsheim (1918). Arch. Anat. Physiol., Physiol. Abtlg, 25.
Trowell. A. (1972). Am. J. Clin. Nutr., 25, 926.
Van Soest, P. J., and J. B. Robertson (1977). Agr. & Food. Chem. Div., Abstr. 38, A.C.S. Animal Meeting, Chicago.
Visek, W. J., and J. B. Robertson (1973). Proc. Cornell Nutr. Conf., 40.
Vock, N. (1982). Diss. Vet. Med. Univ. Vienna.

NUTRITION AND DISEASE

Nutrition of the Rapidly Growing Dog With Special Reference to Skeletal Diseases

J. Grøndalen* and Å. Hedhammar**

*The Norwegian College of Veterinary Medicine, P.O. Box 8146 Dep.
Oslo 1, Norway
**Department of Medicine, College of Veterinary Medicine, University
of Agricultural Sciences, Uppsala, Sweden

ABSTRACT

A short review on endochondral ossification and skeletal lesions in which
under-, mal- and overnutrition seem to play an essential role will be given.
The effects of total food consumption on rate of growth and on the incidence
of skeletal lesions will be discussed. Nutritional requirements in the period
of growth and practical considerations when feeding home-made or commercial
diets will be given.

KEYWORDS

Dog; food consumption; nutrition; skeletal diseases; rate of growth.

INTRODUCTION

The prevalence of skeletal diseases in large and giant dogs is increasing.
Previously, deficiencies in vitamin and mineral supply were considered to be
the main factor in the development of skeletal diseases of nutritional origin;
rickets being the classical lesion in that respect. Today, malnutrition and
overnutrition seem to be essential factors in the development of skeletal
lesions of young, rapidly growing dogs (Hedhammar and others, 1974; Kasstrøm,
1975; Olsson, 1976; Grøndalen, 1981).

ENDOCHONDRAL OSSIFICATION

Except for the bones of the skull which are mineralised directly from connective tissue (mesenchyme), growth takes place by endochondral ossification.
Endochondral ossification occurs in the growth plates but also in the deeper
layer of the articular cartilage. Chondrocytes multiply and form columns
which again degenerate and become vesiculated. The intercellular substance
becomes mineralised. Vessels penetrate from the bone marrow through the
channel formed by the degenerated chondrocytes. Cells from the bone marrow
differentiate into osteoblasts and osteocytes which, together with the

mineralised intercellular substance, form bone. This is a very specialised
process in which multiplication, degeneration, mineralisation, cell differentiation leading to bone formation and bone resorption, have to be coordinated.
The faster the growth, the more disposed this process will be to disturbances
and to skeletal lesions. About 2/3 of the skeleton is composed of inorganic
substances, mostly calcium and phosphorus - tricalcium phosphate $Ca_3(PO_4)_2$ and
calcium carbonate $CaCO_3$. In addition to being a passive locomotory organ, the
skeleton plays an important part in being a reservoir in the mineral metabolism.

TOTAL FOOD CONSUMPTION - ITS EFFECT ON RATE OF GROWTH; SKELETAL CHARACTERISTICS AND SKELETAL DISEASE

To a great extent rate of growth is genetically determined. For a long time
meat-producing animals have been selected according to their growth capacity.
There are also great differences among breeds of dogs as can be seen from the
graphs in Fig. 1. To fully utilise its growth capacity an individual has to
be fed optimal amounts of a balanced diet. If the diet supplies sufficient
amounts of all specific nutrients, the amount of energy, i.e. total food
consumption, regulates rate of growth.

The total amount of energy needed daily by a growing dog increases as long as
the dog is still growing. At the same time the amount of energy per kg bodyweight decreases. To adjust food consumption to an increasing size giving
neither too much nor too little, is sometimes a difficult matter of judgement.
It is nevertheless of prime importance for optimal skeletal development.

The final size of a dog is only to a small degree altered by rate of growth
because it is compensated by length of the growth period.

Both the clinical, histological and physicochemical characteristics of bone
are affected by rate of growth. Broadening of the metaphyseal regions of
long bones is a physiological event during the development necessary to
allow longitudinal growth. During periods of rapid growth, especially in
giant breeds, the broadening is sometimes so pronounced that it is difficult
to distinguish from pathological processes, including rickets.

Bone laid down during rapid growth is less dense, which can be seen on
histological sections and by physicochemical properties. In several studies
it has also been shown now that incidence and severity of skeletal disease
of various kinds are greater at rapid growth.

SKELETAL DISEASES RELATED TO NUTRITION

Nutritional Secondary Hyperparathyroidism, Osteodystrophia Fibrosa (Eng. lit.
Osteoporosis)

A disease caused by low calcium/high phosphorus intake is, in addition to
rickets, a condition in which nutritional supplementation will induce
recovery.

Rickets

It is well known that rickets is closely related to nutrition and that intake
of calcium as well as vitamin D play a role in the development of rickets.

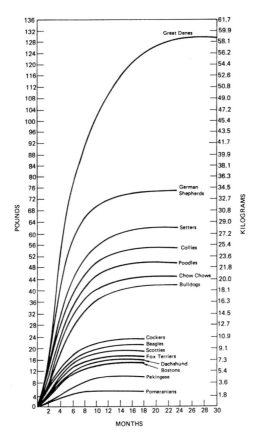

Fig. 1.   Growth curves for fifteen breeds of dogs (courtesy
of R. W. Kirk, Cornell University, Ithaca, New York)

The original works by Mellanby and others showed that they were already fully
aware of the fact that breed and total food consumption as they affect rate
of growth also influence development of rickets (Mellanby, 1921).   Clive McCay,
one of the pioneers on dog nutrition, stated about 40 years ago that "rickets
should be recognised as a disease of rapidly growing animals and that one that
fails to eat enough to grow rapidly will escape" (McCay, 1949).   That statement
also holds true for skeletal diseases seen today that are not as closely
related to nutrition as is rickets.

'Rickets-like' Conditions

Hypertrophic Osteodystrophy (Metaphyseal osteopathy).   In the acute phase the
lesion is characterised by fever, inappetence and unwillingness to move.
The periarticular soft tissues are swollen and the dogs reveal pain when the
metaphyseal areas are being palpated.   Histologically there is a breakdown
and necrosis of bone tissue in the metaphyseal region, appearing radiographically
as a more or less radiolucent area parallel to the growth plate which is of

normal height. In later phases of the disease, new bone formation may appear subperiostally in the metaphyseal region, giving rise to the name hypertrophic osteodystrophy.

The clinical features of the disease resemble scurvy in infants; and it is easily understood that this disease for a long time was recognised as skeletal scurvy in dogs. However, the histological sections from dogs clearly demonstrate that dogs do not exhibit changes typical of vitamin C deficiency as described in man, monkeys and guineapigs. Great variation in the clinical course even without any treatment, explains why clinical effects of vitamin C therapy have been claimed. It has been shown how the clinical course of this disease was more or less unaffected by any treatment, including treatment with megadoses of vitamin C (Gr∮ndalen, 1976).

Retained cartilage in various growth plates is commonly seen among dogs of the giant breeds. In the distal ulna the condition is characterised by a core of retained and more or less degenerated cartilage. In severe cases the condition may cause disturbances of the longitudinal growth, leading to deformation of the legs.

Increased rate of growth aggravates the risk of all metaphyseal osteopathies, including retained cartilage.

Osteochondrosis

Osteochondrosis is defined as a disturbance in the endochondral ossification process. Thus, all lesions concerning regions in which endochondral ossification occurs, should be included in this term. To the clinician, the term osteochondrosis is usually connected with degeneration of the deeper layer of the joint cartilage, leading to cracks, fissures and flaps of cartilage, (osteochondritis dissecans). In dogs the most common location of this disease is the shoulder, the elbow, the stifle and the hock joints.

As in metaphyseal osteopathies, increased rate of growth aggravates the risk of disturbances in the endochondral ossification process of the joint cartilage.

The condition occurs at special predilection sites within the different joints. Osteochondritis dissecans in dogs seems to occur only on joint surfaces of convex conformation receiving weight or pressure from the corresponding joint surface. The etiological factors in osteochondrosis are not clear. It seems to be a disease of multifactorial origin. Mechanical factors including conformation of joints and the weight of the dog must be considered in addition to a generalised predisposition in which increased rate of growth seems to be one factor.

Fissures and Fragmentation of the Coronoid Process

These are frequently diagnosed in young, rapidly growing dogs. The condition may occur as a result of degeneration of the deeper layer of the joint cartilage of the coronoid process (osteochondrosis), but is also frequently diagnosed without findings of any osteochondritic changes by the histological methods available (Gr∮ndalen and Gr∮ndalen, 1981). Weight is transmitted from the medial part of the humeral condyle to the process which is probably not strong enough to bear the loading. Thus, rapid growth/heavy weight are some of the etiological factors which may be discussed in the development of this condition.

Hip Dysplasia, Cervical Spondylopathy (Wobbler-Syndrome) and Enostosis (Panosteitis)

Almost all skeletal disturbances during growth are seen more frequently in larger sized breeds, in males rather than females, (except in hip dysplasia) and in individuals which are fed a free choice of highly palatable diets rather than restricted amounts. It does not mean that the etiology of these diseases is rapid growth in itself. The heredity in hip dysplasia is quite high (Hedhammar and others, 1979) and presumably also in osteochondroses but it does not seem to be directly related to the heredity for rate of growth.

REQUIREMENTS OF SPECIFIC NUTRIENTS

As with energy, the requirements of specific nutrients are also greatest during early life and the period of most rapid growth. Protein, fat, minerals and vitamins are needed to promote healthy development including optimal skeletal characteristics. As total food consumption is quite high due to a simultaneous need for a lot of energy, puppies will usually get large amounts of the specific nutrients, that is if they are fed well composed diets. If the diet is lacking in specific nutrients there is a risk that even a generous supply will create a state of deficiency. In fact, signs of deficiency are easily brought about during growth by generous feeding of diets lacking in specific nutrients; rickets in dogs being one of the classical examples.

The composition of bitches' milk indicates the proper composition of a diet to be fed for optimal development during the very first period in a dog's life (Table 1). Never in a dog's life will there be a demand for a higher level of any nutrient than during that period. Bitches' milk is a complete and balanced diet composed by nature itself. As for all species, the need of the growing puppy progressively diminishes and after weaning a diet less dense in specific nutrients will supply the puppy with all nutrients needed.

TABLE 1   Comparison of Bitches Milk and the NRC Recommendations

	Bitches milk		NRC recommendations
	Dry matter 25%	Dry basis 100%	Dry basis 100%
Protein (%)	8	32	22
Fat (%)	9	36	5
Linoleic acid (%)	1.1	4.4	1
Calcium (%)	0.3	1.2	1.1
Phosphorus (%)	0.25	1.0	0.9

The National Research Council (NRC) of the US National Academy of Sciences has compiled a table on the recommended dietary levels of nutrients in diets for dogs (Table 1). These figures are designed to provide the nutrients required for the entire life cycle of all breeds of dogs (including support of normal growth). There is a tendency to consider these figures minimum requirements rather than recommended allowances and thus believed to be applicable only for adult dogs. When a complete and balanced diet according to NRC is fed to non-pregnant and non-lactating adult dogs, there is an extremely wide margin of safety built into these figures. A comparison to

bitches' milk and studies performed have not indicated a need for a diet more
dense in for example calcium and phosphorus than that recommended by NRC.
Ideally though, these figures should be related to energy rather than to dry
matter. For comparison with the proximate analysis of a commercial diet and
for most other practical purposes, the level of nutrients expressed per 100g
dry matter equals its content per 400 kcal of metabolisable energy (ME).

The publication Nutrient Requirements of Dogs (NRC, 1974) also contains a
table on recommended allowances per kg bodyweight for adult maintenance and
growing puppies. For most practical purposes that table is not very useful.
It is based on the figures on dietary levels and the assumption that calorie
intake during growth is twice that of adult maintenance. Although this holds
true at a certain period of life, it is progressively diminishing. An ambition
to adhere strictly to figures on intake per kg bodyweight would require
changing the diet repeatedly. It is therefore suggested that this table is
only used when reasonable levels of single supplements are evaluated. To
evaluate nutritional adequacy in general the NRC figures on recommended levels
of nutrients per 100g dry matter should be used instead.

Protein

Recommended levels of protein according to NRC (22% protein on a dry matter
basis) will promote normal skeletal development in puppies of all breeds at
all stages of life. Under normal circumstances there are no beneficial effects
of a higher level of protein, although for practical purposes the level of
protein in diets for growing dogs may vary considerably. Due to enhanced
palatability of a diet containing high levels of animal protein and fat, the
risk increases that dogs of larger sized breeds will attain an exaggerated
rate of growth due to enhanced food consumption.

If puppies of large sized breeds are to be fed diets rich in protein, total
food consumption should be restricted, since it is not protein level per se
but rather energy intake that may unfavourably influence rate of growth and
thereby the risks of skeletal disturbances.

Calcium, Phosphorus, Vitamins A and D

Levels of calcium and phosphorus in a diet for growing dogs are naturally of
particular interest with reference to skeletal development. As vitamins A
and D are essential for absorption and handling of calcium within the body
also the dietary levels of these constituents should be monitored.

It is rare today to find growing puppies which are fed diets deficient in
calcium. Recommended levels of calcium according to NRC (1.1% on a dry matter
basis) give even growing dogs of fast growing breeds a wide margin of safety.
Balance studies in German Shepherds as well as in Great Danes at various
stages of life from weaning and onwards have not indicated a need for a higher
level of calcium in the diet (Hedhammar and others, 1980). Diets for growing
dogs should also contain sufficient amounts of phosphorus in balanced proportions to calcium. The recommended amount being 0.9% phosphorus on a dry matter
basis and the optimal ratio between calcium and phosphorus about 1.3:1.0.

Optimal levels of vitamins A and D promote normal skeletal development. The
amount recommended by NRC (5000 IU vitamin A and 500 IU vitamin D per 100g
dry matter) should neither be exceeded nor gone below to any greater extent
because too much vitamin A or D may create disturbed skeletal development as
well as deficiencies of these nutrients.

Vitamin C

Most mammals including dogs have been shown to synthesise their own need for vitamin C, and NRC did not find adequate evidence in 1974 to recommend the addition of vitamin C to the diets of dogs. Since then no reasons have been given to take another point of view, although skeletal diseases of various kinds erroneously have been claimed to originate from vitamin C deficiency.

PRACTICAL APPLICATIONS

Advice on How to Feed Puppies of those Breeds which are Predisposed to Skeletal Disturbances During Periods of Rapid Growth

1. Feed a diet, commercial or home-made, which is complete and balanced according to NRC.

2. Regulate food consumption to promote 'normal' rate of growth; i.e. neither too slow or too fast as compared to littermates or other dogs of the same sex, age and breed.

Advice on How to Feed a Dog with Disturbed Skeletal Development During Growth

1. Check diet for nutritional adequacy by comparing it with the levels recommended by NRC.

2. If deficient - correct it by supplementation. If excessive amounts are supplied - delete superfluous amounts.

3. Decrease rate of growth during the period of recovery by restricted feeding of a complete and balanced diet as indicated above.

ASSESSMENT OF NUTRITIONAL ADEQUACY

1. List all items fed daily to the dog.

2. Check proximate analyses and vitamin content by reading the labels of commercial products and consulting official tables on food composition of other items.

3. Calculate the amount of protein, calcium, phosphorus and vitamins A and D per 100g dry matter and compare it to the levels recommended by NRC.

GUIDANCE FOR SUPPLEMENTATION

1. Most commercial products labelled as complete and balanced do contain sufficient and balanced amounts of all nutrients needed and should not be supplemented.

2. Home-blended diets based only on meat and vegetables have to be supplemented with minerals and fat soluble vitamins.

    (a) The amount of supplements needed can be calculated by comparing the content of calcium, phosphorus, vitamins A and D of the diet on a dry matter basis to the levels recommended by NRC.

(b) If the exact amount of calcium, phosphorus and vitamins A and D
have not been calculated, a good rule of thumb is to add:

1 teaspoon (5 ml) of bonemeal, 500-1000 IU vitamin A and 50-100 IU
vitamin D per 100g dry matter if the diet is composed solely of
ingredients poor in calcium and vitamin D. (That is, 2-3 teaspoons,
10-15 ml, of bonemeal, 2000-3000 IU vitamin A and 200-300 IU
vitamin D per kg of most fresh diets containing 25% dry matter).

REFERENCES

Gr∮ndalen, J. (1976). J. small Anim. Pract., 17, 721-735.
Gr∮ndalen, J., and T. Gr∮ndalen (1981). Nord. VetMed., 33, 1-16.
Gr∮ndalen, J. (1981). Oslo Thesis.
Hedhammar, A., F. Wu, L. Krook, H. F. Schryver, A. Delahunta, J. P. Whalen,
    F. A. Kallfelz, E. A. Nunez, H. F. Hintz, B. E. Sheffy and G. D. Ryan (1974).
    Cornell Vet., 64, Suppl. 5, 1-159.
Hedhammar, A., S. E. Olson, S. A. Anderson, L. Persson, L. Petterson, A.
    Olausson, and P. E. Sundgren (1979). J. Am. vet. med. Ass., 174, 1012-1016.
Hedhammar, A., L. Krook, H. Schryver, and F. Kallfelz (1980). In R. S. Anderson
    (Ed.) Nutrition of the Dog and Cat. Pergamon Press, Oxford.
Kasström, H. (1975). Acta radiol., Suppl. 344, 135-179.
McKay, D. M. (1949). Nutrition of the Dog (2nd ed.). Comstock Publishing
    Company, Ithaca, New York.
Mellanby, E. (1921). Med. Res. Council, Special Report Series No. 61.
Olsson, S.-E. (1976). Gaines Progress (Summer), 1-11. Gaines Dog Research
    Center, New York.
National Research Council (1974). Nutrient requirements of dogs, No. 8.
    National Academy of Sciences, Washington, D. C.

Common Clinical and Nutritional Problems in Racing Sled Dogs

D. S. Kronfeld* and H. L. Dunlap**

*School of Veterinary Medicine, University of Pennsylvania, Kennett
Square, Philadelphia, USA
**Zero Kennel, Bakers Mills, New York, USA

ABSTRACT

Racing huskies are subjected to extreme hard work and stress. They exhibit
several common clinical conditions that have nutritional components of varying
importance. All involve stress, so require a high protein level. Wear and
tear of the feet creates extra demands for SH-amino acids. Lameness may be
associated with pressure sensitive metacarpals. Metacarpal fractures are
more common in males than females and epidemics have been associated with
calcium deficiency. Abnormal locomotion has also been associated with
exertional rhabdomyolysis in dogs fed a high grain diet. These diets are
also associated with rectal bleeding. A little carbohydrate, however,
appears to improve resistance to digestive upsets during severe stress and
the diarrhoea-dehydration-stress-syndrome. Heat stress may lead to fainting
in a race, perhaps due to hyperventilation. Anaemia may be associated with
water retention during early training or pseudopregnancy, or with reduced
red blood cell production due to stress or insufficient dietary protein.

KEYWORDS

Exercise; hard work; stress; feet abrasions; interdigital fissures; toe
dislocations; metacarpal fractures; calcium deficiency; secondary nutritional
hyperparathyroidism; exertional rhabdomyolysis; rectal bleeding; diarrhoea;
heat stress; stress anaemia; dietary protein.

INTRODUCTION

Racing sled dogs or 'Alaskan Huskies' derive mainly from original Siberian
stock with variable infusions of Irish Setter, Alsatian, Labrador, Airedale,
Greyhound and Saluki. Females weigh about 20 kg, males 25 kg, when fit for
racing.

The International Sled Dog Racing Association has active chapters in
Scandinavia and Europe as well as Canada and the USA. Classes in America
are for teams of 3, 5, 7 or unlimited dogs. Unlimited teams usually start
with 10 to 16 dogs. There are also weight-pulls and freight races. Drivers

ride the sled or run behind it. Nordic racers follow the dogs on skis. One
of us (HLD) has been competing for 22 years, the other (DSK) has been studying
the Zero Kennel team for nine years. The team won the ISDRA Gold Medal
(unlimited points championship) in 1976, 1981 and 1982. It races 10 to 12
times, starting in January in Minnesota with races of two heats on successive
days, about 25 to 30 km each. The season continues with races in New England
and Quebec in February, then Alaska in March. Major races in Alaska have
three heats of 40 to 50 km. Zero Kennel has averaged over 35 km/hr in several
races. The best human marathoners, for comparison, are running just over
20 km/hr. A 20 kg dog running at 35 km/hr consumes as much oxygen as a 60 kg
man running at 19 km/hr.

The most common problems are foot injuries and heat stress. Trauma from
fights and auto accidents take a surprising toll that should be partly
preventable. Rectal bleeding is common in dogs fed fibre. Epidemics of
kennel cough or diarrhoea may run through a team. Epidemics of lameness have
been associated with calcium deficiency. Exertional rhabdomyolysis has been
associated with carbohydrate-loading. Other problems are insidious, such as
mild pseudopregnancy and anaemia. These conditions have been addressed by
practical measures based on experience in training and racing, by veterinary
medicine, and by clinical nutrition. Major findings have been the importance
of calcium but not protein in the frequency of lameness and fractures, the
advantage of fat over carbohydrate as a fuel for working muscles, and the
importance of dietary protein in combating sports anaemia which has been
identified tentatively as a form of stress anaemia.

FOOT INJURIES

The most common injuries affect the feet. They depend on work and trail.
Any trail may abrade the balls of the feet if these have not been adequately
cornified by progressive training starting with slow work. Sand and certain
crystalline snows are most abrasive.

Ball abrasions heal quickly if time allows a slackening in the training
schedule. If the dog must train or race at a slow pace, e.g. at a 7 km/hr
trot, it may wear boots (described below). Going faster, the toe may be
taped with durable adhesive tape (e.g. ZONAS porous tape, Johnson & Johnson,
New Brunswick, NJ). The tape is about 10 cm long, 1 cm wide. The middle
goes around the ball of the toe and the ends run around the sides to cross
over the upper surface of the pastern. A better method that requires more
skill is to attach a patch with cyanoacrylate (Krazy Glue, Krazy Glue Inc.,
Chicago, Ill). The patch may be made from strong, light nylon (pantyhose)
or flexible adhesive (e.g. ELASTICON, Johnson & Johnson). The edges of the
latter are bevelled so that the patch blends smoothly with the skin surface.
The patch wears out and drops off in three to five days as the skin re-grows.
Infection has been anticipated but not encountered.

Abrasions also occur at the hair-line, usually on the sides of the toe.
These injuries are prevalent when a thin film of ice or frozen snow on the
surface is insufficient to take the impact, so the foot breaks through
repeatedly. Abraded lateral zones may be covered with adhesive tape that
goes around the ball, as described above. They may be prevented by avoiding
those trail conditions or by wearing boots. These are made from cloth that
is soft as well as strong, e.g. denim. They are designed to fit snug but
not tight, and are closed with Velcro. Boots may be used to cover any injury
at rest or up to 10 km/hr. They are used extensively by teams in long
distance races, like the 1800 km Iditarod Trail race from Anchorage to Nome.

Fissures may develop in the soft underpad between the toes. They occur most
frequently in dry crystalline snow that accumulates between the toes and
abrades the skin. Warning signs are red, thin skin. A fissure can develop
in a single run and persist for the rest of the season. It starts about
0.5 cm long and in a day or two extends for 2 cm, when the split may be
0.5 cm wide. Healing starts from the ends, with ridging of the sides of the
fissure.

Abrasions and fissures may be covered with oily dressings, such as white
ointment (zinc oxide, cod liver oil) and/or boots. Fissures may be treated
once or twice a day with antiseptic, astringent dressing. The best in our
experience are alcoholic solutions of cod liver oil, Juniper tar, Balsam
peru, tannic acid and turpentine (e.g. Pad Kote, Happy Jack Inc, Snow Hill,
NC). Of course, any snow between the toes should be brushed out after each
run.

Toe nails may twist up and bend or break off. A bent or broken nail is
trimmed with clippers. Some dogs run well without part or all of a nail.
Others run tentatively, as if afraid or imbalanced. The nail may be replaced
by a prosthesis fashioned from epoxy glue expressed from a thermo-gun. The
thick glue may be shaped fairly well during its extrusion from the thermo-gun.
It may then be sculptured with a scalpel. The prosthesis wears and drops off
in a week or two as the new nail grows into place.

Dislocated toes are uncommon. They are replaced manually under local anaesthetic. Fibrous tissue around the joint may be increased with sclerosing
agents, e.g. sodium oleate.

Trauma from fights often affects the feet, and this is serious in a running
dog. The racers are conveyed in trucks and the racing sites abound with
vehicles and excited people. Both fights and auto accidents may be minimised
by careful planning of routines.

Nutritional approaches to foot injuries and accidental trauma are general.
They concern metabolic stress and skin conditions. Stress increases demands
for protein mainly, also calcium, magnesium, potassium, copper, iron, zinc,
thiamine, riboflavine, vitamins A and E and perhaps C. Add structural lipids
and emphasise SH-amino acids and the list applies to skin conditioners.
Surprisingly few proprietary preparations approximate this list; one is
Linatone-Plus-with-Zinc (Lambert-Kay Inc., Cranbury, NJ). Less expensive is
the egg. They may be fed raw, despite the common misdirection about avidin
in the white, because this is outweighed by biotin in the yolk.

METACARPAL LAMENESS AND FRACTURES

Sled dog racers have been bothered historically by lameness that has no
apparent cause, 'non-specific lameness' (Stoliker and others, 1976). Careful
examination showed that this is associated with sensitivity in the metacarpal
region more often than the foot. Another not infrequent condition is fracture
of the third or fourth metacarpus. The two conditions became associated by
the development of fractures in dogs that were previously lame.

Careful inspection of radiographs showed indications of small, spiral
incomplete fractures in the metacarpus of certain lame dogs. These observations prompted the hypothesis that the lameness may be due to incomplete
spiral fractures due to torsion as the foot becomes applied to the ground.
These splits would extend with further work. Progressive oblique fractures

in racing sled dogs probably fall in the same family as bucked shins in horses
and march fractures in humans. Torsion may not be the major strain, however,
in the common fracture of the fifth metacarpal in racing greyhounds (Gannon,
1972).

Nonspecific lameness and metacarpal fractures used to be more common in females
than males. Photon absorptiometry showed that bone density was greater in
females than males (Stoliker and others, 1976). No difference was found
between three diets that contained 31, 40 and 53% protein (dry matter)!
These findings do not support the proposition that dietary protein specifically
affects bone density (Hedhammar and others, 1974). The incidence of non-
specific lameness and metacarpal fractures subsided in dogs that were reared
on our experimental diets. Prior to that, the dogs were fed various diets
that often emphasized meat or grain for reasons of economy or attempts at
carbohydrate-loading. So the previous high incidence of bone problems may
have been due to diet, since meat and grain are deficient in calcium.

A few years ago, a prominent racer won the North American Championship race
in Fairbanks, despite the fact that his dominant leader was lame following
the second heat and suffered multiple fractures of metacarpals in both feet
during the third heat. Six of his best team dogs had metacarpal fractures
during the season. The team was fed about one-third dry dog food (Purina
High Protein Meal, Ralston Purina Inc., St. Louis, MO) and two-thirds horse-
meat. The driver had been advised previously (by DSK) to add one cupful of
bone meal to each four-gallon can of this mixture, but this advice was rejected
because the driver had tried calcium before and observed that the dogs ran no
faster. After the tragic victory, while she was on the operating table having
her feet wired, the Athabascan Indian wanted to know more about calcium. In
the light of this experience and others like it, it seems probable that epidemics of metacarpal lameness and fractures may be a manifestation of secondary
nutritional hyperparathyroidism. In view of human osteoporosis, it is ironic
that male dogs seem more susceptible.

HEAT STRESS AND PROSTRATION

Dogs run well in the cold and poorly in the heat. Humidity is equally important;
we do not train when relative humidity (%) or temperature ($^{\circ}$F) exceeds 75, or
both numbers combine to exceed 140.

Dogs that lose their feet during a race and are unconscious or comatose or
severely depressed when picked up have usually been thought to be hypoglycaemic.
Blood analysis has not confirmed this diagnosis. The breathing patterns and
cardiovascular signs of these dogs have suggested heat prostration. Hyperventilation due to the combined stimulation of exercising and overheating may
lead to hypocapnia and vasoconstriction to the brain. This mechanism leads to
fainting in people and, presumably, dogs. Then breathing slows down. This is
an ominous sign in humans. The situation may be different in dogs (Kronfeld,
1975).

Obviously affected dogs are cooled down by rubbing with snow or dousing with
cold water. Rectal temperatures of 35°C have been observed in dogs treated
over-zealously. Thermoregulation may be impaired in these dogs.

Heat stress may be minimized in dogs that are trained to run slowly as well
as fast. This practice is rare among sled dog racers. Veterinarians should
recommend interval training to their racing clients, primarily to improve the
distance over which high speed may be maintained. A secondary benefit is the

capability of running at half-effort in the heat.

EXERTIONAL RHABDOMYOLYSIS

Lameness associated with no apparent injury has also been associated with exertional rhabdomyolysis. Tying-up or cramps are most prevalent in dogs fed grain-based diets. It has been induced by carbohydrate-loading (Kronfeld, 1973). This practice is favoured by human marathoners, despite the fact that it has occasionally resulted in myoglobinuria, ranging from mild to lethal. Red urine following a race is usually regarded as benign in human athletes. It should not be taken so lightly because it might represent haemoglobin or myoglobin as well as red cells. Tan or red urine in a husky with cramps is an indication for a change in management and diet.

The objective of carbohydrate-loading is to avoid muscle glycogen falling below some hypothetical level associated with fatigue by elevating muscle glycogen content before the race. An alternative strategy to achieve the same objective is to adapt the mitochondria to utilise fat, so spare utilisation of glycogen. This is done by training the dog on a high fat diet (Kronfeld and Downey, 1981). Dogs trained on a high fat diet develop a higher plasma free fatty acid concentration after an exhaustive run, and better dogs develop a higher response than poor runners (Hammel and others, 1977). The exhaustion time of Beagles running on a treadmill correlates positively with dietary fat and negatively with dietary carbohydrate (Downey and Kronfeld, 1980).

Although tying-up has been associated only with high carbohydrate diets in racing sled dogs, it is prudent to be alert for other differentials: deficiencies of potassium, phosphorus, selenium and vitamin E; hypothyroidism; malignant hyperthermia; and ionophore (e.g. monensin) intoxication (Kronfeld and Downey, 1981).

'FEEDABILITY' AND 'DDSS'

After our initial experience with tying-up (Kronfeld, 1973) and comparative trials in the field (Kronfeld and others, 1977), we preferred zero-carbohydrate diets for racing sled dogs. Our drivers (HLD, R. L. Downey and T. O. Adkins) developed the opinion that dogs fed zero-carbohydrate were more susceptible to digestive upsets during periods of severe stress. These upsets could be mild or severe, leading to dehydration and further stress, the vicious cycle of the diarrhoea-dehydration-stress-syndrome or 'DDSS' (Adkins and Morris, 1975). Inclusion of 5% rice appeared to improve the dog's resistence to digestive upsets during introduction of the diet or periods of extreme stress. This attribute of the diet was called 'feedability'. The racing diet for Zero Kennel and Dr. Adkin's Iditarod team has included 5% rice for the last two seasons.

To study 'feedability', stools were rated daily in dogs fed a basal diet of pork lung and chicken supplemented with 0, 3, 6 and 9% rice. The dogs raced in the 7-dog and 5-dog classes for two months, each on a single diet, then ran on a treadmill, every dog fed each diet in a 4x4 change-over design. No significant differences were found between diets (Downey and Kronfeld, unpublished data). Nevertheless, our drivers are not convinced by these experimental results, for the dogs may not have experienced sufficiently severe stress.

DDSS tends to ameliorate when stress subsides, i.e. dogs are rested. Affected dogs are often reluctant to drink. They are tempted by flavouring the water with meat juice. The intravenous use of fluids is not allowed on the trail, but electrolyte solutions may be given as a drench. Sterile fluids are easy to administrate subcutaneously in dogs, about 250 ml in each location. Replacement profiles are preferred that include acetate and gluconate instead of lactate.

RECTAL BLEEDING

Dogs may bleed from the anus during a high-speed run. The amount of blood seems to be small, unlikely to be more than 100 ml, though obviously impossible to measure. Blood on white snow or a white coat attracts the attention of spectators and race-veterinarians. Bleeding dogs are usually disqualified from competing in subsequent heats, probably unnecessarily.

The blood is bright red, apparently from capillaries or arterioles in the large intestine or rectum. This bleeding is almost invariably associated with the feeding of dry dog food. The most obvious component that might be incriminated is vegetable fibre, i.e. excessively bulky faeces. Another is the high iron content of these products, that approximates the therapeutic level at maintenance and may provoke gastrointestinal irritation at 3- or 4 times maintenance.

OESTRUS AND PSEUDOPREGNANCY

Bitches do not run well when in heat. Fortunately, oestrus does not usually occur in the racing season and is uncommon during the last month of training, December. So oestrus, a major problem in racing greyhounds, has not been given much attention in huskies that are racing.

After a highly successful season in 1981, Zero Kennel was expected to fare well in 1982. The team placed three times while preparing for two major races at Saranac Lake and Montreal. It performed poorly in both races. The body condition and mental attitude of the five bitches was perplexing. Two were leaders and one ran immediately behind the leaders, so three of the four most important dogs in the team were not running well. After the Montreal debacle, finishing 10 minutes behind the winner, further physical examination brought into question slightly engorged nipples and perhaps water retention rather than too much subcutaneous fat. Blood counts revealed that these five bitches were clustered at the bottom of the team's distribution of red blood cell counts. Then it was recalled that they had all been in oestrus during the second week of December, an unusual event.

A tentative diagnosis of mild pseudopregnancy enabled the prediction of a pronounced improvement in the attitude and running of these bitches in the third or fourth week of February. New records on the training trail in the last week of February were consistent with the termination of pseudopregnancy. The team was taken to Alaska where it won three major races.

Pseudopregnancy may be treated with progesterone analogs or bromocriptine. The latter is a specific inhibitor of prolactin release, but it often causes vomiting and lassitude. Cysteamine has recently been found to suppress prolactin without adverse effects (Millard and others, 1982). Testosterone preparations are used to prevent oestrus or abolish false pregnancy in racing greyhounds.

SPORTS ANAEMIA

Low red blood cell indices in athletes have been called 'sports anaemia' and more recently 'pseudoanaemia' (Dressendorfer and others, 1981). Opinions have differed sharply on its importance as an indicator of over-training or excessive stress. Red blood cells are proving to be valuable indicators of tolerance of stress and adequacy of dietary protein in racing huskies.

Depressed red blood cell indices have been found in dogs fed 28% protein (energy basis) or less but not 32% or more during the ISDRA racing season or the Iditarod Trail race (Kronfeld and others, 1977; Adkins and Kronfeld, 1982). Exhaustive exercise increases the serum glucocorticoids about three-fold (Kronfeld and others, 1977). Anaemia that develops in dogs subjected experimentally to stress is due to diminished production of red blood cells. Regeneration of red blood cells in anaemia due to stress or plasma skimming or standardised haemorrhage is improved by protein supplementation (reviewed by Kronfeld and Downey, 1981).

Retention of water may also lead to a reduction of red blood cell indices, usually during the early stages of training. It is also a response to prolactin release during pseudopregnancy.

The haemogram may be useful, before other signs, in identifying racehorses that have passed the peak of fitness (Steel, 1961). This claim has not been substantiated statistically in horses. Performance rankings of the Zero Kennel team and Dr. Adkin's Iditarod team have correlated significantly with red blood cell indices (Kronfeld and Downey, 1981). Moreover, individuals that appear over-stressed almost invariably have low red cell counts. They improve when reduced to light work for a variable period, usually between 3 days and 3 weeks.

A RACING DIET

Designs of diets for dogs subjected to hard work and stress have emphasised digestibility and energy density, i.e. a high fat content (McNamara, 1972). The protein requirement for hard work was thought to be no greater than for maintenance (Anon., 1974). Protein has not been regarded as a preferred fuel for work. Also, protein supplements appear not to affect the development of muscle during training, except inconsistently when subjects are taking anabolic steroids. The need for a higher protein intake to prevent anaemia in hard working men was proposed in a Japanese report that has been largely overlooked for 30 years (Yamaji, 1951). The most surprising finding in our studies of racing sled dogs has been the need for dietary protein that is higher than the requirement for growth or lactation in dogs (Ontko and others, 1957).

Our current diet for racing sled dogs has 30% protein, 55% fat and 15% carbohydrate on a metabolisable energy basis. It is composed of 5% rice, the remainder equal parts of pork lungs and whole chicken, supplemented with vitamins and minerals about 25% over the NRC recommendations (Anon., 1974). Its dry matter digestibility averages 90%.

REFERENCES

Adkins, T. O. and D. S Kronfeld (1982). Can. vet. J., 23, 260-263.
Adkins, T. O. and J. C Morris (1975). Mod. vet. Pract., 56, 456-461.

Anonymous (1974). Nutrient Requirements of Dogs. National Academy of Sciences,
    National Research Council: Washington, D.C.
Downey, R. L. and D. S. Kronfeld (1980). J. Am. Anim. Hosp. Ass., 16, 273-277.
Dressendorforfer, R. H., C. E. Wade and E. A. Amsterfam (1981). J. Am. Med.
    Ass., 246, 1215-1218.
Gannon, J. P. (1972). Aust. Vet. J., 48, 244-250.
Hammel, E. P., D. S. Kronfeld, V. K. Ganjam and H. L. Dunlap (1977). Am. J.
    clin. Nutr., 30, 409-418.
Hedhammar, A., F. M. Wu, L. Krook, H. R. Schryver, A. DeLahunta, J. P. Whalen,
    F. A. Kallfelz, E. A. Nunez, H. F. Hintz, B. E. Sheffy and G. D. Ryan (1974).
    Cornell Vet., 64 suppl., 5, 1-160.
Kronfeld, D. S. (1973). J. Am. vet. med. Ass., 162, 470-473.
Kronfeld, D. S. (1975). INFO, 5.1, 4-5.
Kronfeld, D. S. and R. L. Downey (1981). Proc. Nutr. Soc. Aust., 6, 21-29.
Kronfeld, D. S., E. P. Hammel, C. F. Ramberg, Jr., and H. L. Dunlap (1977).
    Am. J. clin. Nutr., 30, 419-430.
McNamara, J. H. (1972). Vet. Med. small Anim. Clin., 61, 615-623.
Millard, W. J., S. M. Sagar, D. M. D. Landis, J. B. Martin and T. M. Badger
    (1982). Science, 217, 452-454.
Ontko, J., R. E. Wuthier and P. H. Phillips (1957). J. Nutr., 62, 163-169.
Steel, J. D. (1961). In J. F. Bone (Ed.), Equine Medicine and Surgery. Amer.
    Veterinary Publications: Wheaton, Il.
Stoliker, H. E., H. L. Dunlap and D. S. Kronfeld (1976). Vet. Med. small Anim.
    Clin., 65, 1545-1550.
Yamaji, R. (1951). J. Physiol. Soc. Japan, 13, 484-489.

Food Induced Allergies

G. S. Walton

Department of Veterinary Preventive Medicine, University of Liverpool
Field Station, 'Leahurst', Neston, South Wirral, UK

ABSTRACT

Food allergies are a rare cause of cutaneous enteric respiratory and/or
possibly neurological disease in the dog and cat. Diagnosis requires careful
study of the case history, a detailed clinical examination followed by test
meal investigation and provocative challenge.

KEYWORDS

Food allergy; diagnosis; dog; cat; skin; alimentary tract; respiratory tract;
central nervous system; test meal investigation; provocative challenge.

INTRODUCTION

The purpose of this paper is to describe and discuss the clinical features,
diagnosis and control of allergic hypersensitivity responses to food allergens
as noted in the dog and cat. As these types of response occur infrequently,
it is essential to investigate and eliminate all other possible causes of
cutaneous, enteric or respiratory disorder before considering that the
presenting condition may have been produced by ingested allergens. Prolonged
maintenance of animals on imbalanced or deficient diets may, over a period of
months or years, lead to the production of cutaneous and/or systemic disturbances (Hedhammar, 1982). Severe responses may be noted in individual animals
following the ingestion of specific macromolecules contained in such foods as
shellfish, when that individual possesses an idiosyncrasy to such substances.
Abnormality or deficiencies in the production of individual digestive enzymes
can be responsible for a variety of alimentary disorders. Intolerance is
noted in individual animals to certain food or food products when such items
are either fed in excessive amounts or introduced suddenly into a diet, with
or without the presence of an underlying enzymic abnormality (Meyer, 1982).
Infectious or toxic agents present within the diet can also produce deleterious
effects. Parasitic infestations and certain bacterial conditions may, on
superficial examination, mimic skin changes noted in certain cases of food
allergy.

Throughout life most animals remain refractory to sensitisation by the
multitude of potential food allergens with which they are bombarded daily.
A small number of individuals may, however, after a period varying from a few
weeks to several years, enter a short asymptomatic phase during which allergic
mechanisms become mobilised against one particular food allergen and after
which time any subsequent ingestion of the relevant allergen will result in
a sudden and unexpected exacerbation of symptoms. Thus a food allergy may be
noted for the first time at any age, to one particular allergen that has been
ingested previously either daily or intermittently over many months or years
without adverse effect. Allergic responses to ingested allergens result from
the mobilisation of an immediate anaphylactic and/or arthus type response
which affects one or more body systems. Once established sensitivity is
likely to remain for the remainder of the subject's life, but unlike certain
other types of allergic reaction, subsequent development of allergies to other
food allergens is rare. The response is very specific, cooking or processing
a food allergen may either potentiate or destroy its activity (Walton, 1967).
Cross-reactivity is rare, although cases will be encountered where individual
animals may react to both bovine milk and bovine meat if, for instance, a
serum albumin fraction is involved. Unlike an intolerance a severe reaction
may follow ingestion of minute amounts of the relevant allergen.

Diagnosis must be based on an accurate case history and the presenting clinical
features and confirmed by test meal investigation followed by provocative
challenge.

CASE HISTORY

An accurate case history is invaluable to diagnosis as it will reveal:

1.   A sudden onset of symptoms, affecting only one animal within a community,
     at one time, with no evidence of spread to other in-contact animals or
     to other animals receiving the same diet.

2.   Temporary remission of symptoms during steroid therapy with recurrence
     when therapy is stopped.

3.   No improvement on parasiticidal or fungal therapy and only partial
     improvement on antibiotic therapy, if secondary bacterial infection has
     been a complication.

An accurate case history will also yield valuable information on the diet and
the disease pattern; whether symptoms have been persistent in nature due to
the presence of an allergen in the basic diet, or have been intermittent,
with periods of quiescence, when the relevant allergen has been ingested.
Occasionally it may then be possible, on careful questioning, to ascertain
whether the presenting symptoms involve changes in the skin, alimentary
tract and/or respiratory system.

CLINICAL FEATURES

Close study of the presenting clinical features, having eliminated all
infectious causes, is an invaluable aid to reaching a diagnosis. In cases of
cutaneous involvement, a response will be noted four to twenty-four hours
following ingestion of the relevant allergen and will then persist for a
further one to two days, or for a longer period should further ingestion take
place. The presenting clinical picture will be subject to individual

variation and skin responses can be classified into seven main clinical groups (Table 1) depending on the presence or absence of generalised pruritis, self-inflicted lesions and/or certain other forms of skin change (Walton, 1967).

Generalised Pruritis

Generalised pruritis is a frequent feature and is typified by evidence of a generalised rather than localised skin irritation and is often accompanied by hyperesthesia, an exaggerated scratch reflex and less frequently by involuntary skin twitching. On rare occasions and particularly when a subject is excess-ively nervous, apprehensive or vicious, it may prove impossible to confirm the presence of generalised pruritis. As a sequel to generalised pruritis, self-inflicted skin damage is a common finding and often a major reason for the owner seeking veterinary advice. The distribution of self-inflicted lesions is subject to individual variation and damage is usually noted over an area or areas which are easily accessible and can be most easily rubbed, scratched or bitten. Although in many cases the colour and texture of the skin and coat appears to be macroscopically normal, individual animals may present with evidence of:

1. A generalised urticaria, which in short-coated breeds is manifested by localised tufting of the coat and can be accompanied by oedema of the face and ear flaps. The papules may either be pale and oedematous or hyperaemic in nature.

2. Urticarial plaques of varying size, shape and regional distribution.

3. A diffuse generalised hyperaemia, occasionally accompanied by skin oedema. At initial examination, the presenting picture is often complicated by secondary skin changes including skin thickening, increased skin pigmentation, varying degrees of diffuse hair loss, scaling and seborrhea.

Alimentary system sensitisation

Alimentary system sensitisation may produce changes involving either all or only part of the tract, the symptoms noted following ingestion of the relevant allergen being dependent on the area or areas involved. Upper alimentary sensitisation results in gingivitis and ulceration of the mouth or, when the stomach is involved, symptoms of vomiting and/or abdominal discomfort within a short period following ingestion. Sensitisation of the small or large intestine results in the production of fluid or haemorrhagic faeces some hours after feeding.

Respiratory tract sensitisation

This may result in either nasal irritation or asthmatic episodes being noted either within a few minutes of ingesting the relevant allergen due to inhalation, or asthmatic symptoms some hours later following absorption of the allergen and giving rise to intermittent attacks over a prolonged period.

Although sensitisation involving the central nervous system has not been recognised in the dog and cat, certain animals may, in retrospect, have shown evidence of depression or morbidity when fed the relevant allergen, such symptoms disappearing following removal of the offending substance.

TEST MEAL INVESTIGATIONS

As skin tests and serological ingestigations are unreliable at the present
time in the diagnosis of food allergies, reliance must still be placed on test
meal investigations and provocative testing. If a food allergy is suspected
the subject must be placed on a known diet and all tit-bits excluded. The
choice of diet must be decided taking into account the animal's palate,
economics and convenience to the owner. It is essential to impress on the
owner or handler that a severe response may be noted following ingestion of
minute amounts of the relevant allergen. It is also important for them to
appreciate that any commercial animal and human food products are a conglomer-
ation of different animal and vegetable proteins and thus should be excluded
from any test diet. Unless the owner or handler is intelligent and conscientious and prepared to closely monitor the test meal investigation, the animal
should be hospitalised. In uncomplicated cases, improvement will be noted
within five days of commencing the diet, if the allergen has been excluded.
When marked secondary changes or infection is present, antibiotics and/or
steroid therapy may be required for several days or even weeks, in conjunction
with the test diet, but even in these cases improvement should be noted within
seven days if the relevant allergen is absent. If it is found impossible to
reduce the steroid dose in the complicated case or no improvement is noted
within four to five days in the uncomplicated condition, it is probable that
the relevant allergen is present in the test diet and this should be changed
accordingly. To negate this need certain workers prefer to place the animals
either on a starvation diet for several days or feed only sugar and water, but
this type of regime is unacceptable to most owners. Once improvement has been
achieved on the test diet, a list of substances previously fed to the subject
should be compiled and each added back singly into the basic diet for a minimum
period of five days. If, at the end of that period, no adverse response has
been noted, it can be safely assumed that the substance is not responsible for
the previous symptoms. When a response is observed following addition of a
new substance, the latter should be excluded immediately and when the condition
has become quiescent, reintroduced in a small amount on at least two occasions
to confirm that it was the causative agent. Once the relevant allergen has
been identified and confirmed, it will be possible to compile a balanced diet
excluding this substance.

TABLE 1   Patterns of Cutaneous Response to Ingested Allergens

Group	Generalised pruritis	Self-inflicted skin damage	Other skin changes	Changes in other organs
		Clinical Features		
A	+	−	−	+ or −
B	+	+	−	+ or −
C	−	+	−	+ or −
D	+	+	+	+ or −
E	−	+	+	+ or −
F	+	−	+	+ or −
G	−	−	+	+ or −

COMMENT

Natural hyposensitisation appears to be rare and attempts to produce this
state by addition of minute amounts of allergen included either in the food
or in capsule form have so far proved disappointing. No adequate explanation
can be given as to why sensitisation takes place to only one of the large
number of allergens present within a diet, and often to a substance which does
not consistute a major item in the animal's diet. Cows' milk has been shown
to account for one fifth of the cases included in one series of 200 confirmed
canine food allergies but as this substance is ingested frequently by the
majority and food allergies are comparatively rare within the dog and cat
population no conclusion can be drawn from this finding (Walton, 1982). On
rarer occasions, chemotherapeutic agents, endoparasites, bacterial allergens
and inhaled allergens can produce identical symptoms to those noted in the
food allergy sufferer, but because of their very low incidence they should
only be considered after the possibility of a food allergy has been excluded.

Finally in the young dog a papular urticaria may be encountered which in the
majority of animals appears on only one occasion, resolving spontaneously
within twenty-four to forty-eight hours and for which no aetiological explanation is available at the present time and which requires further investigation.

REFERENCES

Hedhammar, A. (1982). Proc. 1st Nordic Symposium on Small Animal Veterinary
    Medicine, Oslo.
Meyer, H. (1982). Proc. 1st Nordic Symposium on Small Animal Veterinary
    Medicine, Oslo.
Walton, G. S. (1967). Vet. Rec., 82, 204-207.
Walton, G. S. (1982). In press.

Nutrition as it Relates to Dermatoses in Dogs

Å. Hedhammar

Department of Medicine, College of Veterinary Medicine, Swedish
University of Agricultural Sciences, Uppsala, Sweden

ABSTRACT

Nutritional deficiencies are discussed with reference to cutaneous manifestations and occurrence in practice. Recommendations on dietary composition
are presented and interactions between nutrients are indicated when relevant
to effects on coat and skin. Nutritional therapy in canine dermatology is
finally defined as the ensurance of optimal nutrition in general rather than
excessive supplementation of any single nutrient.

KEYWORDS

Dermatology; dog; nutrition; therapy.

INTRODUCTION

Although cutaneous manifestations of nutritional deficiencies of various kinds
are well documented in dogs, it is rare to find simple nutritional deficiencies
as cause of skin disorders in dogs in clinical practice. Consequently few
cases of alopecia, dermatoses, excessive hairshedding and pigmental defects
can be cured by nutritional therapy alone. That excludes dietary changes when
faced with food induced allergies, which are not included within the scope of
this presentation.

CUTANEOUS MANIFESTATIONS OF NUTRITIONAL DEFICIENCIES

It is well known that deficiencies of various nutrients are, among other
symptoms, accompanied by more or less characteristic changes in structure,
colour and function of coat and skin (Follis, 1958). Some of these effects
on coat and skin have been seen in clinical cases although most of them are
only seen when experimentally induced. Simple nutritional deficiencies of
this kind are rare entities in everyday practice today and few changes in coat
and skin are characteristic enough to prove their etiology to be of nutritional
origin (Muller and Kirk, 1976).

103

Energy and Protein

Dogs are rarely fed diets deficient in energy and protein by intention.
However, diseases causing decreased food consumption or malassimilation of
nutrients may induce kwashiorkor- and marasmus-like conditions with effects
also on coat and skin. By feeding highly palatable and digestible diets,
treatment of such diseases are supported.

Fat

Cutaneous manifestations of fat deficient diets are documented in young puppies
(Hansen and Wiese, 1943). The symptoms of a deficiency of unsaturated fatty
acids are quite non-specific. It produces dry hair and dry scaly skin.

Minerals

Severe deficiencies of sodium chloride, iodine, magnesium or zinc may, among
other symptoms, also affect coat and skin but simple nutritional deficiencies
are rare under normal circumstances. The conditions are mostly seen as
multiple deficiencies with emaciation for other reasons or with heavily unbalanced
diets. Regarding interactions with other nutrients and processing of dog foods,
see below under zinc-responsive dermatoses.

Vitamins

Vitamin A is essential for integrity of epithelial tissues. The manifestations
of a deficiency - epithelial atrophy with hyperkeratoses, acanthoses and poor
resistance to infections - are, however, non-specific. When conventional diets
are fed to dogs, vitamin A deficiency is unlikely to occur, but regarding
rancidity, see below.

It should be noted that too generous a supply of fat-soluble vitamins probably
is more common than deficiencies today. Hypervitaminoses A and D may occur by
accidental or intentional oversupplementation with synthetic products as well
as natural sources. Hypervitaminosis A is described to cause pruritus and dry
skin with rashes and hypervitaminosis D to make skin and hair dry and brittle
(Mosier, 1978).

Vitamin E deficiency may occur in connection with rancidity or excessive intake
of unsaturated fat because the requirement depends to some extent on these
features (Hayes and others, 1969). In dogs with steatitis the skin is described
as cold and pale (Anderson and others, 1939).

Experimentally induced deficiencies of vitamins belonging to the B-complex have
been shown to induce alopecia, pigmental defects, hyperkeratoses and acanthoses.
All these symptoms are non-specific unless accompanied by other manifestations
in structure and function of the body. Deficiency of water-soluble vitamins
is unlikely to occur when dogs are fed conventional diets. Most ingredients
commonly fed to dogs are good sources of these vitamins and dogs do not have
any need for dietary sources of vitamin C. Excessive heating, monotonous and
heavily unbalanced diets may, however, create deficiencies of vitamins belonging
to the B-complex under special circumstances. For example, excessive feeding
of meat from certain fishes and raw egg whites will result in deficiencies of
thiamin and biotin respectively.

RECOMMENDED DIETARY LEVELS OF NUTRIENTS

Several nutrients known to be needed by dogs may affect their general condition, including the appearance of coat and skin. Most of them are needed in very small amounts and the requirements are easily met by any conventional diet. The National Research Council of the Academy of Sciences of the USA have compiled information on dog nutrition in their publication 'Nutrient Requirements of Dogs' (NRC, 1974). In Table 1 of this publication recommended contents of all nutrients expressed as percentages or units per kg of food are presented for diets designed to provide the nutrients needed for the entire life cycle including support for normal growth (Table 1).

TABLE 1. Nutrient requirements (and selected recommended allowances) of dogs (percentage or amount per kilogram of food)*

Nutrient		Dry Basis	Dry Type	Semimoist	Canned or Wet
Moisture level (%)		0	10	25	75
Dry matter basis (%)		100	90	75	25
		Requirement			
Protein	%	22	20	16.5	5.5
Fat	%	5.0	4.5	3.75	1.25
Linoleic acid	%	1.0	0.9	0.75	0.25
Minerals					
Calcium	%	1.1	1.0	0.8	0.3
Phosphorus	%	0.9	0.8	0.7	0.22
Potassium	%	0.6	0.5	0.45	0.2
Sodium Chloride	%	1.1	1.0	0.8	0.3
Magnesium	%	0.040	0.036	0.030	0.010
Iron	mg	60	54	45	15
Copper	mg	7.3	6.5	5.5	1.8
Manganese	mg	5.0	4.5	3.8	1.2
Zinc[b]	mg	50	45	38	12
Iodine	mg	1.54	1.39	1.16	0.39
Selenium[b]	mg	0.11	0.10	0.08	0.03
Vitamins					
Vitamin A	IU	5,000[c]	4,500	3,750	1,250
Vitamin D	IU	500[d]	450	375	125
Vitamin E	IU	50[e]	45	37.5	12.5
Thiamin	mg	1.00	0.90	0.75	0.25
Riboflavin	mg	2.2	2.0	1.6	0.5
Pantothenic acid	mg	10.0	9.0	7.5	2.5
Niacin	mg	11.4	10.3	8.6	2.8
Pyridoxine	mg	1.0	0.9	0.75	0.25
Folic acid	mg	0.18	0.16	0.14	0.04
Biotin[b]	mg	0.10	0.09	0.075	0.025
Vitamin B_{12}[b]	mg	0.022	0.020	0.017	0.006
Choline	mg	1,200	1,100	900	300

*Based on diets with ME concentrations in the range of 3.5-4.0 kcal/g of dry matter. If energy density exceeds this range, it may be necessary to increase nutrient concentrations proportionately (see pp. 3,5, and 8 for discussion of nutrient-caloric interrelationships). Recommended nutrient levels selected to meet the requirements of the most demanding life cycle segments, i.e., rapid growth and lactation.
[b]Recommended allowance based on research with other species.
[c]This amount of vitamin A activity corresponds to 1.5 mg of all-*trans* retinol per kilogram of dry diet (One IU of vitamin A activity equals 0.3 *ug* of all-*trans* retinol).
[d]This amount of vitamin D activity corresponds to 12.5 *ug* of cholecalciferol per kilogram of dry diet (One IU of vitamin D activity equals 0.025 *ug* of cholecalciferol).
[e]This amount of vitamin E activity corresponds to 50 mg of *dl-a*-tocopheryl acetate per kilogram of dry diet (One IU of vitamin E activity equals 1 mg of *dl-a*-tocopheryl acetate).

Reprinted from: Nutrient Requirements of Dogs. National Research Council, National Academy of Sciences, Washington D.C., 1974.

Most dogs obviously do quite well on diets which do not strictly follow
these recommendations. During periods of greater demand such as during growth
and lactation, diets close to these figures are needed to ensure optimal
nutrition. Such diets, often referred to as complete and balanced, can either
be a suitable home-made blend or commercially available dog foods of various
types.

The first step when checking a diet for nutritional adequacy is to compare the
estimated content of various nutrients in home-made preparations and the
guaranteed analyses of commercial products which are used to these figures
(Table 1).

It should be noted that there is no 'super-duper' effect on coat and skin by
any nutrient. Superfluous amounts will not do any better than sufficient
amounts. In fact, excessive amounts may upset the nutritional balance and
cause secondary deficiencies of other nutrients. The interaction between
unsaturated fat, selenium and vitamin E should, for example, be observed when
unsaturated fats are added to a dog's diet. Supplementation with vitamin E
is indicated if there is a suspicion of an unbalanced intake of unsaturated
fatty acids and vitamin E or other antioxidants. Note also that for example
wheat germ oil, usually a good source of vitamin E, improperly stored and not
protected by antioxidants is highly liable to rancidity. Another example of
interaction between nutrients is the detrimental effects by excessive calcium
supplementation on availability of zinc and magnesium.

TABLE 2. Comparison of bitches milk and the NRC
recommendations.

| | BITCHES MILK | | NRC RECOMMEN-DATIONS |
	Dry Matter 25%	Dry Basis 100%	Dry Basis 100%
Protein (%)	8	32	22
Fat (%)	9	36	5
Linoleic acid (%)	1.1	4.4	1
Calcium (%)	0.3	1.2	1.1
Phosphorus (%)	0.25	1.0	0.9

NUTRITIONAL THERAPY IN CANINE DERMATOLOGY

Good nutritional therapy in canine dermatology means optimal nutrition rather
than excessive supplementation of any single nutrient. The most appropriate
kind of nutritional therapy is to check the diet for nutritional adequacy and
if necessary change it.

Indications for parenteral administrations of nutrients are extremely rare.
It is only needed when the condition of the dog deems acceptance, absorption
or utilisation of complete and balanced diets impossible or impractical. In
dog breeders' magazines as well as in professional journals dietary supple-

mentation of various kinds are claimed to make wonderful changes in appearance
of coat and skin. However, dietary supplementation as well as parenteral
administration of nutrients will only work when diets lacking a nutrient,
supplied by the product, have been fed for a long time. There is no documen-
tation available proving that conditions not caused by nutritional deficiencies
could be cured by nutritional therapy. Pharmacological dosages especially of
certain vitamins have been used in canine as well as human dermatology, but
have not yet proved to have any effect on coat and skin of non-deficient
animals when administered in excess. Local as well as systematic administration
of vitamin A has been tried on almost all disorders of keratinisation but
topical irritation and systemic toxicity limits its use.

Oral adminstration of more recently invented synthetic derivatives of retinoids
have shown promising results in hyper- and parakeratoses in man (Orfanus, 1978)
but their efficiency on similar conditions in dogs needs further evaluation.

Fig. 1.   Indications for parenteral administrations
of nutrients are extremely rare

UNSPECIFIC DERMATOSES ASSOCIATED WITH FATTY ACID DEFICIENCY

Unspecific dermatoses seen around weaning may be associated with rapid growth
and fatty acid deficiency. Signs of deficiency as manifested in a dry and
scaly skin can be induced when puppies are suddenly changed from bitches'
milk to an exaggerated consumption of diets rich in protein but low in
unsaturated fat. Bitches' milk is extremely rich in unsaturated fat. That
is actually the major difference from complete and balanced diet as recommended
by NRC (Table 2). Therefore, supplementation with sources of unsaturated
fatty acids might be indicated when faced with unspecific dermatoses in
recently weaned puppies. Requirements for fatty acids are much less later in
life and fat supplementation should not be needed for adult dogs fed diets
with more than one per cent linoleic acid on a dry matter basis.

MALNUTRITION AS CAUSE OF IMMUNESUPPRESSION

Malnutrition was earlier claimed as predisposing to generalised demodicosis
in dogs. Even if rather primary immune deficiencies of hereditary origin are
now known as the most likely predispositional factor, it should not be overlooked
that the local host defence mechanism of an intact integumentum can be disturbed by lack of unsaturated fatty acids. Optimal nutrition is an important
aspect of supportive treatment in growing puppies with generalised demodicosis
or juvenile pyodermas although there might be other primary reasons for alter-
ation of the immune response.

TRACE ELEMENTS AND PIGMENTAL CHANGES

Trace element deficiencies are widely appreciated among dog breeders as cause
of pigmental defects. It is true that copper, as well as iron, zinc, certain
amino acids and several water soluble vitamins are essential for normal pigmentation. Most diets do supply these nutrients in ample amounts but heavily
unbalanced and monotonous diets might be deficient in trace elements.

During the last years several cases of pigmental changes of the coat – mostly
in puppies – have been observed in Sweden. As whole litters have been affected,
a thorough anamneses including feeding, immunisation and diseases of both the
dam and the puppies have been obtained by a questionnaire. No relation to the
diet of either dam or puppies nor to status of immunisation has been seen.

ZINC-RESPONSIVE DERMATOSES

Zinc-responsive dermatoses have quite recently been highlighted in the veterinary literature (Kunkle, 1980). Two different syndromes have been seen in
Pennsylvania. Syndrome I: seen in adult sledge dogs, Siberian Huskies and
on occasion in Alaskan Malamutes and clinically manifested in crusting,
scaling and underlying suppuration around the mouth, chin, eyes, ears, elbows
and other joints, have been attributed to increased zinc requirements in these
dogs. Syndrome II: seen in litters of various breeds and clinically manifested
as extreme thickening of the foot pads and hyperkeratotic plaques over portions
of the body with exudative crusts were all attributed to excessive calcium
levels in their diets. See above regarding interference with zinc absorption!

Occasionally in Sweden during the past few years, puppies in litters of
various breeds have been seen with clinical manifestations resembling syndrome
II or parakeratosis as it was seen in growing pigs in the '50s. When tried,
several cases have responded dramatically to zinc supplementation. Most
commonly these puppies have been exclusively fed dry commercial diets. No
single brand is more commonly represented than the other. In a retrospective
perspective it seems as if the history of parakeratosis in pigs, not commonly
seen any longer, is now repeated in dogs. In the '50s parakeratosis was seen
in growing pigs when dry diets with excessive levels of calcium or nutrients
high in phytates were fed exclusively (Worden, 1965). Although nutritional
requirements and interaction with availability certainly are well known to
manufacturers of dog food, changes of recipes, accidental excess of single
nutrients or processing failures, causing nutritional upsets in single batches,
seem to account for at least some cases of zinc responsive dermatoses seen
today. It should be noted, however, that non-dietary exogenenous factors as
well as endogenous factors also may affect zinc availability. For example,
pharmacological dosages of ferrous iron inhibit zinc absorption in humans
(Sandstead, 1981). A negative interaction between glucocorticoids and zinc
has also been reported.

As stressed by Kunkle (1980) it is important that zinc supplementation should not be the new remedy for treatment of all kinds of dermatoses in dogs. Until otherwise indicated, it could be tried in cases of parakeratoses where increased zinc requirements or decreased zinc availability can be suspected. Litters or individual dogs with clinical entities of zinc responsive dermatoses, which have been fed dry type diets exclusively should be discontinued on that particular product until the manufacturer has investigated the possibility of a failure in the recipe, mixing or processing of the product, resulting in decreased availability of zinc.

50 mg zinc per kg diet on a dry matter basis is recommended by NRC (Table 1) but even that zinc level could be considered marginal at high levels of calcium, copper and cobalt, diets rich in phytates such as soy bean meal, high in dietary fibre or low in protein (Sandstead, 1981).

Suitable levels of zinc supplementation have not been established for those instances when zinc responsive dermatoses are suspected. 2 mg zinc/kg body-weight which is the recommended allowance by NRC for growing puppies has been tried with success. Zinc sulphate containing about 22% zinc is a readily available compound which ideally should be given following a meal.

ALOPECIA IN POSTLACTATING BITCHES

Excessive hairshedding even to the point of alopecia is commonly seen in bitches after lactation. Both hormonal and nutritional factors have been implicated. It is therefore advisable to pay special attention to nutritional adequacy of the diet under these conditions.

PRACTICAL CONSIDERATIONS

When faced with severe, generalised or chronic dermatoses in which nutritional involvement cannot be excluded, the anamneses should include a complete dietary history. If the dog is fed an unbalanced diet it should be changed to ensure optimal nutrition. Optimal nutrition is then to feed in adequate amounts a complete and balanced diet which is accepted and tolerated by the dog. A complete and balanced diet includes protein, amino acids, unsaturated fatty acids, minerals and vitamins in amounts recommended by the NRC (1974). It may consist of either commercial dog foods with guaranteed analyses or suitable blends of ingredients from the household or a combination of both.

Change of diet or adequate supplementation is especially important when dogs are fed unbalanced diets during growth and lactation.

REFERENCES

Anderson, H. D., A. C. Elvehjem, and J. E. Gonce (1939). Proc. Soc. exp. Biol. Med., 42, 750-755.
Follis, R. H. (1958). Deficiency Disease. Functional and structural changes in mammalia which result from exogenous or endogenous lack of one or more essential nutrients. Charles C. Thomas, Springfield, Illinois.
Hansen, A. E., and H. F. Wiese (1943). Proc. Soc. exp. Biol. Med., 52, 205-208.
Hayes, K. C., S. W. Nielsen, and J. E. Rousseau Jr. (1969). J. Nutr., 99, 196-209.
Kunkle, G. A. (1980). In Current Veterinary Therapy, VII, Saunders, Philadelphia. pp 472-478.

Mosier, J. E. (1978). Mod. vet. Pract., 59, 105-109.
Muller, G. H., and R. W. Kirk (1976). Small Animal Dermatology, 2nd ed. Saunders, Philadelphia.
National Research Council (1974). Nutrient Requirements of Dogs, No. 8. National Academy of Sciences, Washington, D.C.
Orfanus, C. E. (1978). Dermatologica, 157 (Suppl.).
Sandstead, H. H. (1981). Disorders of Mineral Metabolism, Vol. 1. Academic Press, pp 93-157.
Worden, A. N. (1965). In A. J. Rook and G. S. Walton (Eds.) Comparative Physiology and Pethology of the Skin. Blackwell, Oxford. p 261.

Nutritional Management in Heart Diseases and Diabetes Mellitus

J. Leibetseder

Institute of Nutrition, University of Veterinary Medicine, Vienna,
Austria

ABSTRACT

Dietary recommendations for dogs suffering from cardiac insufficiency are
spacing of meals to avoid excessive filling of the stomach and intestine and
feeding low salt diets because the kidneys tend to retain sodium and water.
The main aims of the dietary management in diabetic dogs are energy balancing,
feeding several meals a day and minimising simple sugar but not polysaccha-
rides.

KEYWORDS

Dietary management; cardiac insufficiency; diabetes mellitus; dog.

INTRODUCTION

One of the most important pre-conditions for health and well-being is adequate
and appropriate nutrition. A healthy organism is endowed with the capacity
to take in adequate amounts of food, digest and absorb the nutrients, to carry
them off by way of blood and lymphatic vessels and to transform these nutrients
into specific substances the organism needs or to oxidise them to provide
energy in accordance with the actual need.

The metabolites which result from this process must be detoxicated and excreted.
Many control mechanisms keep the composition of the blood and extra-cellular
fluids, as well as the individual's body weight within fairly narrow limits.
All these processes have a load capacity to cope with varying food intakes and
changing amounts of various nutrients so as to avoid noxious side effects.

On the other hand disease states are usually accompanied by higher demands for
some essential nutrients as well as an increased requirement for energy. Some
articles about the nutrition of sick animals and many dietetic prescriptions
contain guidance which is no longer tenable at the present level of knowledge.
It is therefore imperative to review the traditional dietetic prescriptions
and select only those which are justified by physiological and pathological
reasons. Some of the traditional diets have to be eliminated whereas well-

founded dietetic measures must be used more strictly in relation to definite indications. This is obvious for the dietetic treatment of metabolic diseases like diabetes mellitus and obesity or of functional disorders of the pancreas or kidney. In diseases of other organs like stomach or liver, in which the diet was the most important part of the therapy in former times, the effects of diabetic treatment could not be verified in exact clinical examinations. All established dietetic measures need to be looked at critically to assess their therapeutic validity if they are to be acceptable to modern medicine.

The relationship between nutrition and disease is in two main areas:

1. Diseases caused by nutritional errors. These can be put into four categories:

    (a) Under-feeding, resulting in a lack of available energy.

    (b) Over-feeding, resulting in an excess of available energy.

    (c) Deficiency disease resulting from a net lack of essential nutrients, e.g. hypo- or avitaminosis.

    (d) Nutrient intoxication, resulting from contamination of food by toxic substances or an excess of essential nutrients where too much is harmful, e.g. an excess of fat soluble vitamins or trace elements such as copper or fluorine.

2. Diseases which can be influenced by dietetic measures but not actually caused by faults in feeding. These conditions can be further classified as:

    (a) Illness where other measures besides dietary adjustment are crucial to successful treatment, e.g. trauma resulting from an accident.

    (b) Distinct metabolic diseases or functional disorders of particular organs which require specific dietary treatment, e.g. diabetes mellitus resulting from endocrine pancreatic failure.

In a few cases there are inter-relations between categories 1 and 2, e.g. in cases of diabetes mellitus where it is associated with obesity. In such cases there may well be several factors which influence dietary therapy, in the case of obese animals with diabetes mellitus calorie restriction may be needed to control obesity and the elimination of simple sugars from the diet to avoid sudden high peaks of circulating blood sugar.

CARDIAC DISEASE

Most cardiac disease leads to functional cardiac insufficiency. As far as nutrition is concerned only chronic cardiac failure is of relevance. For the most part cardiac insufficiency is a consequence of valvular or muscular disease of the heart. The effects develop slowly and eventually involve every organ of the body. Cats with cardiac failure tend to take less rigorous exercise than dogs and so are less affected by the condition.

Causal correlations between nutrition and cardiac diseases are unknown in dogs and cats but there are two reasons for dietetic measures:

1. The intake of large amounts of food can lead to excessive filling of the
    stomach and intestine. As a result the diaphragm is kept in a forward
    position. Cardiac function, already impaired is further hampered mecha-
    nically. The volume of any one meal needs to be restricted to avoid
    unnecessary gastric pressures and to reduce the amount of gas in the
    intestine. Obese animals need to be fed a calorie restricted regime to
    reduce adiposity. The daily amount of food should be divided into
    several small meals.

2. The kidneys of animals with cardiac insufficiency tend to retain sodium
    and water. This gives rise to the clinical picture of ascites (dropsy)
    and local oedema. The basis of this effect is believed to be either
    the reduction in sodium and water filtration or an increase in reabsorp-
    tion of sodium which brings water back into the tubules of the kidney.

Cardiac insufficiency leads primarily to diminished cardiac output and changes
the flow rate in different organs: although some essential organs are still
well supplied, in others, e.g. the kidneys, the flow rate is reduced. The
baroreceptors of the juxtaglomerular apparatus are less stimulated and renin
is released from the apparatus. Renin acts upon a plasma globulin to form
angiotensin 11. Angiotensin 11 constricts the renal blood vessels. It also
stimulates directly the aldosterone-producing cells of the adrenal cortex to
increase the output of the sodium-retaining hormone aldosterone. Aldosterone
then acts to increase sodium retention by the kidney (Fig. 1).

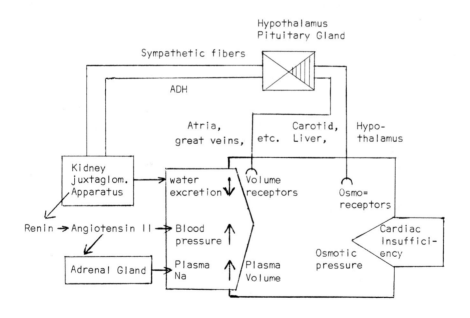

Fig. 1. Formation of ascites in consequence of cardiac
         insufficiency

Normal circulatory dynamics cannot be restored because of cardiac insufficiency, the hormonal mechanism therefore continues to operate and capillary filtrate continues to enter the extravascular pool of fluid. In general retention of sodium produces oedema, not increased concentration of sodium (hypernatremia); in dogs especially, ascites is more common than interstitial oedema. Ascitic fluid may reach 10 to 15% of body weight.

Because plasma sodium concentration changes little, this parameter is not valid for diagnosis, but a sodium concentration of about 300 mg/dl in the ascitic fluid is a definite indicator of ascites.

The reversal of this process can be brought about by desalination. This is achieved by restricting further sodium intake and by diuresis. The more extra-cellular fluid which is lost the more sodium is removed with it.

Attempts to treat canine cardiac failure by feeding low salt diets only are not very rewarding as it takes a very long time to effectively desalinate dogs. Considering the daily endogenous loss of sodium of 3 to 6 mg/kg bodyweight and the possible amount of ascitic fluid (up to 10 to 15% of the bodyweight) with a sodium concentration of 300 mg/dl, desalination takes several weeks, in spite of complete salt restriction in the diet. In addition, dogs enjoy as we do, fairly salt diets and do not usually find low salt regimes very palatable

Salt restriction may, however, be an effective adjunct to other cardiac treatment such as diuresis. A diet may be made up using muscle meat (without added salt), pasta with potatoes and rice as an energy source, with dicalcium phosphat and a salt-free supplement to make up for any mineral and vitamin shortfall.

An example of a simple formula (Table 1) shows that sodium restriction can be achieved with such a diet.

TABLE 1   Sodium Levels in a 'Cardiac' Diet

	mg Na/kg bodyweight	% Na in dry matter of food
Requirement of healthy animals	80	0.4
Recommended Na intake of patients with cardiac insufficiency	8 - 12	0.04 - 0.06
Average Na content of:		
Meat and meat by-products		0.2
Most cereals		0.02
Diet consisting of:		
1/3 meat (30% dry matter)		0.03
+ 2/3 cereals (90% dry matter)		0.017
Contains on average		0.05

Although low sodium diets are not usually very palatable for dogs and cats, it is possible to improve them by adding flavours, by roasting or even frying. If meat and meat by-products are cooked in plenty of water and the liquor is subsequently discarded the total sodium content of the food can be reduced. If this is done a 50:50 volume:volume mixture of meat and cereal will still provide approximately the level of sodium needed.

Table 2 shows the average sodium content of some foodstuffs given to dogs.

TABLE 2   Sodium Content in Foodstuffs (% of dry matter)

MEAT			CEREALS (whole grain)	
Veal		0.27	Rye	0.03
Beef		0.16	Barley	0.03
Pork		0.23	Oats	0.04
Chicken		0.13	Wheat	0.01
			Maize	0.02
Liver:	cattle	0.31	Rice (polished)	0.007
	pig	0.22		
			Flaked oats	0.006
Heart:	cattle	0.21	Wheat grits	0.001
	pig	0.18	Wheat flour	0.002
			Corn flakes	0.97
Lung:	cattle	0.36	Pasta articles	0.008
	pig	0.42	Bread	0.5-1.5
			Salted crackers	2.0
Kidney:	cattle	0.60	Potato	0.004
	pig	0.45	Carrot	0.15
			Soybean meal	0.03
Milk		0.39		
Cottage cheese		0.15		
Egg		0.56		
Sausage		2.00		

Dietary measures must be supported by proper nursing. Exercise needs to be
reduced particularly where the climate is hot and humid. Dogs should be
walked only as far as they can safely tolerate without signs of distress and
all excitement must be avoided. Adequate ventilation of the housing and
cutting the hair on long coated dogs in hot weather are all measures which
can be combined with conventional diuretic therapy in cardiac cases.

In addition to dietary management, medical therapy is indicated in most cases
both to improve cardiac function and to control ascites with the use of
diuretics.

DIABETES MELLITUS

Diabetes mellitus is a very complex metabolic disorder. At present it is
therefore not possible to give a complete synopsis of aetiology and pathogenesis. For over 50 years the metabolic derangements that characterise
diabetes mellitus have been thought to be due to a relative or absolute lack
of insulin. New information, however, incriminates a number of further
hormones like growth hormone, somatostatin (growth hormone release-inhibiting
factor), somatomedines (non-suppressible insulin-like activities), glucagon
and some other hormones, thus making diabetes mellitus a multihormonal rather
than a monohormonal disease. In addition to these endogenous disturbances,
some exogenous factors (i.e. stress) may also be involved in the pathogenesis
of diabetes mellitus.

There is a considerable volume of publications on diabetes mellitus in the
dog dealing with incidence, diagnosis, treatment and prognosis, but there are

few studies on the part that diet plays in the cause or control of this
disease. Because of the scarcity of the veterinary literature one has to
refer to the medical literature. Summarising this literature on the inter-
relation of diet and diabetes, three points seem to be prominent:

1. Obesity markedly increases the likelihood of maturity onset diabetes.

2. An excess intake of total energy, rather than excessive refined carbo-
    hydrate or sugar, is the most important predisposing factor.

3. Increased dietary fibre may be beneficial in reducing blood glucose and
    insulin requirement.

Obesity is probably the commonest dietary disease of dogs in most developed
countries. Surveys suggest that about 25 to 40% of dogs are obese. There
are some indications that obesity is a predisposing factor for diabetes in
the dog also. Breed ranking of obesity and diabetes shows a good corres-
pondence (Table 3).

TABLE 3 Breed Ranking of Obesity and Diabetes Mellitus
         (after Anderson, 1980)

OBESITY (Mason, 1970)	DIABETES MELLITUS (Wilkinson, 1960)	(Foster, 1975)
1. Cocker Spaniel	1. Dachshund	1. Poodle
2. Labrador	2. Terrier	2. Dachshund
3. Terrier	3. Poodle	3. Labrador
4. Collie	4. Spaniel	4. Cairn
5. Poodle	5. Collie	5. Cocker Spaniel
6. Dachshund		6. Collie
		7. Terrier

Animals suffering from diabetes mellitus require very close supervision of
their diet. A balance must be struck between the quantity and type of food
eaten, the level of activity allowed and the dosage of insulin administered.
Where the intake and output of energy is kept fairly constant the dosage of
insulin can be adjusted to keep the plasma glucose level within reasonable
tolerance limits. Hospitalisation may be necessary at the outset to establish
the most suitable dose of insulin for the animal's food intake and level of
activity.

For proper energy balancing the energy requirement for maintenance and exercise
of the adult dog is summarised in Table 4.

In addition to the data on requirement, the dog owner has to have good knowledge about the energy content of the food. Self-prepared food shows in
general a great variation in fat, carbohydrate and protein. For that reason
it is practically impossible to calculate the energy content of this type of
food. It should be changed therefore to prepared foods subjected to quality
control procedures indicating a certain unchanged energy density. Prepared
food has a distinct advantage over more improvised diets as the objective is
to keep the energy intake as unchanged as possible, the most important aspect
of dietary treatment is also to standardise energy intake and output as far
as it is practicable. In case of obesity, reducing diets are recommended

TABLE 4   Energy Requirement of the Adult Dog (from Meyer
          and others, 1980)

	Energy requirement
	$(kJ*/kg\ BW^{0.75})$
Maintenance (per day)	500-600
	$(kJ*/kg\ BW/km)$
Exercise (20-30 kg BW)	
Walk (4- 5 km/hr)	5.0
Trot (8-12 km/hr)	5.5
Canter (12-16 km/hr)	6.0
Full gallop (-60 km/hr)	10.0

* Digestible energy

until the bodyweight decreases to a normal range. Dietary fibre is often an important constituent of this type of diet. Because of the effect of the fibre on decreasing plasma glucose levels after meals, fibre-containing diets are advisable for obese and diabetic dogs. Contrary to a widely held belief, carbohydrate does not increase the need for insulin (unless it is in the form of simple sugars, when it can produce hyperglycaemic peaks), provided that it does not increase the total energy intake. In man the recommended maximum percentage of energy derived from carbohydrate is of the order of 40-45% of the total energy. A dog fed on a canned meat and biscuit diet on a 50:50 volume to volume basis would receive about 35-45% of its energy as carbohydrate, which is not an excessive amount. Dry or canned complete food contains about 30-50% of its energy as carbohydrate, semi-moist food up to 50%, but this food may contain significant amounts of simple sugars, whereas mixers show about 75% of total energy as carbohydrates. The food allowed needs to be divided into several meals to spread the load on the endocrine system. This can be achieved by feeding half the total energy allowed in the middle of the day and the remainder divided up into meals in the morning and evening. Energy output must be controlled as well, compatible with a reasonably normal life. As oestrus in diabetic bitches frequently results in set-backs, spaying is often advisable if this is the case. Diabetes mellitus is usually a progressive disease in dogs so continual surveillance of cases is needed if the animal is to lead a reasonable life for a number of years.

Success can be achieved in maintaining a diabetic dog in good health for a long time but everything depends on the dog having a sensible, patient, cooperative owner who follows the clear explanation of the dietary management by the veterinarian. In most cases written instructions are of considerable help.

REFERENCES

Anderson, R. S. (1980/81). Pedigree Digest, 7, (4), 5-7.
DLG-Futterwerttabellen (1973). Mineralstoffgehalte in Futtermitteln. DLG-
   Verlag: Frankfurt (Main).
Drochner, W. (1978). Report No. 7, 13-22.
Foster, S. J. (1975). J. small Anim. Pract., 16, 295-315.
Holler, K. (1981). Diss. Vet. Med. Univ. Vienna.
Leibetseder, J. and W. Jaksch (1977). Collegium veterinarium, 101-107.

Mason, E. (1970). Vet. Rec., 86, 612–616.
Meyer, H., K. Bronsch and J. Leibetseder (1980). Supplemente zu Vorlesungen und Ubungen in der Tierernahrung, 5 Aufl. Verlag Sprungmann: Hannover.
Oberdisse, K. (1975, 1977). Handbuch d. inneren Medizin, 5 Aufl., Bd. 7, 2A und 2B.
Schall, W. D. (1977). Proc. of the Kal Kan Symp., Ohio State Univ., 13–15.
Souci-Fachmann-Kraut (1977). Die Zusammensetzung der Lebensmittel 1 and 11. Verlag Wissenschaftliche Verlagsgesellschaft mbH: Stuttgart.
Wilkinson, J. S. (1960). Vet. Rec., 72, 548–555.

Nutrition and Kidney Function With Reference to Old Age and Kidney Disease

D. S. Kronfeld

School of Veterinary Medicine, University of Pennsylvania, Kennett Square, Philadelphia, PA, USA

ABSTRACT

Studies have shown that kidney function and resistance to infection are reduced by low-protein diets, and that protein requirements are increased by age and stress. So most older dogs should be fed higher protein diets despite senile degeneration of kidneys. Progressive restriction of dietary protein is contraindicated during old age and the course of kidney insufficiency and mild failure. Instead, dietary protein restriction should begin at some critical point during advanced moderate or severe failure when the disadvantage of reduced kidney function is outweighed by the disadvantage of nitrogenous 'uremic toxins' produced from dietary protein. The timing of sodium restriction, phosphorus restriction, calcium supplementation, and salt substitution or deletion, also require attention. A Basic Recipe is designed to enable modifications as desired. Improvement is needed in the timing of these several dietary interventions during the course of an individual dog's disease.

KEYWORDS

Kidney; chronic interstitial nephritis; renal function tests; renal blood flow; glomerular filtration; tubular reabsorption; senile degeneration; protein; dietary protein restriction; arginine; histidine; methionine; phosphorus; alumina-gel antacids; calcium; salt; sodium; bicarbonate; kidney diets; geriatric diets.

INTRODUCTION

One of the oldest modern concepts of aging relates to loss of growth and regenerative capability of differentiated cells (Minot, 1908). Individual tissues age at rates that relate to their degree of differentiation rather than the body as a whole. Notable are the gonads and their embryonic associate, the metanephros. The kidneys are fully formed at birth or soon thereafter. No new nephrons form after birth, and progressive loss of nephrons occurs after middle age. In most mammals, including man, rat and dog, the kidneys of the aged differ histologically from those of the young, and it is not always easy to distinguish the end results of senile atrophy from those

of pathological injury (Kennedy, 1957). Indeed, the common disease of older
dogs, chronic interstitial nephritis, may represent a continuum from 'normal'
(even though perhaps undesirable) senile changes through insufficiency to
failure of progressively more severe degree.

Purveyors of proprietary dog foods intended for old dogs and those with chronic
kidney disease have emphasised that protein is low in amount and high in
quality. They have correctly identified the senile pathology (Mather, 1979),
then associated this fact with the assumption that a low protein diet will
ameliorate the abnormal situation by diminishing the workload (Morris, 1968).
It would follow that virtually all older dogs should be fed diets that contain
progressively less protein. The key assumption of this rationale has always
been highly questionable, and empirical tests of safety and efficacy of the
products have not been published or required by regulatory agencies. Recent
reports of adverse effects of low-protein diets in experimental models
(discussed below), together with new information on the importance of certain
amino acids, calcium, phosphorus and sodium, have prompted re-evaluation of
the current clinical problems and future research needs. Previous relevant
research and clinical practices will be reviewed briefly to place the present
situation in perspective.

DIETARY MANAGEMENT OF HUMAN UREMICS

The first recommendations of low-protein diets for uremics neglected protein
quality (Fishberg, 1930; Addis, 1948). The amount was about 50 to 60 g/day
or about 10% metabolisable energy in the form of protein. These diets were
not consistently efficacious. Their rationale was based on studies on
partially nephrectomised rats, in which survival was increased by 5% protein
in the diet and decreased by 80% protein.

A breakthrough was achieved by Italian nephrologists who introduced very low-
protein diets, about 12 g/day or 2% energy, composed entirely of essential
amino acids or proteins of very high quality, e.g. egg (Giordano, 1963;
Giovannetti and Maggiore, 1964). Subsequent advances have been the recognition
that histidine may be essential in uremics (Kopple and Swenseid, 1974), and
the demonstration that some keto- or hydroxy-analogues may substitute for
certain essential amino acids (Walser, 1975).

Low-protein diets tend to be unpalatable, so the provision of sufficient food
energy becomes difficult. They also tend to be low in several vitamins, iron
and calcium. Dietary management also concerns phosphorus and the parathyroid
system, as well as salt and hypertension.

A crucial clinical problem remains. The level of renal function at which
protein restriction should begin is difficult to establish in uremic patients.
Current approaches include evaluation of the serum urea/creatinine ratio,
nitrogen balance, urea nitrogen appearance, and creatinine clearance (Anderson
and others, 1973; Kopple, 1981). Determination of this critical point is
even more difficult in uremic dogs, because restriction of dietary protein
reduces renal blood flow and glomerular filtration (Bovee and Kronfeld, 1981).

DIETARY MANAGEMENT OF CANINE UREMICS

A proprietary dog food for canine uremics was introduced in 1948 (Morris, 1960).
It was allegedly low in protein, though actually variable and often over 20%
protein on an energy basis (Kronfeld, 1972). Its objective was "to reduce

nitrogenous wastes, thereby reducing the workload of the kidneys" (Morris, 1968). The workload concept was based on a calculation of work done by the kidney to excrete urea against an osmotic gradient (Addis, 1948). This estimate was erroneous, for urea is excreted passively by a counter-current mechanism proposed by Kuhn in 1942 (Gottschalk, 1964). Moreover, the "Workload Principle" that used to be accepted generally in medicine was limited sharply by findings such as bed rest weakening the venous tree and disuse of bone inducing atrophy.

Proponents of this special 'kidney diet' focussed attention on serum urea concentration as an index of kidney function, distracting from the influence of nitrogen intake (Morris, 1960). They also claimed dramatic clinical improvement, and cited wide acceptance by the veterinary profession as testimony. If this testimony is accepted as provisional evidence of efficacy, then one should look for reasons. The pioneer product was not genuinely low in protein, but it was low in phosphorus and salt. A low-phosphorus intake may mitigate clinical signs of excessive parathyroid hormone, which include anemia, anorexia and lassitude. A low salt intake may reduce extracellular fluid volume, hence diminish polyuria. Improvement in appetite and continence are frequently reported when uremic dogs are fed this product. These uncontrolled clinical experiences have never been supported, however, by comparative trials of efficacy and safety.

Another special dietary product with about half the protein of the first 'kidney diet' was introduced in 1977. It has a high salt content to promote diuresis and palatability. Several changes in the formulas of these two products have occurred in the last few years. The protein content of the second product, for example, started at 10% on an energy basis, decreased to about 5%, then was increased again following reports of adverse effects (Bovee and Kronfeld, 1981; Polzin and others, (1981).

GERIATRIC DIETS

The first canine 'kidney diet' was recommended for the 'geriatric patient' (Morris, 1960). The workload rationale for the canine 'kidney diets' has also applied to the design of special geriatric diets for dogs (Mather, 1979; Mara, 1981). The geriatric products are claimed to contain protein barely sufficient in amount and high in quality. This approach to dietary protein for older dogs runs contrary to well-demonstrated need for about 50% more dietary protein to replete protein reserves in liver and muscle of old dogs than in young adults (Wannemacher and McCoy, 1966).

Casein was used in these repletion studies. Comparison of amino acid profiles in casein and the proprietary geriatric dog foods indicates that they are deficient in protein (Kronfeld, 1982b).

In humans, the daily intake of protein required to maintain nitrogen balance remains undiminished during advanced age when energy intake is diminished by one-third (Zanni and others, 1979). Thus dietary protein on an energy basis should increase by 50% in humans, as it does in dogs. Moreover, older people are more liable to suffer from stress, which involves mobilisation of protein reserves from tissues that depend on prior protein intake. Thus protein requirements are higher in the aged than in young people (Young and Schrimshaw, 1975).

THE PENNSYLVANIA STUDIES

Diets that contain protein at a level twice or more than the 'adequate' level
of 22% on a dry matter basis were proposed to be harmful to the kidneys of
dogs if fed over long periods (Anon., 1972). This proposition was the notion
of an individual (Newberne, 1974), which was accepted by the Subcommittee on
Dog Nutrition (Anon., 1972), even though it contained five inappropriate
citations in succession (Kronfeld, 1974). The National Research Council was
challenged by companies and independent nutritional scientists, and it could
not bring forth evidence to support the proposition. Instead, it deleted the
questionable section on high protein diets (Anon., 1972) from another revision
of the Nutrient Requirements of Dogs (Anon., 1974).

The proposition that a diet containing 44% protein is bad for dogs is absurd
physiophyletically because dogs evolved on diets that contained this much
protein. Nevertheless, it received support from the highest scientific
authority in the USA. So it prompted a series of studies in the University
of Pennsylvania. Two experimental models were used to reduce the number of
active nephrons, because a study of the natural process of aging was expected
to be too expensive. These models were partial surgical ablation and induced
infection.

Experimentally induced pyelonephritis was the lesser model for the original
purpose (Bovee and others, 1979b). It showed, however (Bovee and others, 1979a),
that peripheral white cell counts and urinary shedding of bacteria persisted
at higher levels much longer in dogs fed a 19% protein diet (k/d^R, Hill's Pet
Products, Topeka, Ks) than in dogs fed a 27% protein dry food (Wayne Dog Food,
Wayne Pet Feeds, Chicago, Il) or a 56% protein canned food (ALPO Beef Chunks
Dinner, Allen Products Co., Allentown, Pa).

The partial nephrectomy reduced renal function to 25 to 50% of usual level
for young adults without inducing signs of failure during 48 months (Bovee and
others, 1979b). Renal blood flow and glomerular filtration were reduced by
about 25% more in dogs fed 19% protein than in those fed 27 or 56% protein.
The tubular maximum of para-amino-hippuric acid was 67% lower in the dogs fed
the 19% protein diet. The 56% protein diet did not produce a 'trophic effect'
that would have been expected according to the workload hypothesis.

More severe partial nephrectomy induced azotemia and other signs of renal
failure (Bovee and Kronfeld, 1981). Four proprietary products were fed in a
cross-over design with periods of 14 days. Protein contents on a dry matter
basis were 8% (u/d, Hill's), 18% (k/d, Hill's), 26% (Wayne), and 54% (ALPO).
Renal blood flow rate was 28% lower an glomerular filtration rate was 23%
lower when dogs were fed the two special 'kidney diets' than when they were
fed the two ordinary dog foods. The 18% protein diet had the lowest salt
content but, paradoxically, depressed tubular reabsorption of sodium. Moreover,
fractional reabsorption of phosphate was higher when dogs were fed this diet
than when they were fed the two ordinary diets, even though these three diets
contained the same level of phosphorus. Serum concentrations of creatinine
were not significantly different between diets, and serum urea concentrations
were significantly lower only when dogs were fed the 8% protein product. These
findings suggest that the safety as well as the efficacy of the two special
dietary products, especially k/d, is highly questionable.

Inspection of the analyses of the diets for differences that might account for
the observed effects was not rewarding in regard to previous concepts. Protein
score and essential amino acid index were appreciably higher in u/d than the
other three products. Further inspection revealed that arginine intakes were

108, 233, 423 and 753 mg/day/kg$^{0.75}$ when dogs were fed the 8, 18, 26 and 54% protein diets, respectively. Arginine is not regarded as essential in healthy adult dogs, but it appears to be essential in pups, kittens and adult cats (Milner, 1979).

Arginine is the only amino acid that is synthesised in the kidney rather than the liver. Total kidney capacity for synthesising arginine may be reduced as the number of functional nephrons is reduced. Thus dietary arginine may need to be increased when total protein or amino acid intakes should be reduced during chronic renal failure.

THE MINNESOTA STUDY

Following preliminary reports of the success of the partial nephrectomy model in Pennsylvania, similar studies were begun in Minnesota (Polzin and others, 1981). Hill's k/d^R and u/d^R were compared to an ordinary canned product, Kennel Ration^R (Quaker Oats Co., Chicago, Il). These products contained 8, 18 and 44% protein, respectively. Kennel Ration was an unfortunate choice, since it has a poor amino acid profile (Kronfeld, 1978).

Beagles were fed these diets for four weeks then subjected to arterial ligation and partial nephrectomy. Several dogs fed Kennel Ration developed anorexia, diarrhoea, hypothermia, then died. Survivors fed this product developed poor coats and high blood urea concentrations.

Dogs fed the 8% protein product manifested several signs of protein insufficiency: low serum concentrations of albumin and haemoglobin, reduced hindleg circumference, and slow re-growth of hair. They also developed severe metabolic acidosis, hypercholesterolemia, and an 88% reduction in glomerular filtration rate. Dogs fed the 18% protein product developed mild metabolic acidosis and an 80% reduction in glomerular filtration rate.

The authors concluded that their "studies revealed no evidence of adverse effects from dietary associated reduction in glomerular filtration rate" (Polzin and others, 1981). This conclusion emphasised the fact that the dogs apparently fared better on k/d and u/d. Moreover, they attributed the deaths of dogs fed Kennel Ration to diet rather than ligation and ablation, whereas previous investigators have regarded the model as being valuable only after the dog has reached a steady state following stress and duress of surgery.

The Minnesota workers recommend that "excessive quantities of dietary protein should be avoided since catabolism of excessive protein will augment production of catabolic waste products which contribute to uremic manifestations" (Polzin and others, 1981). This recommendation re-emphasises the interpretation of serum urea concentration as an index of renal function and a sentinal of toxic nitrogenous waste products (Morris, 1960; Morris, 1968).

The most important Minnesota result in this author's opinion was confirmation of the Pennsylvania finding that reduced dietary protein reduces glomerular filtration rate in uremic dogs. This finding should re-direct attention back to the critical point when restriction of dietary protein becomes more beneficial than disadvantageous.

IMPLICATIONS OF RECENT RESEARCH

The concept that dietary protein should be restricted progressively in all

older dogs and through successive stages of renal insufficiency and failure
should be seriously reconsidered in view of the above studies (Bovee and
others, 1979a, 1979b; Bovee and Kronfeld, 1981; Polzin and others, 1981).
The 48-month experiment invalidates the hypothesis that a low protein diet
improves the excretory functions of kidney reduced experimentally to 25 to
50% of normal capacity - the range found in older dogs that have senile
degeneration of the kidneys but show no clinical signs. The study also
indicates that low-protein diets, like the geriatric products, are unsuitable
for older dogs with a force that depends on how well the experimental model
simulates the natural condition of aging. Supporting this view are calculations of protein quality of commercial special geriatric dog foods and
comparisons with the protein requirements of old dogs (Kronfeld, 1982b).

Once clinical signs of renal failure become manifested, the same contention
becomes intensified. Should dietary protein be restricted progressively?
Or should dietary protein remain unchanged until the critical point is reached
when limiting the production of postulated nitrogenous toxins, as yet unident-
ified, becomes more important than reduction in renal functions? In my view,
the studies in Pennsylvania and Minnesota (reviewed above) strongly support
the critical point approach to dietary intervention in chronic kidney disease.

For improvement of clinical practice, convenient and error-free ways are needed
to determine the critical point. The 24-hour creatinine clearance requires a
metabolic crate (Bovee, 1979). Serum concentrations of urea and creatinine
are more readily obtained but have limited utility in uremic dogs (Finco and
Duncan, 1976). Their value is liable to increase appreciably through the
application of more powerful statistical methods, e.g. discriminant analysis.
Inclusion of dietary protein as a factor, as well as serum concentrations of
urea and creatinine, may allow further resolution of the critical point
(Cowgill, 1981).

Further nutritional research should be conducted with semi-purified diets
containing known mixtures of amino acids. Especially interesting are arginine
and histidine, which may not be essential in healthy adults but may be required
during uremia (Kopple and Swenseid, 1974; Bovee and Kronfeld, 1981). Also,
methionine is interesting because it has been used as a supplement for uremic
diets (Anderson and others, 1973), but oxidation of its sulphur may contribute
to metabolic acidosis, an undesirable characteristic of uremia.

                    DIETS FOR UREMIC DOGS

Commercial interests have usually confined diets for uremic dogs to one or,
recently, two formulas (Table 1). Some clinical investigations have deplored
the single formula approach because the course of chronic kidney disease calls
for different dietary modifications at different times, i.e. for many diets,
not just one (e.g. Bovee, 1972). Moreover, intercurrent diseases, such as
congestive heart failure, may influence the diet of a uremic dog.

The Basic Recipe described in the companion article on Optimal Regimens is
modified readily for dogs with renal disease. For a 10 kg adult dog, it
comprises 2/3rds cupful rice, 1/3rd cupful medium fatty meat, 30 g chopped
liver, 8 g bone meal, 5 g corn oil, 3 g iodised salt and 500 ml water. It
contains about 18% protein on an energy basis, which would be regarded as low
by most standards for dogs, together with 1.4% calcium, 1.3% phosphorus and
0.5% sodium on a dry matter basis.

TABLE 1   Average Analysis of Two Special Dietary Products
intended for the Dietary Management of Canine
Renal Failure (personal communication from M. L.
Morris, Jr., September 1981)

	Dry Matter (%)	
	k/d	u/d
Protein	16.1	9.1
Fat	27.3	20.0
Carbohydrate	53.5	67.8
Calcium	0.52	0.48
Phosphorus	0.26	0.21
Potassium	0.34	0.27
Sodium	0.25	0.27

A low-phosphorus diet, about 0.3%, is obtained by substituting calcium
carbonate for bone meal in the Basic Recipe. This may be the first modification needed, because a reduced excretion of phosphorus is common in the early
stages of clinical kidney failure. The consequent increase in plasma phosphorus
concentration may tend to suppress plasma calcium concentration, hence release
parathyroid hormone. The hormone will tend to correct the change in plasma
calcium concentration, but at the same time, exert adverse effects such as
suppression of red blood cell production. Anaemia is accompanied by lassitude
and loss of appetite, some of the signs of uremia that are most difficult to
treat. Further control of hyperphosphatemia may be achieved with certain
antacids, e.g. alumina-gel, that bind phosphorus and prevent its absorption
from the gut.

Calcium carbonate has other desirable attributes. The carbonate tends to
counteract metabolic acidosis. The calcium is absorbed efficiently, so tends
to prevent hypocalcaemia and hyperparathyroidism. Later in the disease,
failure to synthesise the active metabolite of vitamin D in the kidney may
impair calcium absorption from the digestive tract. At this point, additional
calcium carbonate may be included in the diet to achieve a calcium-rich diet.
Any supplementation with vitamin D should be cautious.

Low-protein diets are obtained by exchanges of meat with rice and egg. The
Basic Recipe has 2/3rds cupful of rice and 1/3rd cupful of meat for a 10 kg
healthy dog. Changing the proportions to 5/6ths cupful of rice and 1/6th
cupful of meat reduces the protein content to 13% of the metabolisable energy.
This should be enough for most cases that require protein restriction. Addition
of one or two teaspoonfuls of chicken fat or turkey fat will improve the
palatability and further decrease the protein content on an energy basis.
Substitution of the 1/6th cupful of medium fatty meat (125 kcal, 40 grams wet
weight, 10 grams protein) with one egg (6 g protein and 80 kcal) and 1 tea-
spoonful of chicken fat (45 kcal) will achieve a protein level of 10% on an
energy basis.

The sodium content of the Basic Diet is about 0.5% on a dry matter basis.
This is about the level of the salt recommended by the National Research
Council (Anon., 1974). On the other hand, dogs evolved on diets that contained
about 0.16% sodium or about 0.4% salt, so the physiophylic or evolutionary
approach would suggest that this level may be close to optimum for healthy
dogs (Kronfeld, 1982a). The salt content of commercial dog foods is high in
the interests of palatability, for salt is a major contributor to the taste
of meat. A low-salt diet, by most standards about 0.05% sodium, is obtained

simply by leaving out the salt from the Basic Recipe. This may be desirable
in uremic dogs that have concurrent congestive heart failure and oedema or
elevated blood pressure (Cowgill, 1981). The iodine of the iodised salt may
be replaced by tincture of iodine, about 0.001 ml for a 10 kg dog. For
convenience, the tincture may be diluted with vodka. If a dog is being
treated with a diuretic that depletes body potassium, the salt in the Basic
Recipe may be replaced by an iodised mixture of potassium and sodium chlorides
(e.g. Lite Salt^R, Morton-Norwich Inc., Chicago, Il).

A low-chloride diet may be obtained by substituting all or part of the iodised
sodium chloride in the Basic Recipe with sodium bicarbonate. The bicarbonate
will diminish any tendency towards metabolic acidosis. The sodium may be
needed if tubular reabsorption is greatly depressed in advanced stages of
chronic renal failure. Again, iodine should be replaced.

The timing of each of the above dietary modifications should be based on an
integrated evaluation of clinical signs, blood analysis and other specific
tests when available (Cowgill, 1981). Experimental progress has broken down
massive complacency in this field but not achieved the resolution needed to
simplify the task of the clinician.

REFERENCES

Addis, T. (1948). Glomerular Nephritis: Diagnosis and Treatment. Macmillan,
    New York, NY.
Anderson, C. F., R. A. Nelson, J. D. Margie, W. J. Johnson and J. C. Hunt
    (1973). J. Am. med. Ass., 223, 1, 68-72.
Anonymous (1972). Nutrient Requirements of Dogs. National Academy of Sciences,
    National Research Council, Washington, DC.
Anonymous (1974). Ibid.
Bovee, K. C. (1972). J. Am. Anim. Hosp. Ass., 8, 246-253.
Bovee, K. C., D. A. Abt and D. S. Kronfeld (1979a). J. Am. Anim. Hosp. Ass.,
    15, 9-16.
Bovee, K. C. (1979). The uremic syndrome: patient evaluation and treatment.
    Compend. Contin. Educ. Vet. Pract., 1, 279-283.
Bovee, K. C., D. S. Kronfeld, C. F. Ramberg, Jr. and M. Goldschmidt (1979b).
    Investig. Urol., 16, 378-384.
Bovee, K. C. and D. S. Kronfeld (1981). J. Am. Anim. Hosp. Ass., 17, 277-285.
Cowgill, L. D. (1981). Disease of the kidney. In S. J. Ettinger (Ed.),
    Textbook of Internal Veterinary Medicine, 3rd ed. W. B. Saunders,
    Philadelphia, Pa.
Finco, D. R. and J. R. Duncan (1976). J. Am. vet. med. Ass., 168, 593-601.
Fishberg, A. M. (1930). Hypertension and Nephritis. Lea & Febiger, Philadelphia,
    Pa.
Giordano, C. (1963). J. Lab. clin. Med., 62, 231-246.
Giovanetti, S. and Q. Maggiore (1964). Lancet, i, 1000-1003.
Gottschallk, C. W. (1964). Am. J. Med., 36, 670-685.
Kennedy, G. C. (1957). Br. med. Bull., 13, 67-70.
Kopple, J. D. (1981). Nutr. Rev., 39, 193-206.
Kopple, J. D. and M. E. Swedseid (1974). Am. J. clin. Nutr., 27, 806-812.
Kronfeld, D. S. (1972). Some nutritional problems in dogs. In D. S. Kronfeld
    (Ed.), Canine Nutrition. University of Pennsylvania, Philadelphia, Pa.
Kronfeld, D. S. (1974). Cornell vet., 64, 466-475.
Kronfeld, D. S. (1978). J. Am. vet. med. Ass., 172, 1144-1146.
Kronfeld, D. S. (1982a). Pure-Bred Dogs and Kennel Club Gazette, 99, 5, 8-10.
Kronfeld, D. S. (1982b). Compendium on Continuing Education of Practicing
    Veterinarian, in press.

Mara, J. L. (1981). Pure-Bred Dogs and Kennel Club Gazette, 98, 10, 10-11.

Mather, G. W. (1979). The consideration of renal pathology as a basis for protein levels in the nutrition of dogs. Gaines Professional Services, White Plains, NY.

Milner, J. A. (1979). J. Nutr., 109, 1161-1167.

Minot, C. S. (1908). The Problem of Age, Growth and Death. Putnam, New York, NY.

Morris, M. L. (1960). Nutrition and Diet in Small Animal Medicine. Mark Morris Associates, Denver, Co.

Morris, M. L. Jr. (1968). Nutrition. In E. J. Catcott (Ed.), Canine Medicine. Am. Veterinary Publications, Wheaton, Il.

Newberne, P. M. (1974). Cornell Vet., 64, 159-177.

Polzin, D. J., C. A. Osborne, D. W. Hayden and J. B. Steves (1981). Minn. Vet. J., 21, 16-29.

Walser, M. (1975). Clin. Nephrol., 3, 180-186.

Wannemacher, R. W. and J. R. McCoy (1966). J. Nutr., 88, 66-74.

Young, V. R. and N. S. Schrimshaw (1975). Nutrition Notes, Am. Inst. Nutr., 11, 4, 6-7.

Zanni, E., D. H. Calloway and A. Y. Zezulka (1979). J. Nutr., 109, 513-524.

Part 2 — Behaviour

INTRODUCTION

Methods Used to Describe the Normal and Abnormal Behaviour of the Dog and Cat

R. A. Mugford

10 Ottershaw Park, Ottershaw, Chertsey, Surrey, UK

ABSTRACT

No one discipline provides a rounded description of the complex interactions between man and companion animals. Reliable data on dog and cat behaviour can now be collected from laboratory, domestic, feral and wild situations, but it may be difficult to integrate this within comparative psychology. Ethology and social psychology provide concepts and terminology more relevant to understanding the human-companion animal bond.

KEYWORDS

Companion animal bond; ethology; behavioural problems.

INTRODUCTION

Since ancient times, man has shared his hunts, house, table and, in many instances, his bed with dogs and cats. These animal companions are an integral part of our European folklore, literature and leisure. Little formal instruction in canine or feline language is given to our children and yet most become fairly accurate interpreters of their pets' behaviour, their needs and their next move. Understanding and sympathy for dogs and cats seems to be as much about human intuition as about scientific knowledge. The dog in particular shares so many attributes of social behaviour and organisation with man that it is quite reasonable that we shamelessly anthropomorphise about our pets.

Communication is a two-way street and one wonders which parts of our anatomy, vocalisations or chemical signals are attended to by our domestic animals. Does a dog read a human smile as we read a wagging tail, for instance? These issues have interested philosophers from Descartes to Hume, and later Darwin took up the challenge in his remarkable essay 'The Expression of the Emotions in Man and Animals' (1873). The experimental tradition which came to dominate scientific effort after Darwin was probably not so successful, and certainly not so interesting in its attempts at describing animal communication.

One of the great drawbacks of the biological tradition in the 19th and early 20th Century has been a concern for control or removal of extraneous variables from animals undergoing systematic testing or observation. As Katcher (1981) has pointed out, Pavlov put his dogs into a chamber, Freud isolated his subjects under hypnosis and modern medicine invariably isolates its patients in hospitals away from the community. The majority of behavioural studies upon the dog and cat have been conducted with this same tradition of 'scientific' control, the consequence being that many of the more interesting aspects of intra-specific and interspecies social interactions have been ignored. However, the post-war influence of biologists like Lorenz, Tindbergen and Thorpe initiated a fundamental shift away from the experimental traditions of physiology and towards the more extensive, naturalistic study of animal behaviour. In a word, ethology.

The practising veterinarian, dog trainer or animal psychologist quickly finds that the real world of dogs, cats and their owners presents them with behavioural phenomena that scientific theory and reliable investigation have not dealt with. However, that is no excuse for ignoring the published scientific literature on, say, learning theory, as the majority of dog trainers have tended to do. One need not invent a pseudo-science of dog training (e.g. Woodhouse, 1973) when sources such as the present volume offer the framework for a rational understanding of our companion animals' behaviour.

BLACK BOX BEHAVIOURISM

The American psychologist, Watson, is credited with having ushered in a long and, some would say, wasted era of studying animals' reactions to events within highly contrived laboratory situations. No student instruction in animal behaviour used to be complete without that symbol of behaviourism, the Skinner box: rat, pigeon, or primate model. Within this apparatus, the experimenter could control every detail of the environment together with contingencies between various stimuli (S) and responses (R). Ever more complex learning schedules or temporal associations between S and R could be manipulated to tax the animals' enterprise or persistence. Specialised terminologies evolved amongst different schools of pigeon-pecking and rat-running theorists to complete the isolation of comparative psychology from the real world of animals living the free life (see Catania, 1968).

In Russia, Pavlov's studies of the conditioned reflex in dogs provided the main ideological theme for research into learning, sensory processes and even psychology (Corson and O'Leary Corson, 1976). His original discovery of the classical conditioning paradigm arose from an accident in his experiments on gastric physiology: his laboratory dogs salivated at the sound of technicians preparing food and well in advance of it being offered. Pavlov utilised a variety of conditioning situations and unconditioned responses, but almost all of his research concerned isolated and usually harnessed dogs.

There is no doubt that the classical conditioning methodology can be applied to the specialised aspects of dog training: for instance, in inducing a stereotyped escape response to an innocuous stimulus or verbal command. However, most learning situations encountered by companion dogs or cats require that the animal retains considerable flexibility of response to stimuli, depending upon their social and ecological context. Too stereotyped a response to a given stimulus would leave the animal vulnerable to environmental change. If the behavioural tradition of learning theorists such as Skinner (1966) has had relatively little to offer dog training, it has

still offered useful techniques to explore specialised issues such as the
measurement of olfactory thresholds (Moulton, 1973), food preferences
(Kitchell and Baker, 1972) or meal patterning (Kanarek, 1975).

ETHOLOGICAL STUDIES

Ethology can be defined as the study of animals within their total environment,
both physical and social. For the committed ethologist, understanding of
behavioural phenomena should naturally follow from careful observation and
recording, irrespective of pre-conceived theory. Early ethologists such as
Lorenz and Tindbergen eschewed the laboratory for the field, but there remains
plenty of scope for applying the same uncommitted approach to data collection
from animals in artificial settings. For instance, Leyhausen (1978) can be
credited with providing the most comprehensive picture of the social life of
cats, and his conclusions are of practical relevance to resolving behavioural
problems. Much of this work was done by observing the social interactions of
free-roaming pet and feral cats near his home. Equally important ethological
data on the more restricted topic of play in cats were provided by Barrett and
Bateson (1978), based upon laboratory investigation.

Considerable practical difficulties and even discomfort may have to be
faced by the observer who wants to study dogs, cats and their wild relatives
in natural conditions. Mech (1970) and his co-workers were able to provide
a well-rounded picture of the wolf in North America by developing sophisticated
radio-tracking techniques, by following packs from helicopters, and by patient
tracking on the ground. Beck (1973) tackled the feral dog in an American city,
his main source of data being 'capture' on camera in order to time sample his
subjects' movements around their urban environment. Photographic methods of
monitoring an animal's movements and behaviour are ideal for those interested
in following dogs and cats because individuals tend to have unique coat
markings.

One of the irritating characteristics of photographic film is that time
passes as it waits to be developed, and that can mean days from shooting to
inspection of film. The arrival of video has dramatically eased the
observation and analysis of visual behaviours. Relatively cheap and portable
VTRs are now available that can be used for time lapse recording with rapid
review or slow motion replay. The author became an enthusiast for video-
based data collecting procedures when studying feeding behaviour of groups
of dogs and cats (Mugford and Thorne, 1980). We used infra-red sensitive
cameras so that day and night activity could be recorded without any special
environmental impositions being made upon the animals. Modern equipment is
sufficiently compact to be carried in a briefcase and used to provide
detailed information on unusual behavioural sequences. Dog fights usually
happen so fast that the most alert observer can miss important information
on who does what and when: information vital to defining the behavioural
problem, designing treatment and evaluating results of therapy. A video
record may be to the animal behavioural specialist what the comprehensive
diagnostics laboratory report is to the clinician.

THE ANIMAL IN THE FAMILY

Pet owners are very willing to talk about the relationship they have with
their dog or cat; indeed it can sometimes be difficult to change the subject!
The ease with which people converse about animals in general and their own
pets in particular has been noted by several authors (see Fogle, 1981) and

recently has found application in psychiatric settings. Dialogue between
habitually withdrawn and mistrustful patient and psychotherapist seems to
occur more readily when a bond has formed via an intermediate pet (Corson,
O'Leary Corson and Gwynne, 1974); people seem not to be so stressed by
strange, potentially threatening situations when in the presence of a pet
(Mugford, 1980). This phenomenon facilitates the work of professionals like
veterinarians probing people about their relationship to companion animals.
A social worker seeking frank information about a parent's attitudes to their
spouse or child has no such advantage.

A variety of styles can be adopted by interviewers probing sensitive aspects
of the pet-owner relationship. In the author's practice, an open or non-
structured approach to information-gathering is applied. No pre-arranged
questionnaire or check-list is used except for preliminary questions to
gather basic demographic data, e.g. sex, age, breed of dog; number, age and
names of children, etc. The objective throughout the interview is that the
owner should not be subjected to value judgements or criticisms about the
care of their pet, even when such criticisms are actively sought. It is
remarkably common to find that owners of 'problem' pets harbour an acute
sense of guilt about their animals' problematic behaviour. Such self-blame
can prove a handicap when constructive strategies are being proposed to
overcome the animals' behavioural problems.

The environment in which questioning occurs can be a critical factor in
eliciting reliable information. The author prefers to see pet owners in
their own home so that habits and critical events can be demonstrated or
re-enacted. However, there are also powerful practical and economic
arguments for seeing clients in a practitioner's clinic which is strange to
animal and owner. In this situation the interviewer must be particularly
skilful in his or her line of questioning and comment. It is very likely
indeed that the behaviour being discussed will not be witnessed in a strange
setting: most cats only spray or bite within their territory. The apparent
innocence of the animal away from home can easily be used to undermine the
owners' credibility and self-esteem. Thus, care should be exercised not to
jump to conclusions about the owners' truthfulness or sanity.

                    NORMAL VS. ABNORMAL BEHAVIOUR

If one studies the behaviour of animals such as laboratory mice, having
relatively little genetic variability and raised in rather standardised,
even impoverished environments, one still encounters large individual
differences. A heterogeneous species such as the dog, raised in a multitude
of environments and social situations presents even greater variability.
Thus, one generalises about the behaviour of cats or dogs at one's peril,
and the greater one's knowledge of the two species, the less appropriate
seems the term 'abnormal'. For instance, 'whirling' is a commonly occurring
stereotypy in kennelled dogs, but is unusual in free-roaming or home
situations. If one examines the behavioural options available to a kennelled
dog, one finds that restricted movement and reduced social contacts have made
whirling a highly appropriate behaviour in this environment. It brings
vestibular stimulation and attention from kennel staff, and in that setting
is certainly not an abnormal behaviour. However, to the compassionate
observer, it can fairly be described as undesirable behaviour.

The great majority of behavioural problems encountered in companion animals
are quite normal in the sense that they concern acts commonly performed by
other members of the species in other contexts. The obvious examples are

barking dogs or spraying cats: both species-typical communicatory patterns,
but not acceptable in many homes. Such behaviours are undesired rather than
abnormal, though that assessment does not mean that they cannot be modified
(see later chapters by Voith and Mugford, present volume). Nevertheless, in
veterinary and behavioural practice, certain highly damaging and inappropriate
behavioural patterns are encountered that justify the description 'abnormal'.
For instance, self-mutilation due to stereotypic tail chasing, flank sucking
or persistent licking is sometimes seen in both dogs and cats. It may be
possible to relate aberrant behaviours such as inappetance, narcolepsy or
sudden aggression to disease processes of the CNS or endocrine systems, but
in other cases (e.g. phobias) there may be no organic cause.

TERMINOLOGY

In this brief review of methods for describing the behaviour of dogs and cats,
the author has tried to avoid the use of unnecessary jargon that has developed
within psychology and ethology just as in other disciplines. There is a core
of behavioural terminology which the informed reader should be familiar with
and a comprehensive glossary such as the Oxford Companion to Animal Behaviour
(McFarland, 1981) is a useful possession. The nice feature of ethological
writing about animal behaviour is that most of the terms are descriptive and
self-explanatory. By contrast, many terms used in comparative psychology
(e.g. reinforcement, condition, extinction, etc.) have quite different
meanings from their usage in everyday English. However, specialised terminology need not deter the curious pet owner, animal trainer or veterinarian
from making valid observations and contributing to our wider understanding
of the human-companion animal bond.

REFERENCES

Barrett, P. and P. Bateson (1978). Behaviour, 66, 106-120.
Beck, A. M. (1973). The Ecology of Stray Dogs: a study of free-ranging
    urban animals. York Press, Baltimore.
Catania, A. C. (1968). Contemporary Research in Operant Behaviour. Scott,
    Foresman and Company, Illinois.
Corson, S. A. and E. O'Leary Corson (1976). Psychiatry and Psychology in the
    U.S.S.R. Plenum Press, New York.
Corson, S. A., E. O'Leary Corson and P. H. Gwynne (1974). In R. S. Anderson
    (Ed.) Pet Animals and Society. Bailliere Tindall, London.
Darwin, C. R. (1873). The Expression of Emotion in Man and Animals.
    Appleton, New York.
Fogle, B. (1981). Interrelations Between People and Pets. Charles C. Thomas,
    Illinois.
Kanarek, R. B. (1975). Physiol. Behav., 15, 611-618.
Katcher, A. (1981). In B. Fogle (Ed.), Interrelations Between People and
    Pets. Charles C. Thomas, Illinois.
Kitchell, R. G. and G. G. Baker (1972). In H. Swan and D. Lewis (Eds.),
    Nutrition Conference for Feed Manufacturers. Churchill Livingston,
    Edinburgh.
Leyhausen, P. (1978). Cat Behavior: the Predatory and Social Behaviour of
    Domestic and Wild Cats. Garland STPM Press, New York.
McFarland, D. (1981). The Oxford Companion to Animal behaviour. Oxford
    University Press, Oxford.
Mech, D. L. (1970). The Wolf. Doubleday Natural History Press, New York.
Moulton, D. G. (1973). In W. I. Gay (Ed.), Methods of Animal Experimentation,
    4. Academic Press, New York.

Mugford, R. A. (1980). In S. A. Corson and E. O'Leary Corson (Eds.), Ethology and Non-verbal Communication in Mental Health. Pergamon Press, Oxford.
Mugford, R. A. and C. J. Thorne (1980). In R. S. Anderson (Ed.), Nutrition of the Dog and Cat. Pergamon Press, Oxford.
Skinner, B. F. (1966). In W. K. Honig (Ed.), Operant Behaviour: Areas of Research and Application. Appleton, New York.
Woodhouse, B. (1973). Dog Training My Way. Barbara Woodhouse, Herts., UK.

PHYSIOLOGICAL AND
SOCIAL

Neurophysiology of Behaviour

H. Ursin

Institute of Physiological Psychology, University of Bergen, Bergen,
Norway

ABSTRACT

The brain (CNS) is a complex system of self-regulating networks, rather than
a system of reflex chains. Self-regulating nets operate by comparing a preset
value for the variables that are controlled with the actual value for each
such variable. When there is a discrepancy, regulating processes are initiated.
These include behaviour, and not only the traditional homeostatic mechanisms.

In particular threatening situations the brain elicits defensive behaviours.
Particular CNS structures are involved. These 'emotional' types of behaviour
represent instrumental strategies, which may be used to solve the underlying
problem. The activation and effect is then reduced.

KEYWORDS

Activation; affective behaviour; coping; emotions; expectancy; instrumental
aggression; instrumental fear; neuroethology; networks.

REFLEXES, GENETIC PREWIRING AND LEARNING

Any student of behaviour is struck by the extreme degree of variance between
individuals, responding to one and the same stimulus. For anyone trained in
the classical biological sciences, this may lead to frustration, but since
multivariate principles now are accepted also within classical medicine, and
veterinary medicine, we should be able to accept this variance as an interesting
phenomenon in itself.

There are two main sources of variance in biology, genetic variance and
variance due to individual storage of information, which depends on the central
nervous system. The latter source of variance, which is learning or memory,
is an important aspect of adaptation to the environment. The capacity to store
information is of two main classes. Brains may store information about
relationships between stimuli (one stimulus or event is followed by another
event), the typical case is classical conditioning. Pavlov's dogs learned
that the bell was followed by a meatball. We also refer to this type of

learning as stimulus expectancy. The second type of information storage or
learning is about the relationship between responses and events or stimuli.
Skinner's rats learn that if they press a lever food will appear. This is
referred to as instrumental conditioning or response outcome expectancy
(Bolles, 1972; Dickinson, 1980).

In addition to being able to store information, the brain also organises the
responses, or the options for behaviour in any situation. An individual is,
therefore, dependent on his genetic equipment or his prewired brain programmes
when he is to react to the environment. These programmes may be simple
reflexes, monosynaptic or polysynaptic, with a limited variance in the response.
However, even for monosynaptic reflexes there is the possibility of bias from
the central nervous system, which may inhibit or facilitate the alpha motor
neuron. The more complex the reflex chain, the more variance dependent on
'higher' functions.

There are also complex programmes wired into the central nervous system, which
ethologists have referred to as 'fixed action patterns'. These patterns are
not as fixed as we believed earlier. They are also modifiable by individual
learning. In insects and simpler forms of nervous systems the plasticity is
limited, but the programmes are not necessarily simple. Very complex data
analyses are possible, as for example when a frog analyses the flight pattern
of an insect, and calculates where it will be when the tongue reaches it (see
Ewert, Capranica, and Ingle, 1982). There is, however, little individual
variance in these programmes, which is unfortunate for the insect.

This symposium deals with small animals, but the brains of these species are
comparatively large. Therefore, we must expect a large individual variance
even in whatever fixed action patterns they might have. In particular, the
stimuli that 'release' these fixed action patterns show a considerable lack
of stereotypy.

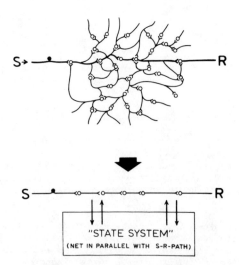

Fig. 1.   Relationship between the network and possible
          S-R pathways (from Ursin, 1980).

Another way of stating that variance is to be expected in behaviour is to refer to the fact that the brain is organised as a complex network. Even the most simple anatomical and physiological investigation of the central nervous system reveals that it is a system of networks rather than a system of straight reflex chains. One useful approach to the analysis of networks is to select a pathway through the network, and regard the rest of the circuitry as a state system, wired in parallel with the S-R pathway and with reciprocal relations with S-R pathway at all points (Fig. 1.). The S-R system is fairly rigid, but may contain habituating synapses (Kandel, 1970). The state systems shows much more plasticity, and also contains sensitising synapses (Thompson and Spencer, 1966). The general principles for the plasticity and variance in responses to a given stimulus, therefore, are known, even on the cellular level, but we still do not know the circuitry of complex behaviours. We are left with fairly crude experiments investigating the behavioural importance of populations or nets of nerve cells, defined either anatomically, or more recently, bio-chemically.

SELF-REGULATING NETWORKS: MOTIVATION, DRIVE, AND ACTIVATION

The network organisation is the structural basis for the self-regulating principles for brain function, realised in traditional physiological theory as the principles of homeostasis and in psychology as general control theory formulations covering all brain functions (Vickers, 1973). The main rule is that brains respond whenever there is a discrepancy between the set value and the actual value for any of the variables that are monitored and controlled by the central nervous system. In all situations with a marked discrepancy between important set values and their corresponding actual values the organism reacts with a general, non-specific response affecting all autonomic responses, somato-motor responses, and endocrine responses. The brain activity itself as measured by the electroencephalogram (EEG) also changes. This response pattern is referred to as 'activation'.

The CNS substrate of activation is the mesencephalic reticular formation. There is currently concern over how important biochemically specific ascending fibre systems are for activation. The dopamine and the noradrenergic fibre systems arising in the brain stem and affecting large parts of the CNS are of particular interest. The substrate for the control of homeostatic variables like osmotic pressure and feeding is the hypothalamus, where the comparison of the set values and the actual values takes place. For more complex set values the circuitry is more complex, but limbic structures like the hippo-campus and the amygdala are definitely involved in acquisition of set values, and in recording discrepancies between the expected outcome of a stimulus or response and what really happens.

Activation persists until the set value and the actual value again become equal, or that motivational system is switched off. Activation also affects the responses, and responses are emitted until the activation is eliminated. Activation, therefore, will tend to eliminate itself. The same concept may be referred to as 'drive' or 'energy'. It is, however, not a hydraulic system, and may be stopped or inhibited ('switched off') without pathogenic effects. This is an important difference from the old and untenable 'instinct' concepts, which still may be found among some naturalists and in some psychodynamic traditions.

The bodily processes during activation have delayed feedback effects on the state of the central nervous system. The old theories of emotions cover different aspects of this brain/body feedback loop. The Cannon-Bard position

dealt with the efferent loop from the brain to the body, while the James-Lange
position covered the feedback from the body to the brain. Cannon-Bard stated
that fear led to activation within the sympathetic system. Their model did
not deal with all the other somatic changes. James-Lange stressed the importance of the experience of this peripheral body effect for emotions. The
experience of these changes was the 'true emotion'. Both positions cover
parts of our present position. Emotional behaviour is characterised by the
activation-processes, and the experience of these processes is important for
emotions. Schachter and Singer (1962) found filtering processes affecting the
sensory feedback part of the loop. The individual makes an appraisal of the
feedback dependent on the expectancy and interpretation he makes of the
situation he is in. There is also evidence of direct humoral feedback which
affects the state of the brain. This feedback consists of catecholamines,
and peptides with behavioural effects(DeWied, 1974; Hole and others, 1979).

Psychology may be referred to as the systematic study of the variables that
produce the variance in the responses to stimulation. The variables that are
intervening between the stimulus and the response have been referred to as
'intervening variables' (Tolman, 1932). Emotions are but one example of such
factors. Other classes are motivation, attention, and the activation level
itself. In this paper emotional behaviour will be used as the main reference,
since this is one type of behaviour which is fairly well described and also
relevant for this particular conference.

ETHOLOGY AND PSYCHOLOGY

The traditions in this field derive mainly from psychology, but also from
ethology, which is the study of animal behaviour by zoologists, with particular
preference for 'naturally occurring behaviour'. While the psychologists were
mostly concerned with learned behaviour, the ethologists were most concerned
with genetic programmes. However, presently there are no clear border lines
between the two traditions and it is no longer necessary to operate with a
distinction between these two disciplines. The nomenclature and positions
outlined in this paper are intended to be as non-controversial and as much
based on consensus as possible, but opinions do differ on several crucial
issues. Readers interested in the current theoretical issues are referred to
The Behavioral and Brain Sciences, an international journal of current research
and theory with open peer commentary. This particular format offers a unique
opportunity of becoming familiar with current research and theoretical problems
and positions.

NEURAL SUBSTRATE OF BEHAVIOUR

As mentioned above, the neural substrate of behaviour may be explained on the
cellular level as habituation, sensitisation, and plasticity due to learning
or memory storage. It is also possible to account for more complex behaviour,
but this requires analyses of populations or nets of nerve cells. These may
be studied by stimulation or ablation techniques, and the attempt is to
understand which parts of the brain are involved in or necessary for a particular behaviour. This will explain how the brain works and will also offer an
opportunity of studying units and mechanisms in behaviour.

The aspects of behaviour which have been studied in most detail for neural
substrate in higher animals are connected with emotional behaviour, in
particular, fear and aggression. These behaviour patterns have similarities
within each species and across species, and are generally assumed to have

genetic components, even if there is individual variance. Therefore, emotions constitute a very interesting model for the interaction between programmes wired in the brain and learning factors.

NOMENCLATURE

There is no standard nomenclature based on any international agreement or convention for psychological terms, or for classification of emotional behaviour. It is possible that even if it were tried, no agreement would result. However, there is still considerable agreement, and enough standard textbooks used to ensure professional communication.

The term defense is sometimes used to cover all types of threat-induced behaviour, regardless of whether the behaviour has an offensive or a defensive character, or whether it represents fear. In the present paper the term will be used in a rather strict ethological sense. It then refers to the particular behaviour shown by intruders when faced with the territory owner. This behaviour may also be elicited by pain or electrical shocks. The behaviour is clearly aggressive and threatening to the opponent, and has been referred to as 'deimatic' (I threaten). It is also the behaviour shown against any large and dominating enemy, for instance an experimenter, or a veterinarian.

These strategies depend on separate structures in the brain and the important contribution from neuroethology for these complex types of behaviour has been the demonstration of subunits within larger classes of behaviour. For instance, for aggressive behaviour neuroethological research had demonstrated convincingly that it is not possible to regard aggression as any unitary type of behaviour. Aggression must be subdivided into several independent categories. In addition to the categories already treated, defense and offense, we must also recognise prey-killing behaviour and, perhaps, male sexual behaviour. All categories depend on separate structures within the brain.

NEUROETHOLOGY AND NEUROPSYCHOLOGY

Before we conclude that a structure plays a crucial role for a certain behaviour, several criteria must be satisfied (Ursin, 1981):

1.   The particular behaviour must be readily identifiable in the naturally occurring behaviour of the animal.

2.   The behaviour should be elicited by stimulation of that particular structure and be reduced by lesion to the structure.

3.   Units in the structure should change their activity during execution of that particular behaviour.

4.   Lesions should also produce a handicap in learning problems where this particular behaviour is important for the execution for the instrumental response.

5.   Electrical or chemical stimulation should 'jam' (block) the ordinary stimulus control of the behaviour.

6.   Pharmacological manipulations of the area should also interfere with this type of behaviour.

7.   Some phylogenic homology should exist across species, and the behaviour change produced should be fairly specific for this particular response.

When these strict criteria are used, the amygdala complex, and possibly the septal complex, are the only limbic structures that are involved in any type of aggressive or fear type of behaviour. Since these are the only limbic structures that are not a part of the celebrated Papez circuit, an updated version of the Papez 'theory' of emotions may be the inversion of the original statement. In fact Papez listed the limbic structures that are without any important influence on any emotional behaviour studied in man or animals. It is therefore also unacceptable to assume a homogenous 'limbic system' role for emotional behaviour (see Ursin, 1981 for expansion of argument and references).

NEUROPSYCHOLOGY OF INSTRUMENTAL BEHAVIOUR

It is also possible to study the neural substrate of problem solving and learning itself. As mentioned above, it is possible to account at least for the most probable changes for habituation and sensitisation on the neuronal level, but we do not yet know any details in what happens when a synapse in the brain becomes more or less effective as a consequence of reward, that is, as a consequence of what happens when a particular response is emitted. However, we have substantial knowledge of which structures are involved in problem solving and instrumental learning. Again, the limbic structures play a crucial role, and the activation and motivation systems in the brain stem and in hypothalamus are also necessary for learning to occur. Cortex, which was assumed to be the highest level in traditional neurology, seems to have a more limited function as a storage area, in addition to its importance for sensory discrimination.

The septo-hippocampal and the entorhinal-hippocampal loops (Gray, 1982) are of particular importance for learning, either because of their role for understanding or recognising complex stimuli, or through a general memory mechanism. It has also been postulated that all learning of space depends on these structures, that is how the individual learns how the world is organised regardless of his own location in space. This was referred to as a cognitive 'map' in previous theories, and is now an important element in our thinking about the function of these structures.

When animals are trained, there is often a conflict between the trainer and the animal. The animal has a motivational state which differs from what the trainer wants to elicit. The outcome of this conflict depends on the principles for learning, which again depend on limbic structures. If the trainer is able to introduce a stronger approach system to the animal than what the animal is engaged in, there is only an approach/approach conflict with relatively modest activation. However, if the possible reward is less rewarding than what the animal is engaged in, punishment is the only way out, with high degrees of activation, and possible development of defensive strategies which may be unwanted. However, if there is an alternative response pattern open to the animal, punishment may be an effective strategy. The high affect and emotional level may then gradually be transferred to relaxed and adequate behaviour, if the limbic structures are intact. If the conflict remains unsolved, the high affect remains, with possible ill effects on the somatic and psychological health (Ursin, 1982). This also depends on intact limbic structures, and possibly also on the frontal lobe. Without these structures the individual may tolerate more problems and conflicts, but the price is a reduced ability to cope with the environment. Psychosurgical

adventures constitute no practical solution to behavioural problems, in man
or beast.

Affective and Instrumental Behaviour

The particular behavioural pattern selected by a subject will increase in
probability in a given situation if it has the desired instrumental effect.
If the behaviour chosen brings the reward or helps in avoiding punishment
that behaviour is reinforced. Since this means that the problem is now
reduced or eliminated, we will also expect it to have a reducing effect on
the activation response, and therefore on the somatic state of the organism.
This particular effect of instrumental behaviour has been referred to as
coping (see Levine and Ursin, 1980 for references).

There are therefore always two stages in emotional behaviour, at least for
fear and aggressive behaviours (Ursin, 1980). Initially, there is an affective
phase with high activation. This is gradually transferred into an instrumental
phase with low activation. Aggressive acts, therefore, may be performed both
under high and low levels of activation.

According to this theoretical position, emotional behaviour should be accepted
as potentially instrumental behaviour, which is regulated by the same laws of
reinforcement as all others types of behaviour. It also affects the activation
response itself, as do all others types of instrumental behaviour. It has been
shown that rats that are given the opportunity to fight as a response to shock
show a reduction in their corticosterone response as compared with rats that
receive the same amount of shocks, but without this 'coping' possibility
(Conner, Vernikos-Danellis and Levine, 1971). In social structures, there are
numerous examples of a lower activation level (higher coping level) in the
dominating subjects as compared with the submissive ones. This is probably
due to the coping mechanisms, and not what determines the position. For
instance, even if high testosterone levels may produce aggression, the high
testosterone level in the dominating male in a colony is probably not the
reason for his dominance, but a consequence of his position. This explains
why his cortisol levels are lower than the competition. Also, the establish-
ment of the social structure seems to represent a coping response for the
whole group (see Myhre, Ursin and Hanssen, 1981, for data and discussion).

CONCLUSION

These response-classes emerge as strategies that are innately organised and
based on CNS prewired structures. However, it is also important to realise
that the behaviour strategies we have dealt with are subject to learning both
for stimulus and response aspects. All the behaviours we have described have
clear instrumental effects and may be effective strategies in dealing with
dangerous and threatening situations. Even if we have not yet reached any
clear understanding of the units in behaviour or in anatomy, the neuroethological tradition has been a very useful tool, but should not be used as the
only tool when one tries to understand the complex neural and behavioural
mechanisms involved in emotional behaviour in animals and, also, in humans.

Behaviour also depends on the prewired diagrams in the brain, and some of the
data treatment that goes on in brains may be accounted for on the cellular and
subcellular levels. This should not lead to naive and reductionalistic
positions. The brain may not be anything else than a complex data handler,
but it is an extremely complex device which tells us that any simplistic

146 H. Ursin

attempt to explain its function, be this philosophically or quasiscience, is
doomed to failure.

Bolles, R. C. (1972). Psychol. Rev., 79, 394-409.
Conner, R. L., J. Vernikos-Danellis, and S. Levine (1971). Nature, 234, 564-566.
DeWied, D. (1974). Pituitary-adrenal system hormones and behavior. In F. O.
  Schmitt and F. G. Worden (eds.) The Neurosciences Study Program. 3. MIT:
  Boston, USA.
Dickinson, A. (1980). Contemporary Animal Learning Theory. Cambridge University
  Press: Cambridge.
Ewert, J.-P., R. R. Caprancia, and D. J. Ingle (eds.). Advances in Vertebrate
  Neuroethology. Plenum Press, London/New York. In press.
Gray, J. A. (1981). The Neuropsychology of Anxiety: An Enquiry into the Function
  of the Septo-Hippocampal System. Oxford University Press: Oxford.
Hole, K., H. Bergslien, O.-G. Berge, J. Jørgensen, K. L. Reichelt, and O.
  Trygstad (1979). Neuroscience, 4, 1883-1892.
Kandel, E. R. (1970). Sci. Am., 223, 57-70.
Levine, S., and H. Ursin (1980). Coping and Health. Plenum Press: New York.
Myhre, G., H. Ursin, and I. Hanssen (1981). Z. Tierpsychol., 57, 123-130.
Shachter, S., and J. E. Singer (1962). Psychol. Rev., 69, 379-399.
Tolman, E. C. (1932). Purposive Behavior in Animals and Men. Appleton-Century-
  Crofts: New York.
Thompson, R. F., and W. A. Spencer (1966). Psychol. Rev., 73, 16-43.
Ursin, H. (1980). In M. Koukkou, D. Lehmann, and J. Angst (eds.) Functional
  States of the Brain: Their Determinants. Elsevier/North Holland Biomedical
  Press: Amsterdam. pp 119-130.
Ursin, H. (1981). In P. F. Brain, and D. Benton (eds.) A Multidisciplinary
  Approach to Aggression Research. Elsevier: Amsterdam. pp 269-293.
Vickers, G. (1973). Behav. Sci., 18, 242-249.

Human/Animal Relationships

V. L. Voith

Clinical Studies, School of Veterinary Medicine, University of
Pennsylvania, Philadelphia, PA, USA

ABSTRACT

People indicate they are attached to their dogs and cats in a variety of ways.
Throughout the year 1981, over 700 dog owners either completely or partially
filled out a questionnaire concerning the person's attitude toward and how
s/he interacted with the pet. The vast majority of respondents consider their
dog to be a family member (99%), talk to their dog once a day or more (97%),
believe they are aware of their dog's moods (99%), believe that the dog is
aware of their (the owner's) moods (98%), share table food (64%), and snacks
(86%), with their dog. Fifty-six percent allow the dog to sleep on the bed
and get on furniture; 54% celebrate their dog's birthday, 91% had photographs
and 9% had paintings or drawings of their dog. Respondents owning cats
answered similarly.

Most people who sought help for behaviour problems of their pets said they had
kept the animal despite the problem because they were attached to it or because
it would be inhumane to euthanise the animal.

KEYWORDS

Attachment; pet owners; dogs; cats; behaviour problems.

INTRODUCTION

Humans have always been interested in, aware of, and responsive to the behaviour of other animals and vice versa. After all, we evolved together. In
the beginning the interactions may have been predator/prey relationships;
sometimes we were the predator and other times the prey. With some species
we may have developed an early symbiotic relationship involving predator
detection, defence, food detection and scavenging. Eventually, we began
domesticating animals and selecting for specific behavioural and morphologic
traits. Domestication allowed a maximum utilisation of animals for food,
shelter (housing and clothing material), transportation, protection (defence,
an early warning signal, a means of escape), mechanisms of pursuit or domin-
ation over other people, symbols of value, hunting abilities, pest and predator

control and, at some point in history, companionship. Throughout the course
of domestication, we have selected for traits considered desirable for the
above qualities. In general, behavioural traits such as aggressiveness and
roaming have been selected against; tractability and reproductive efficiency
selected for. Paedomorphic (infant-like) morphological and behavioural traits
have often been selected for in companion animals. In fact, dogs may have
become neotenised (Frank and Frank, 1982).

No one is quite sure when and how animals became companions and pets. But it
is apparent that today, many people have companion animals and are quite
attached to them.

People demonstrate that they are attached to their pets in a variety of ways.
People take measures to keep pets in their proximity. Pets are often kept in
the home, are taken on trips, accompany the owner throughout the day, and
sleep with the owner. Some owners return home sooner than otherwise because
they have left a pet at home and are worried that the animal is becoming
lonely or that the animal 'misses them'. Or perhaps the owner misses the pet.
Not infrequently owners may sever a relationship with another person because
s/he does not like their pet. Many owners share their main meals with their
pets, and even more frequently share snacks with their pets. Owners engage
in varying degrees of time investment and financial expenditures to ensure
that their pet is healthy, happy, and enjoys a long life. Many owners endure
misbehaviours and inconveniences caused by their pet rather than separate
themselves from their companion. Such owners are not masochists; they have
searched for ways to correct the problem but solutions generally are not
readily available. Consequently, the owners keep the problem animal despite
the problem behaviours. Finally, most owners experience grief over the loss
of a pet and there have been reports of profound grief when a pet dies
(Keddie, 1977; Quackenbush, 1981).

REVIEW OF 100 ANIMAL BEHAVIOUR CASES

In an attempt to learn more about the attachment of people to pets, despite
serious behaviour problems, specific data were collected in a series of 100
cases seen over 4 months, December 1980 - March 1981, at the University of
Pennsylvania, Animal Behaviour Clinic (Voith, 1982). These cases involved
both dogs and cats and the range of problems usually seen by animal behaviourists. The duration of these problems ranged from several months to
several years. None was as short a duration as a few weeks. Ninety-nine
percent of the clients indicated that they considered the problem either very
serious or serious.

The majority of dog problems involved aggressive behaviour, primarily toward
people. The second most common problem involved separation anxiety behaviours
which were manifested as destructive behaviour, excessive vocalisation, or
eliminative behaviours in the owner's absence. The third most common canine
behaviour problem was some form of fear or phobia unaccompanied by aggression.
These fearful behaviours were primarily responses to loud noises, such as
thunderstorms, but sometimes to people or novel environments. Overactivity
or hyperactive behaviour was the fourth most common complaint. Neurological
disorders were the least common causes of behaviour problems.

The most common reason cats were presented was because they were not using
the litter box for elimination behaviours. The second most common complaint
involved aggression towards other cats. Other complaints involved hyperactivity
aggression to people, excessive chewing or inappropriate ingestive behaviours.

Sixty-two percent of these cases were classified as primarily dog cases, and thirty-eight percent as cat cases. This ratio is compatible with the percentage of dogs and cats seen for behaviour problems at other locations in the United States and for dogs and cats seen for medical and surgical reasons at the Veterinary Hospital, University of Pennsylvania.

The majority of people who brought a pet to the Behaviour Clinic lived with other people and had another pet at home. Most had owned a pet of the same species before.

During the course of the interview, the clients were specifically asked:

- why they had kept the pet this long despite the problem?
- had they considered euthanasia?
- did they have any other pets at home?
- was this their first pet?
- had they told any friends that they were going to bring their pet to an animal behaviourist or animal psychologist and what was the friend's response?

Additionally, it was noted whether the person indicated at any time during the interview that s/he felt guilty about having caused the problem or whether the person referred to the animal as a human being in some context.

The responses to the question of why the person had not got rid of the pet because of the behaviour problem fell into ten categories:

- A statement of affection, such as "I love (like) him/her", or that another person (e.g. the children, the wife) was attached to the animal.
- A humanitarian reason, such as "no one else would take this animal". Therefore the owners felt they had to keep the animal or it would be put to death. Typical statements depicting this reason were "I feel that people have a responsibility to a pet", "I have already saved his/her life once before" (the animal had already been rescued by the person in another situation). In some cases, the person expressed feeling sorry for the animal.
- Another response category was simply that getting rid of the animal was not a consideration: they had not or were not going to consider getting rid of the animal.
- Sometimes an owner responded to the question by referring to the animal as a person or with the statement that the pet was a member of the family.
- Not infrequently, the owner would answer with the statement that the animal had positive attributes that outweighed the behaviour problem's negative qualities. Owners would say that the pet is good, sweet, or lovable most of the time or that s/he was really not a bad animal.
- Some owners answered that they thought that the behavioural problem was curable; therefore, they kept the animal because they thought the problem could eventually be resolved.
- Occasionally owners answered that an animal had a monetary value.
- Twice people answered that they could not live without the animal.
- Some owners believed that the animal could not live without them. This answer was different from the answer that the animal would have to be put to sleep if this person didn't keep it because no one else would take it.

- Three dog owners indicated that the protective value of the dog
  was a reason for having kept it. However, this was never a first
  response.

Overwhelmingly the first response (55% of both dog and cat owners) was a term
of affection. The second most common first response (16% of both dog and cat
owners) was a humanitarian reason. If a person's first response was a humanitarian reason, their second response was generally one of affection. The
third largest category of first responses was the statement that getting rid
of the animal was not a consideration.

There were no statistical differences between any of the first responses of
dog and cat owners. Except in one instance, there were no correlations between
category of responses and whether the person was from a single or multi-person
household or whether the person had other pets. The two people, one cat and
one dog owner, who answered they could not live without the animal were people
living alone without other pets in the household. Not all persons living alone
without other pets answered as such; however, those that did answer so were
living alone without other humans or pets in the household. Mr Jamie Quackenbush
(1981), a social worker on the staff at the Veterinary Hospital, University of
Pennsylvania, has also observed a correlation between a dependency upon an
animal and a solitary living situation.

There were no significant differences between the cat and dog owners as to why
they kept behaviour problem animals, whether they had considered euthanasia as
a solution to the problem, or whether they felt guilty about having caused the
problem. Sixty percent of both dog and cat owners endured some social ridicule
by their friends who were aware they were bringing their cat or dog to see an
animal behaviourist. There was, however, a large percentage difference whether
or not the owners referred to the animal as a person at some time during the
session. More dog owners than cat owners (45% vs. 34%) referred to the pet
as a person at some time during the interview. Perhaps this is because dogs
have, as do people, a wider range of and/or more easily recognised facial and
postural expressions than do cats which causes people, consciously or
unconsciously, to identify more with dogs than with cats.

The above cases indicate that the attachment people have to their companion
animals can be quite strong. Owners can recognise their attachment to the
pet and at the same time acknowledge that the animal is causing them
inconvenience, financial or social expenses, or emotional pain. When most
owners come to the conclusion that the cost or disadvantages of keeping the
pet outweighed the benefits, they will decide to no longer keep the pet.
However, this is rarely done without regret and sorrow.

An incident that dramatises the profound attachment a person can feel for an
animal, while being fully aware of the negative attributes of the pet,
involved a woman whose three-day-old baby had been killed by her dog (Voith,
1982). The woman was well composed and at ease during the interview which
took place about one week after the incident had occurred. She appeared to
be coping with the situation very well. She was still grieving over the loss
of her child and cried for a while every night. She viewed the incident as
an accident, neither her fault nor the dog's. She did not want to keep the
dog nor did she think she would ever get another dog. She said "Bernie (the
dog) was very close to me, but I don't know if I could ever have another one."
Towards the end of the session she said "... an absurd thing to me. I feel
the loss of my pet. Now, how can I feel that way after Bernie killed my baby?"

People often acknowledge their attachment to a pet while simultaneously being cognizant of the negative impact the animal has or had on their lives. Like the mother in the above case, this attachment puzzles the owners who realise the disadvantages of the pet. Owners of behaviour problem animals may say, "I know that it is just an animal, but I feel as though it's my child". And that is the crux of the matter. People tend to relate to an animal as having both human and animal characteristics and owners seem to define their relationship with their pet as having both human and animal qualities. For example, most dog and cat owners indicate that they consider the pet an 'animal' member of the family, yet will talk to it as though it were a person (usually a child) rather than a 'pet' (Voith and Danneman, 1982; Ganster and Voith, 1982).

Why The Attachment?

Attachment, whether defined as an emotion (an affective state) or defined strictly in terms of objective behaviours (e.g. attempts to maintain proximity) serves to keep individuals together. As such, attachment is a mechanism for social cohesion. Attachment and/or attachment behaviours are essential for social animals and are inherent in social groups in animals such as people, many canids, equids, etc. The benefits of sociality are related to survival for individuals in these groups. Part of the adaptive strategies of Homo sapiens are attachment behaviours.

As attachment is a mechanism to maintain social contact, there also are factors that encourage and maintain attachment. Behaviours and other factors that may encourage attachment between people are social sign-stimuli involving facial expressions, vocal and eye contact, the length of time in proximity with another individual, sharing of experiences (especially happy or life threatening), 'feelings' such as joy, happiness or love which are evoked by the behaviours of another, dependency, responsibility, cooperative behaviours and tactile stimulation. On the whole, a person's survival is enhanced by cooperative behaviours with other people. Since attachment enhances survival, it should be fairly easy to elicit among people and particularly strong between parent and child.

People are primed to become attached to other people, especially their own children. The activities that serve as attachment mechanisms between people also occur between people and their pets, such as sharing meals, sleeping quarters, spending time together. The pet engages in behaviours that are interpreted by the owner as indicative of attachment. The pet appears happy when the owner returns, sad when the owner departs, demonstrates a desire to be touched or cared for by the owner, etc. Companion animals enthusiastically seek out and greet people. The pet often maintains physical contact with the owner for prolonged periods of time. Animals are capable of making the owner feel happy, good, or loved.

Many of the attributes of children and interactions between people and children are shared by pets. Cats and dogs are usually raised by a person and are quite dependent, even in adulthood, upon that individual. Dogs, in particular, have been selected for infant and juvenile morphological and behavioural traits. Some breeds appear to have been neotenised.

Attachment can be emotional responses or behaviours that adhere individuals. The activities and sign stimuli that serve as attachment mechanisms between people also occur between people and their pet animals. In fact, pets fit very well into this system. Therefore, it should not be surprising that people become attached to pets and relate to them as people, particularly as children.

It is as many owners verbalise "I know it's just an animal, but I feel about it as though it were my child".

RESULTS OF A SURVEY OF DOG OWNER'S ATTITUDES AND INTER- ACTIONS WITH THEIR PET

Throughout the year 1981, an 81-item questionnaire was available to any person entering the Veterinary Hospital of the University of Pennsylvania. The questionnaires were stacked beneath a sign stating: 'If you have a dog, would you mind filling out a questionnaire?' The questionnaires took 15 to 30 minutes to complete. The questions involved behaviours on the part of the animal and behaviours and attitudes of owners towards the animal. The respondent's identity was not required and the questionnaires could be returned by putting them into a box or handing them to a hospital staff member. Over 700 of the dog questionnaires were either partially or completely filled out and the frequencies of responses tabulated. Cross-tabulations of the responses have not yet been done (Voith and Danneman, 1982). Some respondents elected not to answer certain questions and others appeared not to have finished the questionnaire. Therefore, when the terminology 'a percentage of respondents answered ...' is used, it refers to the percent of people who answered that specific question. There were at least 500 specific responses to each question. Table 1 includes representative samples of the questions and the type of responses available.

TABLE 1   Representative Question

How often does your dog sleep in or on the bed with a member of your family?

    1.   Always?
    2.   Usually (5-6 nights per week)?
    3.   Frequently (2-5 nights per week)?
    4.   Sometimes (less than 2 nights per week)?
    5.   Never?

Do you celebrate your pet's birthday?

    1.   Always?
    2.   Frequently (every other year or more)?
    3.   Sometimes (less than every other year)?
    4.   Never?

Many of the responses were indicative of attachment between owner and pet. Ninety-nine percent of the respondents considered the dog to be a member of their family. When asked what kind of family member, the most frequent single response indicated an animal member (57%), a child (28%), and a brother or sister (10%). Many respondents indicated more than one answer. When multiple responses were tabulated, 65% indicated they considered the dog an animal member, 38% as a child, and 18% a brother or sister.

Ninety-seven percent of the respondents indicated that they talked to their dogs frequently (once a day or more). When asked how they talked to their dog, the most frequent single responses were as a child (52%), as an adult human (29%), and with 'pet talk' (16%). At least once a month, 45% of the owners talked to their dog about problems and events important to them;   16% did so once a day or more.

Ninety-nine percent of the respondents thought that they were aware of their dog's moods and 98% believed that the dog was aware of the owner's moods. Eighty-five percent of the owners believed that they were aware of the dog's moods over 80% of the time and 73% believed that the dog was aware of the owner's moods over 80% of the time.

Fifty-six percent of the owners allowed the dog to sleep on the bed of a member of the family. Fifty-six percent also allowed the dog to sleep on other pieces of furniture.

Owners shared their food with their pets. Sixty-four percent gave titbits from the table to their dogs while eating, and 86% shared snacks with their dog other than at mealtimes.

Eighty-three percent of the owners took their pets with them when they went on errands and 72% took their dogs with them when they left home one night or longer.

TABLE 2   Some Data from Dog Questionnaire

Percent of respondents who indicated whether their dog always, usually (80-90% of the time), frequently (30-70%), sometimes (less than 30%), never sleeps on bed with family member, is fed from table, fed snacks, taken on errands and trips.

	Sleeps on bed (n=727)	Fed from table (n=709)	Shares snacks (n=709)	Taken on errands (n=710)	Taken on trips (n=699)
Always	26.00	10.01	11.00	4.23	24.46
Usually	8.25	9.17	13.40	12.82	28.47
Frequently	7.98	14.81	19.75	25.49	11.44
Sometimes	13.61	30.04	42.03	40.28	18.60
Never	44.15	35.97	13.82	17.18	28.17

Most of the owners (68%) indicated that they spent more than an hour each day talking to, playing with, exercising, training, or caring for their dog. Fifty-four percent of the dog owners celebrated their dog's birthday. Nine percent had paintings of their dogs and 91% had photographs.

Another reflection of attachment is that owners kept dogs despite inconvenient behaviours. Twenty-three percent of the owners indicated that once a week or more their dog disobeyed, ran away, stole food, got into the garbage or otherwise behaved in an independent manner. Twenty percent of the owners answered that their dogs never engaged in such behaviours. Forty-two percent of the respondents answered that their dog engaged in behaviour they considered a problem. How serious they considered the problem was not determined, but the owners were asked to briefly explain the problem. The most frequently cited

problems were some form of aggression (15%), eliminative behaviour (13%),
destruction (12%), or excessive noise/vocalisation (12%). Twenty-five
percent of the owners indicated that the dog had received some obedience
training either at an obedience school or by a professional obedience trainer
(how many successfully completed obedience sources has not yet been determined).

Despite the fact that some aggression and noisy behaviour was a problem for
the owners, many owners may have appreciated such behaviours. Seventy-five
percent of the respondents considered their dogs protective, "a good watch
dog", of themselves or their home. Ninety-nine percent of the dogs barked on
at least 30% of the occasions when people came to the owner's home; 47%
always barked.

Thirty-two percent of the respondents were men and 68% were women. The largest
single group (40%) of respondents were part of a nuclear family (two adults of
opposite sexes with children). Twenty-nine percent of the respondents were
one of a couple (two adults of the opposite sex). Eight percent were single
adults. The most common source of the dogs was a professional breeder or kennel
(30%) followed by a friend, neighbour or relative (23%), advertisement of a
non-professional (home environment) (12%), and an SPCA or similar agency (8%),
or a pet shop (8%). Eighty-five percent had owned the dog more than one year;
74.5% for more than two years. The majority (87%) had obtained the dog when it
was under a year of age. Fifty-five percent acquired the dog when it was 10
weeks old or younger.

Sixty percent of the respondents indicated that they had other pets; of those
who listed the type of other pet, 61% indicated that they had at least one
other dog and 53% had at least one other cat. Incidentally, 14% also had fish,
7% birds and 3% owned amphibians and/or reptiles. Forty-six percent of the
answers referred to male dogs and 54% to female dogs.

RESULTS OF A SURVEY OF CAT OWNERS' ATTITUDES AND INTER-ACTIONS WITH THEIR PETS

A questionnaire containing similar questions was filled out by 53 owners of
male cats (23 presented for urethral blockage and 30 for minor medical disorders
or vaccinations) (Ganster and Voith, 1982). This was part of the questionnaire
developed as a preliminary survey aimed at determining correlations between
environmental events and urethral blockage in male cats.

All but one of the respondents considered their cat to be a member of the family;
this was regardless of the number of adults, children or other pets residing in
the household. When asked what type of family member they considered the cat
to be, 57% (30) considered the cat only an animal member, 32% (17) chose only
a human category - either parent, sibling, child or good friend, 42% (22) chose
a combination of human and animal member, and 36% (19) viewed their cat as a
child member of the family either exclusively or in combination with another
answer.

All of the respondents talked to their cat either a lot or sometimes and 41%
indicated that they confided in their cat to some extent about problems and
events which were important to the owner. When asked to indicate how the owners
talked to their cats, tabulation of single answer selections revealed that 34%
of the owners selected only "as a child", and 30% chose only "pet talk", and
15% chose "as to an adult". The response frequencies, exclusively plus in
combination with other answers, were as follows: 51% chose "as to a child",
49% chose "pet talk", 23% chose "as to an adult", and 2% chose "other". It was

interesting to note that although many owners viewed their cat exclusively an animal member of the family, many of the same owners indicated they talked to their cat as they would to a person rather than talking to it as an animal. The reciprocal relationship was also found: those that viewed the animal as a person often talked to it as an animal.

Most owners included their cat in some routine daily activity as well as special events. Forty-nine percent shared food during or after mealtimes and 43% shared snacks with their pet. Thirty-two percent of the respondents indicated that some portion of the cat's diet was comprised of food that the owners prepared specially for the cat or shared with the cat from their meals. Many owners regularly celebrated their cat's birthday (34%), often by giving it a toy or a favourite food such as tuna, ice cream, turkey, or cheese; sometimes by singing to it and occasionally by having children draw or paint pictures of the cat. Twenty-five percent of the respondents indicated that they had drawings or paintings of the cat and 91% had photographs of their cat. When asked to indicate where these pictures are kept, 36% answered that they were organised (such as albums) (and this was correlated with whether or not there were children in the family), 25% had them displayed somewhere, 3 owners even carried a picture of the cat in their wallets and 57% answered that these pictures or photographs were placed in drawers, closets, or other storage areas.

Ninety-six percent of the respondents felt that they were aware of their cat's moods, some or most of the time, and 92% felt that their cat was also aware of their (the owner's) moods to a similar extent.

Fisher's exact probability statistics were performed on numerous cross tabulations of these variables. Few statistically significant results were found, undoubtedly because of the small sample size. However, the trends were interesting. People who did not have children in the household tended to consider the cat a child member of the family whereas those with children tended to chose animal member. However, an interesting reversal was found when the same individuals indicated how they talked to their cats. More of the respondents with children indicated they spoke to the cat as they would to a child (67%), compared to a smaller percentage (43%) of people without children who indicated that they spoke to their cat as a child. A greater percentage of owners without children talked to the animal as a pet than did owners with children. Interestingly, 50% of the respondents who had children indicated that they would spank the cat for misbehaving. This was more than 3 times the frequency of spanking by respondents who did not have children.

People from multi-member households tended to interact with their cat more frequently than did owners that lived by themselves. Respondents who belonged to a multi-person household shared table food and snacks with the cat more often and celebrated their cat's birthday more frequently than did those who lived alone with their cat. All of the owners from multi-member households felt that they were aware of their cat's moods at least some of the time whereas only 80% of the owners living alone felt the same. When asked how often they talked to their cat, 78% of the persons from multiple member households answered "a lot", and 22% answered "sometimes", compared to persons living alone who answered 60% to "a lot" and 40% to "sometimes". There was no significant difference between these two groups when asked to indicate what type of family member they considered their cat to be or how they talked to their cat. When differences did occur regarding these answers, it was correlated with whether or not children were in the family.

There were no differences, statistically or in trend, between male and female respondents' answers. An unpublished survey of 82 dog owners (35 men and 47

women) (Katcher, Friedmann, Goodman and Goodman) revealed no statistical
differences between the men and women regarding responses to similar attachment
questions, attitudes or activities. In this survey positive responses were
slightly more frequent in women than in men but the differences were not
significant. Another study by the same group of investigators involving 110
randomly chosen subjects that were observed unobtrusively during the time they
waited in the Veterinary Hospital at the University of Pennsylvania revealed
that there were no differences in the way in which men and women touch their
animals or the amount of time they spent in physical contact.

COMPARISON OF DOG AND CAT ANSWERS

The population of respondents and phraseology of the questions were too different in the surveys to place great validity in comparison of the responses.
(Another cat survey comparable to the dog survey has been conducted and is in
the process of being tabulated.) However, one cannot help comparing the
responses of the dog and cat owners in the already completed studies; although
one must be cautious about generalising the comparisons to all dog and cat
owners. Responses to similar questions indicate that both dog and cat owners
are very attached to their animals and tended to respond similarly to many of
the questions. An identical percent (98) considered the animal a family member,
and the most frequent single response (57%) of both dog·and cat owners was as
an animal member. Approximately the same percent of dog and cat owners talked
to their animals about problems, believed that they were aware of their animal's
moods and vice versa, and an equal percent (91) had photographs of their pets.
There were differences in the percentage of responses as how the owners talked
to their animals. More dog owners talked to their pet as a person than did
cat owners, and a lower percentage of dog owners talked to their dog with pet
talk than did cat owners. Dog owners tended to share meals and snacks more
often with their pet than did cat owners. Dog owners celebrated their pet's
birthday more frequently than did cat owners. However, a greater percent of
cat owners had paintings and drawings of their pet than did dog owners. Cat
owners also differed from dog owners in that when the questionnaires in the
waiting room ran out and only the sign asking people to fill out questionnaires
was left, cat owners often asked the receptionists where the questionnaires
were so that they could fill them out. Some even requested that the questionnaires be sent to them, and occasionally notes were attached to a returned
questionnaire indicating the respondent would be happy to participate in other
surveys. If any dog owners asked where questionnaires were or spontaneously
solicited a questionnaire to fill out, I was unaware of their requests.

REFERENCES

Frank, H., and M. G. Frank (1982). Appl. Anim. Behav., 8, 507-525.
Ganster, D., and V. L. Voith (1982). Attitudes of Cat Owners Toward Their
    Cats: A survey. Submitted for publication to Feline Practice.
Katcher, A. H., E. Friedmann, M. Goodman and L. Goodman. Men, Women and Dogs.
    Unpublished manuscript.
Keddie, K. (1977). Br. J. Psychol., 131, 21-25.
Quackenbush, J. E. (1981). The Compendium on Continuing Education, 3, 764-770.
Voith, V. L. (1981). Attachment between people and their pets. In B. Fogle
    (Ed.) Interrelations Between People and Pets. Charles C. Thomas, Spring-
    field, Illinois.
Voith, V. L. (1981). Mod. vet. Pract., 6, 483-484.
Voith, V. L. (1982). The attachment of owners to pets despite behaviour problems
    of the animal. Submitted for publication to J. Amer. vet. med. Ass,
Voith, V. L., and P. Danneman (1982). Manuscript in preparation.

Scandinavian Pet Environment

B. Klamming

Masterfoods Scandinavia, Malmo, Sweden

ABSTRACT

Dog and cat populations in the Nordic countries are presented in relation to other European countries. Typical feeding habits of prepared petfoods and the veterinarian's relationship to the pet owner are described.

KEYWORDS

Dog ownership; cat ownership; dog feeding; cat feeding; dog population; cat population; visits to veterinarians; information sources.

PET POPULATIONS

There is a wide range of different animals being kept as pets in Scandinavia* but to save time I will restrict my presentation to the two most popular species, dogs and cats. Before talking about the Scandinavian dog and cat population, it is worth having a look at our ranking in relation to some other European countries on which we have reasonably reliable data (Table 1).

Most of the countries in Western Europe are represented in Table 1 and as perhaps can be expected the highest ownership of dogs and cats exists in typical agricultural countries as France, Denmark, Belgium and Holland. None of the European countries comes near the dog and cat ownership of Australia, Canada and the United States.

The dog and cat population for the countries listed is about 133 million and a third of all households in the European Community and a quarter of all households in Scandinavia owns a dog or a cat.

Since two important demographics, when comparing pet population, are size of households and number of pets per owning household a better comparison might be the number of dogs/cats per 100 people (Table 1).

---

* For the purpose of this paper, 'Scandinavia' includes Finland as well as Norway, Denmark and Sweden.

B. Klamming

TABLE 1   Comparative Data on Pet Ownership

		Percentage of households owning		Ratios of pet animals per 100 people	
		Dogs (%)	Cats (%)	Dogs	Cats
1.	Austria	15.8	23.2	6.0	13.3
2.	Belgium	29.5	18.2	11.8	8.3
3.	Denmark	26.0	22.0	13.3	16.7
4.	Finland	22.0	16.0	8.6	9.0
5.	France	36.3	22.7	17.2	12.5
6.	Germany	12.5	8.2	5.5	5.2
7.	Italy	20.5	17.0	8.0	8.3
8.	Netherlands	25.6	20.0	9.1	10.0
9.	Norway	16.0	20.0	6.8	9.9
10.	Sweden	20.0	16.0	9.6	9.5
11.	Switzerland	15.0	15.0	5.3	9.0
12.	United Kingdom	22.8	18.2	10.4	9.4
Weighted average (Scandinavia)		21.0	19.1	9.7	10.6
Weighted average (Overall)		21.3	17.1	8.3	8.3

The difference between the two methods of comparison is not very dramatic, but Sweden, for instance, with the smallest number of people per household in Europe, moves from a ranking of 8 for percentage of households owning dogs to 5th place for the ratio of dogs per 100 people.

TABLE 2   Dog and Cat Populations in Scandinavia

	Denmark		Finland		Norway		Sweden		Total	
	%	'000	%	'000	%	'000	%	'000	%	'000
Dogs										
Weight range (kg)										
-10	22	150	31	130	27	75	37	300	30	655
11-20	21	145	32	135	32	90	26	210	27	580
20-	57	385	37	150	41	115	36	290	43	940
	100	680	100	415	100	280	100	800	100	2175
Average (weighted)	21		18		20		18		19.5	
Dogs/100 people	13.3		8.6		6.8		9.6		9.7*	
Cats	850		435		405		795		2485	
Cats/100 people	16.7		9.0		9.9		9.5		10.6*	

* weighted average

If we look at Scandinavia in more detail (Table 2) we find that there are roughly 2.2 million dogs in the four countries together, and this population has been more or less static during the past 10 years, in other words the 'dog explosion' that was expected in the early '70s never took place.

The major change in the population has been in the size break-down where it has become increasingly popular to own larger breeds.

With the exception of Sweden, Scandinavia has more cats than dogs. The size of cat populations is to a large extent dependent on the degree of urbanisation. In Denmark, for instance, roughly 25% of the cats are pure farm cats which are not likely to be fed prepared cat food, nor taken to a veterinarian.

TABLE 3   Percentage of Households Owning one or more Dogs
or Cats (1982)

	Denmark		Finland		Norway		Sweden	
	1	2+	1	2+	1	2+	1	2+
Dogs	86	14	90	10	91	9	84	16
Cats	55	45	69	31	77	23	82	18

The number of dogs per household does not vary greatly between the countries. Sweden has a slightly higher percentage owning more than one dog and there are slight indications that having more than one dog is becoming more popular. The differences on cats only reflects the various degrees of urbanisation. Available information suggests that the Swedish figures reflect the future situation in the other countries, with a marked decline in total cat population as a result.

FEEDING HABITS

How are those 4.5 million dogs and cats fed? Man has kept pets as his companions for several thousand years. In the past, they were fed exclusively on either table scraps or meals prepared from everyday human food. It was in 1868 that an Englishman, James Spratt, introduced the first dog biscuit in England. Around 1930 the first canned dog food appeared in Europe. However, it was only in 1950 that pet food was commercially introduced in a wide scale.

The tradition of mixing biscuits with meat, fish or canned pet foods still prevails in countries such as England, whereas the Scandinavian countries tend to follow the 'complete' food pattern established in the USA. Even here, however, pet owners tend to mix prepared complete foods with table scraps, fresh food and other prepared dry or wet pet foods. Very few pets are fed solely on one type of food.

One way to compare the relative importance of prepared foods is to calculate the calorie coverage, which is 'the total estimated yearly prepared calories sold, expressed as a percentage of the theoretical calorie requirement of the total population'. On this basis Scandinavia, with a calorie coverage of 22% on dog food and 16% on cat food, is on the average European level for dog food whilst cat food is only half of the European average. Scandinavia still has a long way to go before they reach the American figures of 72% for dogs and 70% for cats.

TABLE 4   Percentage of dog owners having
served ..... last week

	Prepared dog food			Fresh Food	Table scrap	Have used prepared last year	kcal coverage	weighted coverage
	Wet	Dry	Other					
Denmark	10	49	16	76	84	58	12.5	21.6
Finland	52	35	6	N/A	77	84	18.0	21.4
Norway	30	55	18	15	77	87	20.1	23.1
Sweden	31	76	15	18	84	90	33.0	36.7
Scandinavia (weighted average)	29	57	14	-	82	79	22.1	28.0

Table 4 shows the relative usage of various types of food fed to dogs during one week.

Dry food is the most common prepared food in all countries except Finland where wet food is the dominant prepared food fed. Even though wet food appears to be less frequently used, it is still used by 1 out of 3 dog owners. Other prepared foods include deep frozen food, semi-moist, dry fish and biscuits. Of all types of food, household scraps remain the most common.

Even though most dog owners in all four countries use prepared foods, they use them at a very variable degree as demonstrated by the huge difference in calorie coverage for dog owners using prepared foods.

TABLE 5   Dog and Cat Food Usage in Sweden (1981)

	DOGS		CATS	
	Prepared food users %	Total consumer expenditure %	Prepared food users %	Total consumer expenditure %
Only cans	15	5	28	15
Canned and dry	55	65	64	82
Only dry	30	30	8	3

What Table 5 shows is that 15% of the Swedish dog owners who use prepared dog food, buy nothing but cans. Those 15% account for 5% of the total consumer expenditure on prepared dog food. 55% of all users use both canned and dry and they account for 65% of money spent. The remaining 30% only buy dry products and they also account for 30% of the money spent.

If dogs are mainly fed dry foods the situation on cats is somewhat different. The frequency of usage between wet and dry foods is about 50:50 (Table 6), and scraps are not as popular for cats as for dogs.

The majority of cat owners feed their cats prepared cat food but the volumes used vary greatly from country to country, with Finland showing the lowest percent market penetration of all Western European countries.

TABLE 6   Percentage of cat owners having
served ..... last week

	Prepared cat food			Fresh food	Table scrap	Have used prepared last year	kcal coverage	weighted coverage
	Wet	Dry	Other					
Denmark	42	41	4	55	77	55	12.4	22.6
Finland	39	14	5	N/A	61	59	4.2	7.1
Norway	29	43	N/A	69	70	70	15.4	22.0
Sweden	78	65	1	35	60	95	26.0	27.0
Scandinavia (weighted average)	52	45	–	–	65	74	16.4	22.2

If the frequency of usage of dry and wet foods are roughly the same, the
actual volumes consumed are by no means equal as demonstrated in Table 5.

THE PET AND THE VET

In our continuous Pet Ownership Surveys we only have two standard questions
which refer to the veterinary profession. They are 'How many times have you
visited a veterinarian during the last two years?' and 'What is your main
source of information when it comes to feeding your pet?'

TABLE 7   Times visited Veterinarian during
the last Two Years

	Denmark		Finland		Norway		Sweden	
	Dog %	Cat %	Dog %	Cat %	Dog %	Cat %	Dog %	Cat %
0	17	68	47	80	32	75	23	52
1	25	20	30	15	30	16	25	32
2+	58	12	23	5	38	9	52	16

One interesting fact is that, with the exception of Danish dogs, there is a
strong correlation between pet owners visits' to veterinarians and the
penetration of prepared pet foods. The more developed the pet food market
is, the more pet owners see their vet. This is not a cause and effect
relationship(!), but an indication of the growing awareness of the importance
of safety, hygiene and a balanced nutritious diet not only for the family,
but also for the animals in its care is only one part of the total revaluation
of the health concept in its widest meaning, including jogging and yearly
medical check-ups.

Only in Denmark is the veterinarian ranked as the major source of information
(correlating with the higher rate of visits to the vet). In Norway and Sweden
the figures for veterinarians seem reasonable considering that many dog owners
have little or no contact with the veterinary profession.

As can be expected few cat owners seek feeding advice from veterinarians. Their
main sources of information are 'on-pack information' and 'other cat owners'.

SUMMARY

Certainly, the Pet Food Industry is no better than any one else at foreseeing
the future, but based on the figures presented here and the development in
Sweden during the past 10 years, we can anticipate some possible developments.

Dog ownership will continue to be static or even decline, but larger breeds
are tending to become more and more popular as is owning more than one dog.
Dog owning households will seek to optimise the economy of feeding their dogs.
This will possibly lead to a stagnation in wet food penetration and a further
growth of complete dry foods. It can also be a temptation to feed inferior
food for cost reasons.

Cat ownership will decline as will the number of cats per owning household as
cat owning becomes more and more urban. This will further speed up the
development of prepared cat food, particularly in the wet form.

Other developments of importance to the future are:

The growth of the prepared petfood industry will continue to take place
along with developments of the human food processing technology, and
changes in human food habits, i.e. 'human food processing technology'.

Smaller family units will result in a decrease in the total consumption
of food in each household, coupled with an increased usage of convenience
human foods with a corresponding decline in the amount of leftovers and
household scraps.

A continued development of self-service stores will take the place of
the local butcher, grocer and fishmonger, who formerly provided a source
of cheap special cuts for pets which could be used for the preparation
of home-made pet food.

BEHAVIOURAL
DEVELOPMENT

Behaviour Development of the Puppy in the Home Environment

P. L. Borchelt

Animal Medical Center, 501 East 62nd Street, New York, USA

ABSTRACT

During the early life of the puppy in the home environment, the owner must
manage behaviours such as elimination, attachment and separation, investigation, play, fear and, sometimes, aggression. The development of these
behaviours during approximately the first 6 months is outlined and a variety
of management techniques is presented.

KEYWORDS

Development; elimination; attachment; separation anxiety; investigation;
play; fear; aggression; space management.

INTRODUCTION

The average dog owner hopes for a long-term relationship with an affectionate,
playful and obedient pet. But the owner soon discovers that a variety of
species-typical behaviour systems, including elimination, attachment,
exploration, play, fear and aggression must be managed appropriately within
the constraints of the human environment. The fact that many dog-owner
relationships are only of short duration attests to the widespread
difficulties in coordinating human and animal requirements.

Can the animal behaviour literature be of any help? The pioneering work on
behavioural genetics and social behaviour of dogs by Scott and Fuller (1965)
contributed significantly to our understanding of the development of
behaviour in general, and the process of socialisation in particular. Since
then, researchers in canid behaviour have investigated topics such as social
and communication signals (Fox, 1970, 1971 a&b), scent marking (Bekoff, 1979),
play (Bekoff, 1974), sexual behaviour (Beach, 1969), social attachment and
separation (Scott, Stewart and DeGhett, 1973) and learning (Stanley, Bacon
and Fehr, 1970; Bacon and Stanley, 1970). These data tell us much about
the behaviour of dogs, but little about the management of behaviour of pet
dogs living in the human environment.

In this chapter, I will briefly outline some results obtained in the process
of diagnosing and treating behaviour problems encountered by owners of pet
dogs. The focus will be on those behavioural systems of most concern during
the first 6 months of the dog's life. Working with dogs of varying genetic
and experiential backgrounds in diverse home environments has all the
advantages and disadvantages associated with field studies. Although control
of relevant variables and specification of past histories is difficult, and
sometimes impossible, after many hundreds of cases, patterns begin to emerge
from seeming chaos.

CLASSIFICATION OF DOG BEHAVIOUR

It is helpful to begin with a structure for classifying dog behaviour.
Table 1 is a second approximation to classification of behaviour systems,
combining elements of classification systems proposed by Scott and Fuller
(1965) and Denny and Ratner (1970). The dog owner is confronted with
managing, to a greater or lesser degree, all of these species-typical
behaviour systems. For each of these systems, a large scientific literature
exists which encompasses comparative descriptions, controlling variables,
and in some cases, physiological mechanisms. This information, combined
with the extensive literature on animal learning and behaviour modification,
can all be brought to bear on the management of dog behaviour. Most of the
time successful management by the average owner is a combination of good
luck and the dog's adaptability to living in the human environment.
Unsuccessful management is often the result of inaccurate information (see
any popular dog book!) and the unavailability to the average person of
relevant information about animal behaviour and learning.

TABLE 1 A Classification of Dog Behaviour Systems
(Systems below the dotted line are social behaviours
whereas those above may be non-social)

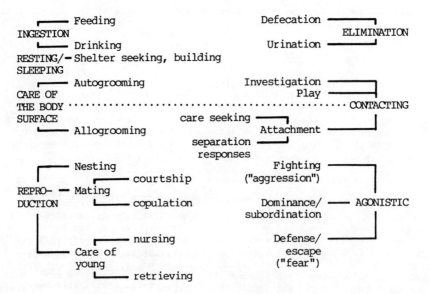

During the first 6 months, the critical management decisions relate to feeding (including destructive chewing during teething), elimination, separation responses, play, investigation and occasionally aggression. All of these behaviour systems interact to some extent. A change, or management problem, in one behaviour system may influence another. Table 2 illustrates some of the interactions to be discussed. The following sections describe the typical problems encountered and discuss some appropriate and inappropriate management decisions. A critical tool for effectively dealing with some of these behaviour systems is proper management of the space available to the puppy.

TABLE 2   Critical Behaviour Systems of the Puppy

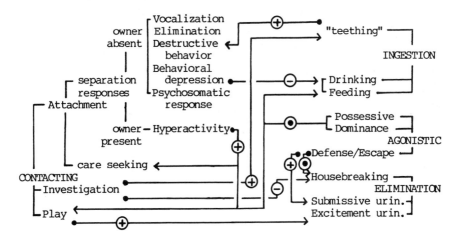

SPACE MANAGEMENT

Because the new puppy has not learned appropriate elimination and chewing behaviour, most owners manage these behaviours by initially restricting the space available to the puppy in the home. In providing space to the pup for ingestion, resting/sleeping, elimination, investigation and play a proper space management programme fulfills 3 functions: first, it meets the pup's current needs for these behaviours; second, it meets the owner's need for protection of furniture, carpets, and household objects; and third, it provides a basis so the puppy can easily learn to adjust to the human environment as its various behaviour systems mature. A proper space management programme eases the owner's task of managing both separation and elimination behaviours. The concept of proper space management will be embedded in the discussion of most of the following behaviour systems.

ELIMINATION

1.   Paper Training and Housebreaking

Elimination behaviour must be managed soon after the dog is obtained. Usually, the pup eliminates soon after eating, after awakening, or after excitement, play or any vigorous activity. Some pups do and other do not display characteristic behaviours such as sniffing or circling prior to elimination. An early management decision is whether to paper train or

housebreak the puppy. If the owner is home all or most of the time and the
outside can be reached quickly, housebreaking can be initiated immediately.
If the young puppy and owner live in an apartment on the upper floors of a
high-rise building, the decision to initially housebreak is not wise.
Because the puppy eliminates frequently and unpredictably, paper training is
required until the dog can control its elimination behaviour so that a
reasonably small number of walks outside on the street is sufficient.

Descriptions and observations of successful and unsuccessful management
techniques (Voith and Borchelt, 1982a) indicate that several factors can
influence the process of the dog learning where to eliminate. Puppies tend
to move away from their eating and sleeping places to eliminate, if given a
chance. Obviously preventing a puppy from soiling its sleeping and feeding
areas requires that it have enough room to get the preferred distance from
these areas. Some pups readily eliminate several feet or less from these
areas but other pups prefer greater distances. Thus, the common recommendation of crate training young puppies works sometimes but fails when the
puppy prefers to move more than 1-2 feet from its resting and feeding area.
Furthermore, many dogs rapidly develop preferences for elimination in
specific locations and/or on specific surfaces.

Many owners restrict the pup to a room (usually one with an easily cleaned
floor) and, at first, put newspapers over most of the floor area, particularly
away from the food and water bowls. Sometimes the pup eliminates on the paper
only in one area (location preference). In this case the papers in the other
areas can be safely removed and the pup will continue to eliminate on the
paper in its preferred location. The strength of location preferences can
vary. A pup with a strong location preference can be induced to change its
preferred location only if the papers are moved gradually (perhaps as little
as a few inches per day) to a more appropriate location (from the owner's
point of view). A weak location preference can be changed much more quickly.

Sometimes the pup prefers no specific location but instead prefers a specific
surface. Some pups develop preferences for surfaces in the home that are
hard and smooth (linoleum, tile, hardwood floors), or coarsely textured
(carpets, throw rugs). These preferences can be learned as a result of a
position preference other than the one the owner has chosen. In other cases,
the puppy might have an initial preference for a non-paper surface or an
aversion for a paper surface. An aversion to paper surfaces can arise from
unusual elimination postures (Sprague and Anisko, 1973) or unusual behaviours
associated with elimination. For instance, if the puppy consistently circles
intensely before defaecating or walks forward while defaecating, the paper
may become aversive because it slips under the puppy's feet.

Successful management of elimination behaviour can be quite seriously
complicated by punishment techniques. It is 'common knowledge' that the
owner must demonstrate to the dog that 'mistakes' are not to be tolerated.
The average dog book recommends taking the pup to the elimination site,
pointing out the 'mistake', and then yelling, hitting it, administering
leash corrections, or frightening it with the sound of rolled up papers.
Sometimes the above methods are augmented by giving the puppy an aversive
gustatory stimulus such as alcohol, hot sauce, etc. and then placing this
substance on the elimination spot. Although these techniques may work, at
least in some cases of inappropriate location preferences, they risk
eliciting defensive and escape behaviours, inducing the pup to withdraw from
or even to avoid the owner. In extreme cases, submissive urination can be
elicited, as well.

Other aversive or frightening stimuli can also negatively affect a housebreaking problem during its initial stages. For instance, if the puppy is
frightened by city noises, traffic, strangers, etc. when first exposed to
the out of doors, then elimination behaviour may be inhibited and the pup
will only eliminate in the house. If the owner, in an attempt to hasten the
transition from paper training to housebreaking, exposes the puppy too
rapidly to the frightening stimuli outside, the puppy may become sensitised
and a severe phobia may develop. In these cases, the phobia must be treated
before housebreaking can succeed. Desensitisation and flooding techniques
for fear related problems are discussed in Tuber and Hothersall (1982).

Another common reason for puppies not eliminating outside during the transition from paper training to housebreaking is investigatory behaviours that
inhibit elimination. Some puppies spend considerable time sniffing all over
the environment during the walk, much to the frustration of the owner who
may recommend obedience procedures such as placing the puppy in a heel
position at all times. In some cases, this is effective. Other times, the
puppy escalates its investigatory behaviour and constantly pulls on the
leash. Leash corrections or other punishment techniques at this point may
induce defensive behaviour or fear of the owner (or walking outside!).

A more effective alternative is to habituate the puppy's investigatory
behaviour to one particular area, where elimination is appropriate. The
puppy is taken to the area where it remains until investigatory behaviour
has ceased and elimination has occurred. Since investigatory responses
habituate rapidly (Ratner, 1970), this usually only requires a few minutes.
Then, walking to other areas will re-elicit investigatory behaviour which
serves as a reward (Timberlake, 1980) to the puppy for eliminating in its area.

2.   Submissive Urination

Some puppies respond to any gesture of the owner that even remotely resembles
a dominance posture by urinating, either by squatting or while displaying
species-typical submissive behaviour, such as roll over, inguinal presentation,
submissive grin (Fox, 1971b). When the owner yells, strikes, or threatens
the pup, submissive behaviour is elicited to a great or lesser degree
depending on the strength of the eliciting stimuli and the pup's threshold
for displaying submission. Rarely, a pup will have such a low threshold that
any approach by the owner, even slow and with a soothing voice, will elicit
submissive urination. Submissive urination is more likely when the owner
approaches the puppy while standing and bending over the pup (similar to
'standing over', a dominance signal, Fox, 1971a).

Obviously, any threatening or aversive technique used in an attempt to solve
this problem is likely to exacerbate it. Paradoxically, rewarding the pup
by feeding it, for instance, while the owner approaches is often effective
in decreasing the problem. The effect is to substitute one behaviour system
(submissive urination) with another that inhibits it (feeding), then gradually
presenting stimuli that tend to elicit submissive urination. This technique
is called counterconditioning and is described extensively in the behaviour
modification literature. An alternative technique is to totally ignore the
occurrence of submissive urination and habituate the pup to the eliciting
stimuli.

3. Excitement Urination

Young puppies urinate readily after any vigorous activity, but slowly develop
inhibiting mechanisms as they age. Occasionally, a puppy will have difficulty
with bladder control and consequently urinate during play. Of course, any
circumstance that tends to escalate play or increase activity level (see below)
will tend to intensify this problem. Punishment techniques are usually
unsuccessful since the puppy is incapable of responding appropriately.
Moreover, punishment may result in submissive urination or other negative side
effects such as defensive or escape behaviour. Usually the best solution is
to encourage play or high activity levels in locations where urination is
acceptable and minimise such activity in locations where it is not.
Discounting physical pathology, puppies outgrow an excitement urination
problem eventually.

CONTACTING: ATTACHMENT AND SEPARATION

The dog is a highly evolved social animal that shows intense attachment to
conspecifics and to humans. Generally, the puppy is obtained soon after it
has been weaned. At this time the natural process of learning to tolerate
separation from the dam is just beginning and the pup's attachment shifts to
include littermates. Puppies separated from the dam and litter at this time
typically display vocalisations at a high rate - up to 100 per minute
(Elliot and Scott, 1961). Usually, vocalisation decreases within a few days
or so as the puppy adjusts to the home environment.

Experiments have indicated that this separation distress or anxiety can be
alleviated, at least in some breeds, by antidepressants (Scott, Stewart and
DeGhett, 1973). Pettijohn and others (1977) found that food and toys have
little or no effect on alleviating distress vocalisations, whereas social
stimuli were effective. Human contact was more effective than contact with
other dogs. In the typical home situation, drugs are not usually practical
or desirable, but social contact usually cannot be provided at all times
either.

Furthermore, as indicated in Table 2, vocalisation is only one of a number
of responses elicited by the absence of the owner. Some pups eliminate as
a separation response. Most popular dog books do not describe separation
elicited behaviour and the owner may mistake such elimination as a failure
to housebreak. If the puppy is young and has not yet been fully housebroken
or papertrained, then the owner faces the difficult task of differentiating
the two problems. This is critical because techniques used for housebreaking
do not usually solve separation problems.

Other puppies chew and dig as a response to separation. Again, it is sometimes difficult to distinguish separation elicited destructive chewing from
normal 'puppy chewing' or 'teething' behaviour and the two behaviours are
managed differently. A behavioural depression, usually manifested by a lack
of feeding or drinking behaviour in the owner's absence, or a psychosomatic
response such as diarrhoea, may occur in puppies but is more likely in older
dogs.

Rarely, as a result of separation anxiety, a puppy will display intense and
prolonged activity (hyperactivity) when the owner is present. This is
usually indicated by frequent and easily elicited greeting, play behaviour,
or other care-seeking behaviours such as following, close attention to the
owner, maintenance of body contact, etc. This heightened arousal and

activity level, at least in its early stages, can be rewarding for the owners. In these cases, the increased attention the puppy receives from the owner can serve to maintain or escalate the problem. Sometimes, this escalated activity can induce an excitement urination problem.

Frequently, the very space management techniques used to successfully manage elimination behaviour will cause or escalate a separation problem. For instance, a 6-8 week old puppy is generally confined to some extent, particularly at night. Usually, the resultant separation-elicited vocalisation ceases in a few nights or so. However, the rapidity with which the dog adjusts to separation is influenced by many variables. Firstly, there are individual differences, of unknown causation. Secondly, the amount and quality of time spent with the owner can either decrease or increase the problem. In the worst case, an owner who obtains a new puppy and then goes to work for 8-10 hours, 5 days a week, is likely to have a serious problem. This situation is usually difficult to manage because it provides frequent separation of long duration which does not allow the puppy to gradually learn to tolerate separation. At the other end of the continuum is the owner who is at home all day (every day) with the puppy and never leaves it alone, even at night. This prevents the elicitation of separation behaviour, of course, but also prevents the puppy from ever adjusting to separation of even a short duration.

In the more usual situation, at least one of the owners is initially at home with the puppy for at least some part of the day to provide social contact. With a proper space management programme the puppy is confined to some extent to manage elimination behaviour, but also receives an adequate level of social contact, play and investigation to keep separation behaviour at a minimum. Ideally, periods of social contact can be timed properly with feeding and elimination behaviour so that resting and sleeping are likely during the periods of social isolation. Judicious observation will also allow social contact to serve as a reward for progressively longer periods of social isolation without signs of separation behaviour. This is easy if the owner has time available during the day so separation behaviour is not elicited, but is difficult otherwise.

A third variable influencing separation behaviour is the puppy's previous experience with attachment and separation. A puppy obtained at the age of 3-4 months or so from a pet store, adoption shelter or a breeder may either have experienced little or no attachment during this time, or have experienced attachment and subsequent loss from a previous owner. In experimental settings, puppies deprived of attachment or social contact with humans exhibit extreme fear responses to human and other novel stimuli (Freedman, King and Elliot, 1961; Fuller, 1963). Puppies for sale or adoption to the public are rarely maintained under such extreme social deprivation. Rarely, they are restricted in social contact to one or a few people. It is common for puppies to be exposed to many people frequently, but not to one person consistently. In general, attachment to the new owner (once it occurs) is strong and consequently separation-elicited behaviour is likely (Borchelt and Voith, 1982).

A common recommendation for separation-elicited behaviour problems (referred to incorrectly as 'spite') is to confine the puppy to a crate frequently described as just large enough to allow the puppy room to stand and turn around. The average dog book refers to dogs as 'den dwelling' animals and presumes that confining imparts a feeling of security to a puppy. Dogs, in fact, are not den dwelling animals, although in a variety of canids the dam will construct a nest (often underground) for the pups. The nest is a defense against predators and protection against inclement weather. The pups use it as a 'home base' from which they explore, investigate and play.

There is no door on the den which encloses the pups for many hours.

In many cases, 'crate training' a puppy will attenuate vocalisation and elimination, and prevent chewing. Unfortunately, it may also exacerbate these behaviours and sometimes leads to psychosomatic signs or hyperactivity elicited by the owner's return. Although a psychosomatic response is probably rare in puppies, a common manifestation when it does occur is diarrhoea. A disease state is then assumed as the cause but remains elusive. Crating or other confinement (e.g. isolating in a small room) is highly likely to exacerbate a separation problem once it has occurred for any length of time, or for a puppy with a previous attachment and separation problem.

If the owner uses punishment techniques in an attempt to suppress separation behaviour, a likely result can be either the elicitation of defensive/escape behaviours or a paradoxical increase in attachment and subsequent escalation of the separation problem. A number of studies have shown that averse stimuli can intensify attachment responses in chicks (Hess, 1973), puppies (Stanley and Elliot, 1962), and monkeys (Harlow and Harlow, 1971). Moreover, punishment can lead to a shift in the form of expression of separation anxiety. For instance, if a puppy whines or barks when it is alone, and the owner immediately returns and punishes the vocalisation (by yelling, hitting, etc.), the puppy may cease vocalising and begin to exhibit elimination or destructive behaviour. In some cases, the puppy simply learns to delay the onset of vocalising!

CONTACTING: PLAY AND INVESTIGATION

A common form of play in puppies involves mouthing and biting. This is particularly true when play is escalated by separation problems or by play deprivation. Usually, play behaviour is directed at the owner, and at parts of the body that move, e.g. hands and feet. Owners inadvertently may form a positive feedback loop if they try to correct the puppy or shoo it away with hands or feet. The result is often an escalation of mouthing to biting and chasing, followed by further attempts of the owner to prevent the problem by striking at or threatening the puppy with hands, feet or an object such as a rolled-up newspaper or magazine. Physical or auditory aversive stimuli intense enough to suppress play are likely also to elicit defensive and escape behaviours.

Instead, since play behaviour in young puppies usually can be easily exhausted, it is more effective to redirect the puppy's play behaviour to a toy which moves. Toys, particularly chew toys, are frequently provided for the puppy but the key elements of movement and interaction with the owner are usually missing. In most cases, a tug of war game can be instituted when the puppy solicits play. Many dog books argue against tug of war games since 'they make the dog aggressive'. Although most puppies do growl during these games, it is a 'play-growl' of quite different tone, intensity and significance than growls exhibited in an aggressive context. Conducted properly, the tug of war game will exhaust play behaviour and teach the puppy that mouthing and biting occur only with the toy in its mouth. Moreover, the interaction with the puppy (holding and pulling on the toy) eventually can be presented in brief bursts such that play is used to reward short durations of quiet, non-play behaviour.

AGONISTIC BEHAVIOUR

The most common type of aggressive behaviour exhibited by young puppies involves growling, baring the teeth and/or biting when the owner approaches the puppy during feeding, or tries to take away food or bones. This 'possessive aggression' is often correlated with dominance aggression (Borchelt, in press; Voith and Borchelt, 1982b) in older dogs. The amount of time in possession of a bone has been used commonly in laboratory studies as a measure of dominance in pairs of puppies (Scott and Fuller, 1965; Fox, 1971a).

Most owners confronted with a new puppy that exhibits such aggression use a punishment technique, usually hitting or yelling at the puppy when it growls. This is often successful in permanently suppressing the aggression, particularly if the food or bone is presented to the puppy several times in a row, with aggression punished and non-aggression rewarded. The effect of punishment is to establish a dominance relationship with the owner relatively dominant and the puppy relatively submissive. If punishment is to work in tis situation, it will do so in a few trials, assuming that the level of punishment is sufficiently high. Too high a level, however, may elicit defensive responses.

Occasionally, a puppy will become more aggressive when punished. The puppy may continue to escalate to the highest level that owners can reasonably deliver. Some puppies also become possessive of toys, or steal household objects such as clothes, pens and pencils, tissues, etc. and guard them. In these cases, a counterconditioning programme is generally effective (Voith and Borchelt, 1982b). A number of stimulus situations that elicit aggression are defined, then gradually presented as the puppy is rewarded (food, play, or whatever behaviour system works for the individual puppy) for non-aggressive behaviour. For instance, play behaviour can be structured so that tug of war or chase and fetch occur only after the puppy has relinquished possession of the toy. If necessary, play behaviour can be deprived for a period of time to increase the reward value of subsequent play.

ACKNOWLEDGEMENT

I would like to express my gratitude to hundreds of puppy and dog owners who let me (for fair exchange of fees) enter their lives briefly to learn and teach about dog behaviour problems. Their need and desire for information allowed me to satisfy mine also, without financial support from any governmental agencies or private foundations. Thanks are also due to William J. Kay, DVM and Victoria Voith, DVM, PhD, for their encouragement and friendship.

REFERENCES

Bacon, W. E. and W. C. Stanley (1970). J. Comp. Physiol. Psychol., 70, 344-350.
Beach, F. A. (1969). Am. Psychol., 24, 971-987.
Bekoff, M. (1979). Biol. of Behav., 4, 123-139.
Bekoff, M. (1974). Am. Zool., 14, 323-340.
Borchelt, P. L. (in press). App. Anim. Ethol.
Borchelt, P. L. and V. L. Voith (1982). Symp. on Anim. Behav., Vet. Clin. N. Amer. W. J. Saunders, Philadelphia. pp. 625-635.
Denny, M. R. and S. C. Ratner (1970). Comparative Psychology: Research in Animal Behaviour (revised edition). Dorsey, Homewood, Ill.
Elliot, O. and J. P. Scott (1961). J. Genet. Psychol., 99, 3-22.

Fisher, A. E. (1955). Doctoral Diss. Penn. State Univ.

Fox, M. W. (1971a). Behavior of Wolves, Dogs and Related Canids. Harper and Row, New York.

Fox, M. W. (1971b). Z. Tierpsychol., 28, 185-210.

Fox, M. W. (1970). Behavior, 36, 49-73.

Freedman, D. G., J. A. King and O. Elliot (1961). Science, 133, 1016-1017.

Fuller, J. L. (1963). World Cong. Psychiat., 3, 223-227.

Harlow, H. F. and M. K. Harlow (1971). Experimental Psychopathology. Academic Press, New York. pp. 287-334.

Hart, B. (1969). Comm. Behav. Biol., 4, 237-238.

Hess, E. H. (1973). Imprinting. Van Nostrand, New York.

Pettijohn, T. F., T. W. Wong, P. D. Ebert and J. P. Scott (1977). Dev. Psychobiol., 10, 373-381.

Ratner, S. C. (1970). Current Issues in Animal Learning. Univ. of Nebraska Press, Lincoln. pp. 55-84.

Scott, J. P. and J. L. Fuller (1965). Dog Behaviour: The Genetic Basis. University of Chicago Press, Chicago.

Scott, J. P., J. M Stewart, and V. DeGhett (1973). Separation and Depression: Clinical and Research Aspects. AAAS, Washington D.C. pp 3-32.

Sprague, R. H. and Anisko, J. J. (1973). Behavior, 47, 257-267.

Stanley, W. C., W. E. Bacon and C. Fehr (1970). J. Comp. Physiol. Psychol., 70, 335-343.

Stanley, W. C. and O. Elliot (1962). Psych. Reports, 10, 775-788.

Timberlake, W.((1980). In: The Psychology of Learning and Motivation, Vol. 14. Academic Press, New York. pp. 1-58.

Tuber, D. S. and D. Hothersall (1982). Symp. on Anim. Behav., Vet. Clin. N. Amer. W. J. Saunders, Philadelphia (in press).

Voith, V. L. and P. L. Borchelt (1982a). Symp. on Anim. Behav., Vet. Clin. N. Amer. W. J. Saunders, Philadelphia. pp. 637-643.

Voith, V. L. and P. L. Borchelt (1982b). Symp. on Anim. Behav., Vet. Clin. N. Amer. W. J. Saunders, Philadelphia. pp. 655-663.

Social Behaviour in Free-ranging Domestic and Feral Cats

O. Liberg

Department of Animal Ecology, University of Lund, Ecology Building,
223 62 Lund, Sweden

ABSTRACT

The paper is a review of social behaviour in the domestic cat. House-based cats form groups, where permitted, in which females are closely related to each other as they usually stay for life, while foreign females are not tolerated. Males compete intensely for females and go through typical social stages. Many are expelled by competitors from their natal homes. Cats are active both at day and night and rest about 50% of their time. Activity types are influenced by social and domestic status. Home range sizes and utilisation are very variable and influenced by both environmental and social conditions. Aggressive and amicable behaviours are described as well as marking behaviour and frequency. Sexual behaviour is described with special emphasis on interactions between males during courtship. The paper is concluded with some evolutionary reflections on evolution of domestic cat behaviour.

KEYWORDS

Domestic cat; feral cat; social behaviour; social organisation; home range; activity; Felis catus; Felis silvestris; reproductive success.

INTRODUCTION

The domestic cat (Felis catus) originated through domestication of the African wild cat (Felis silvestris) in North Africa and the Middle East some time between 3 and 5000 years BC. It is now spread over all continents. Most domestic cats all over the world maintain a peculiar intermediate status between a purely domestic animal and a completely wild creature. This intermediate status of the cat naturally influences its behaviour, which has been only slightly modified through domestication.

A number of studies of cat behaviour have been performed. In the 1950s and 1960s students of cat behaviour concentrated on specific motor patterns or rather pure ethological experiments performed under laboratory conditions (e.g. Leyhausen, 1956; Baron and others, 1957; Ewer, 1961; Cole and Shafer,

1966). In the late 1970s a few studies of behaviour and social interactions
in free ranging cats appeared (Laundre, 1977; Macdonald and Apps, 1978;
Dards, 1978; Panaman, 1981). This brief and very superficial review of cat
behaviour is partly based on these and other published studies, and partly on
my own work for the last eight years with a rural free ranging cat population
in the Revinge area in Southern Sweden.

The review first deals with general social and behavioural patterns including
social organisation, activity patterns and home ranges. The last part
describes some individual behaviour patterns such as amicable and aggressive
expressions, marking behaviour and sexual behaviour and interactions. I will
not deal with predatory behaviour which has been described in detail by
Leyhausen (1956; 1979). Neither am I including behavioural stages of growing
kittens, or mother/young interactions (see Caro, 1981 for references).
Generally the review concerns cats that are free ranging, i.e. cats that are
allowed to move around at their own will most of the time. I will use the
term 'domestic cat' for cats that have regular connection with at least one
human household where they are provided with food and cover. Cats without
such a connection, and which instead are self-dependent, are called feral cats.

SOCIAL ORGANISATION

When describing social organisation of domestic cats, I will first deal with
females and then with males, as the sexes differ widely in this aspect.

Females

In the Revinge area female cats were generally based at human households.
When more than one adult female lived in the same household, the animals
usually were related to each other, as they normally were recruited from
inside the group. Foreign female cats were not tolerated. Most female cats
born in the group, and not killed by the owners at an early age, stayed for
life. This was in contrast to male cats, where dispersal was a common trait
(see below). However, a few female cats emigrated from their natal group.
They usually settled at a new human household where, for the time being, no
other adult female cats lived. Releasing factors for the emigration were
conflicts with other females in the original group, or disturbance by for
example dogs, especially during the breeding season. Emigrating females
rarely moved further than to a place just outside the home range of the natal
group.

Normally all adult females in a group were breeding. In exceptionally large
groups, some females failed to breed successfully. In extreme cases with
strong food competition, and probably also a high level of 'social stress',
very few, if any, females managed to bring up a litter.

A similar pattern of female cat organisation has been found in other areas as
well, where check of offspring was not complete and where the cats had access
to a concentrated food resource, such as a dairy farm, or, usually in urban
areas, one or several open garbage bins or dumps (Macdonald and Apps, 1978;
Laundre, 1977; Dards, 1978). In pure feral populations, where the cats
maintain themselves on their own hunting of natural prey, they usually live
solitary with the exception of mothers with immature offspring (Jones, 1977;
van Aarde, 1979).

Males

Conflicts between individuals had a much more prevalent bearing on male/male relationships than could be discerned within female groups. The ultimate cause for conflict between males was competition for access to females. In the Revinge area I recognised four development stages in adult male cats. First the young maturing male entered the stage of 'Novices'. The transformation of a sub-adult male to the Novice stage was marked by sudden occurrence of aggressive behaviour towards the young male on behalf of older and dominant male competitors. Usually this event coincided with, or closely succeeded the sexual maturation of the young male. The harassment of the Novice by stronger males continued, especially if female cats occurred in the household of the Novice. In response to this repeated persecution, a large proportion of the Novices emigrated, and usually settled in an area with low activity of dominant males. As this normally also meant in an area with no or few households with female cats (the foci of social life in domestic cats) I called these males 'Outcasts'. Because any 'vacant' but appropriate human households quickly got occupied by a female cat, these dispersing young males usually had no alternative but to settle as feral cats. In the Revinge area, this social expulsion of young male cats from their natal homes was the most important cause for the occurrence of feral cats, or 'wild cats' as they are popularly called. Typical of the behaviour of both Novices and Outcasts was their watchful appearance whenever travelling or in unknown surroundings, and their avoidance of other male cats. Thereby, they also failed to participate in courtship of females in oestrus.

With increasing age, the subordinate male cat, either directly from the Novice stage, or via a period as an Outcast, entered the 'Challenger' stage. It no longer avoided male competitors, and participated regularly in courtship of females. The Challenger stage usually only lasted a short time, at most one breeding reason, after which the cat, if still alive, turned into a 'Breeder'. The criterion of a Breeder was total male dominance and, therefore, mating priority in at least one household with female cat(s). Rarely a cat became a Breeder before the age of three, and usually not before it was four years old.

Breeders could not completely monopolise the females, as subordinate males applied sneaking strategies. Reproductive success, however, calculated on the basis of a combination of genetic (inheritance of coat colours) and behavioural evidence, in Breeders was double that of the average Challenger and four times that of Novices and Outcasts.

ACTIVITY PATTERNS

On an annual basis, the average cat in the Revinge area was active about 50% of the time, evenly distributed over day and night. When activity data were analysed seasonally it was shown that cats were more diurnal in winter and more nocturnal in summer. This probably had to do with a dislike of being out in the cold nights in winter and during the hottest part of day during summer. When different categories of cats were analysed separately, certain differences appeared. Domestic females and Novices had the lowest activity (41 and 45%, respectively), and Outcasts had the highest (65%). Females and Novices also usually had shorter periods of activity (1-3 hours) interrupted by periods of resting, than did feral males and dominant males. In all seasons there was an activity peak between 1800 and 2100.

As expected, feral cats spent longer time hunting (33% of total time) than did house-based cats (15%) that had an almost ad libitum food supply 'at home'. Among domestic cats, females and subordinate males (Novices) spent more time hunting than dominant males. The most probable reason for this was that the dominant males (Challengers and Breeders) instead used more of their time for social activities, 14 and 22% respectively, as compared with 5 and 7% for females and Novices. However, a lot of the time that female cats spent with their kittens, they were recorded as passive by the radio receiver because they didn't move, although they might have been performing active social behaviour like suckling. Social behaviour in males consisted of courtship of females and conflicts with competitors.

In a study of a group of female cats at a Welsh dairy farm during winter, the cats were sleeping 40% of the time and resting (without sleep) in 22%. They spent 15% hunting, 15% grooming, 3% travelling, 3% feeding and 2% on other activities (Panaman, 1981). These figures correspond surprisingly well with the Revinge figures for corresponding season. An exception was that the Welsh females spent around 80% of their time in the immediate surroundings of their home, while the Revinge females only spent around 60% 'at home'. However, the Revinge cats often had a 'second home', an outlying barn or some other unoccupied building, where they spent considerable time.

HOME RANGES

Domestic females and Novices in the Revinge area had comparatively small home ranges (20-150 ha) where most of the activity was performed at and near the home household and in a few favoured patches with good prey habitat. Feral cats naturally moved over larger areas, as they had to include in their home ranges enough prey habitats to support themselves over the year. The few feral females that were recorded had home ranges of 2-300 ha, while some feral males had home ranges covering up to 900 ha. Challengers and Breeders, whether domestic or feral, covered varying areas, from 100 and up to 800 ha, depending on distribution and density of households where female cats lived. Obviously these dominant males had large enough home ranges to cover an optimal number of female cats. In the non-breeding season they only utilised a small part of their ranges, which supports the notion that the determining factor for dominant male range extension is female cat distribution.

Cats in urban areas naturally have much smaller home ranges than those of the Revinge cats, usually below 10 ha (Dards, 1978).

Female cats belonging to the same group shared their home ranges, but they did not overlap the ranges of other female groups. Male cats overlapped both the ranges of females and of each other's home ranges extensively, and so were not considered to be territorial.

AGGRESSIVE BEHAVIOUR

An encounter between two individual animals can be classified as either agonistic, amicable or neutral. Within a cat group consisting of adult females, juveniles and a single male, it was shown that during the non-breeding season about half of the encounters were agonistic, and the rest about equally shared between neutral and amicable encounters. Amicable behaviour includes such friendly interactions as allogrooming, reciprocal headrubbing, playing with each other and sleeping together, but also close sniffing including nose contact. Neutral behaviour includes the close approach of the animals which then apparently ignore one another, or exploratory sniffing without nose contact. In female-female and adult-kitten encounters, agonistic behaviour usually consisted only of mild defensive threats in the form of hisses or growls, with ears flattened to the sides, and occasionally they might direct a blow towards the opponent with a front paw.

With the exception of females defending kittens, more serious aggressive interactions usually only occur between adult male cats during the breeding reasons. In an encounter between two competitors one might observe a sequence of escalated steps, starting with mild offensive threatening at a distance with ears erect and turned round to expose the back sides. If the threat intensifies the cats get closer to each other, stretch their legs which makes the rear end higher as the hind legs are longer than the forelegs. The base of the tail is held at the same angle as the back, but then with a sharp turn so that the rest of the tail is hanging straight down. The opponents look straight into each other's eyes, the pupils are narrowed and the head is held obliquely at a 45° angle towards the vertical plane. The next step is what I call the vocal duel, i.e. both opponents start howling in a tone that goes up and down (caterwauling). If an attack follows, the howl rapidly goes up to a high pitch scream. The attacker aims a bite towards his opponent's nape, but the defender meets this by throwing himself on his back, fending off the attacker with all four feet and open mouth. The cats might roll around for a few seconds, then separate. The process might then start again with close range threats. At any stage one of the participants might break the session by either departing with typical slow and stiff movements, or by adopting the extreme defensive posture by lying on his side or back and refusing to leave this position. The attacker then usually will leave the place after some circling around the defender. A fight, however, might be ended with an immediate full speed flight by the inferior animal. Most conflicts never escalate to fights, and fights are usually short and rarely result in serious wounds, but superficial incisions like ripped ears and skin wounds on chins, shoulders and elbows are regularly found on male cats during the breeding season.

Cats seem to have no specific means of inhibiting attack, such as can be found for example in the more social canids. A subordinate cat, especially a male, avoids dominant rivals. In a sudden encounter, where it is cornered and cannot get away it will adopt a typical defensive posture, crouching, protecting its neck by 'pulling in' the head, flattening the ears, hissing and, if the attacker comes too close, striking out with the front paw. In extreme cases it will throw itself on its back, as described earlier. This might or might not deter the aggressor. If possible the defensive animal will try to get up higher than the attacker. In most cases where an adult cat has gone up in a tree it is to avoid an attack, either from a conspecific or from some predator, like a dog or even a human being.

MARKING

Communication by scent is common and important in most mammals. The most common way of scent marking in all felids, including the domestic cat, is by ejecting a small amount of urine backwards onto an object in the environment. During the marking the cat raises the tail straight up, and a short rapid trembling of the tail can be seen. Both sexes mark in the same way, but males mark much more frequently than females, and socially high ranked males more than low ranked. Marking occurs the year round, but is more prevalent in the breeding season.

The meaning(s) and adaptive value of marking is still obscure. A number of functions have been suggested, such as sexual signalling, territorial defense and self-assurance, but most questions in this field are yet to be answered. At present it seems most likely that urine marking in cats serves many purposes. That sex is involved can be inferred from the fact that cats don't mark until they have reached puberty, and that marking behaviour decreases and usually ceases completely in neutered cats. As a urine mark of one cat usually does not immediately deter another cat, it has been argued that marking has no territorial function. But we do not know what psychological effect the presence of a mark or a number of marks of a resident cat has on a newcomer that, for example, could predispose it to withdraw without further violence in a subsequent encounter with the resident.

Cats also mark by the use of faeces (that in these cases are not buried), and by claw marking, rolling and head rubbing. Virtually nothing is known about the functions of these types of marking and their relations to each other, although a lot of speculation has been put forward.

SEXUAL BEHAVIOUR

Female cats are usually seasonally polyoestrus. In the northern hemisphere most matings occur in February–July. Cats are induced ovulators, and it usually takes more than one copulation to achieve conception. If the female conceives, the oestrus will last 4–6 days, but if not, it might be prolonged up to at least 10 days.

The oncoming oestrus is marked by the female becoming increasingly restless. Crying, loss of appetite, rolling, head rubbing, and finally presenting of the vulva with raised hindquarters and lowered shoulders and head follow en suite. Receptiveness can be checked by gently pressing the hand down on her back, whereupon the receptive female cat raises her tail and hindquarters and 'presents'. Detailed descriptions of the female oestrus behaviour and the tom cat's response, as well as precopulatory, copulatory and post-copulatory behaviours are given by Leyhausen (1979).

Often several males are courting a female cat in oestrus simultaneously. Usually one of the suitors maintains a position much closer to the female than his competitors. This I have called the Central Male position (CM). The other males hold Peripheral Male positions (PMs). Usually the CM position is held by the local dominant Breeder, and the PMs are other Breeders and Challengers. It is usual in this situation that the status of the local Breeder is challenged and tested, and it is here that most escalated conflicts occur. Still, for the main part, the courtship is a rather peaceful business, where the participants can be lying for hours without anything special happening. It is only the CM that mates with the female. Matings occur with a frequency of around 15 per 24 hours.

It has been proposed that the female cat is very selective with regard to sexual partner, and might choose a male even if he is socially subordinate (Leyhausen, 1956). In the Revinge cats I found no evidence of this, neither is it, from a theoretical viewpoint, easy to see why this should occur. However, there were indications that at least some females tried to avoid being courted and mated by males closely related to them.

CONCLUSIONS

In basic behaviour patterns, like aggressive expressions, mode of fighting and reproductive behaviour, the domestic cat has changed little from its wild ancestors. In other aspects, especially concerning the high degree of intra-specific tolerance, it differs widely from the original stock of wild cats. This tolerance allows cats to live in large groups at farms and other places with a concentrated food resource. This, however, affects males less than females. In the male cat the competition for breeding opportunities functions as a spacing mechanism. The great flexibility in cat behaviour is shown by its adaptation to different environmental situations, producing large variations in traits like home range size and activity patterns, and even in social organisation (social versus solitary ways of life). This great flexibility is typical for most carnivores. It is therefore not known at present whether the cat's adaptations to a co-existence with man are genetically fixed as a result of natural and/or artificial selection or just examples of behavioural plasticity.

REFERENCES

Baron, A., C. N. Stewart, and J. M. Warrer (1957). Behaviour, 11, 56-66.
Caro, T. M. (1981). Behaviour, 76, 1-23.
Cole, D. D., and J. N. Shafer (1966). Behaviour, 27, 39-53.
Dards, J. L. (1978). Carnivore Genet. Newsletter, 3, 242-255.
Ewer, R. F. (1961). Behaviour, 17, 247-260.
Jones, E. (1977). Aust. Wildl. Res., 4, 249-262.
Laundre, J. (1977). Anim. Behav., 25, 990-998.
Leyhausen, P. (1956). Z. Tierpsychol. Beiheft, 2, 1-120.
Leyhausen, P. (1979). Cat Behaviour. Garland Press, New York, London.
Macdonald, D. W., and P. J. Apps (1978). Carnivore Genet. Newsletter, 3, 256-268.
Panaman, R. (1981). Z. Tierpsychol., 56, 59-73.
Van Aarde, R. J. (1978). Carnivore Genet. Newsletter, 3, 288-316.

Inheritance of Behaviour in the Dog

L. Fält

The Swedish Dog Training Centre, Box 2101, S 881 02 Solleftea,
Sweden

ABSTRACT

There are big differences in behaviour between and within breeds of dogs.
Some of the physical features in the standard of a breed might influence the
behaviour in several ways, e.g. pattern of movement or success as a sender
of signals. Breeds have - or have had - different functions based upon
behaviour specialisation - sheep dogs, hunting dogs, etc. - that breeders
have developed and stabilised during centuries. Scott and Fuller (1965)
demonstrated many differences in behaviour among the five breeds they studied.
For institutions that breed and train service dogs it is important to know if
it is possible to get a population more adapted to the work of guide dogs,
police dogs, etc. by selective breeding. Examples of breeding programmes
and some results are given from an institute for guide dog training
(Pfaffenberger and others, 1976) and from the Swedish Dog Training Centre
(guide and police dogs). These studies have shown that it is possible to
make testing programmes for analysis of the heritability of behaviour and
that it should be possible to improve populations by selective breeding.

KEYWORDS

Dog; behaviour; breed differences; heritability.

INTRODUCTION

As Scott and Fuller (1965) pointed out in their now classical book on Genetics
and Social Behavior in the Dog, the dog is a veritable genetic gold mine.
There are big differences between breeds and all sorts of individual differences appear.

PHYSICAL FEATURES AND BEHAVIOUR

The physical variation is obvious. The range of size is incredible. Saint
Bernards and Pyreneans weigh about 40 times as much as Chihuahuas. Greyhounds
have long, graceful limbs while the Dachshunds have very short legs. Bulldogs

have foreshortened heads and undershot jaws while Salukis have long, narrow
heads. There are also variations in length, texture and colour of their hair.
The Mexican Hairless and the Chinese Crested Dogs are almost bald breeds,
while the hair is continuously growing in the Poodle.

Some physical traits might have a direct influence on behaviour. For example,
the patterns of movement are not the same in Bulldogs as in Borzois.

The dog is an extremely social animal. It has a complicated communication
system. Some physical features may influence the understanding of signals
between individuals. In the visual part of the communication system the dog
uses its face, ears, body positions, movements, etc. In the ideal model of
the breed, the standard, we often include features that work against those
that were developed during natural selection in the ancestor, the wolf. The
black lips that contrast to the white cheeks, the bushy tail, the erect ears,
etc., are the structures that maximise the efficiency and reliability of the
signal.

It is obvious that some features such as long hair on the face, docked tail,
pendent ears, black colour, etc., influence the transferring of information.
They may alter the information content of the signal between the sender and
the receiver. At least they create a disturbance, a noise, in the trans-
mission. Thus some physical features in the standard of a breed may influence
behaviour in several ways.

BEHAVIOUR DIFFERENCES BETWEEN BREEDS

Different breeds have different functions based upon behavioural specialisation:
sheep dogs, hunting dogs, greyhounds, companion dogs, etc. Some of these
functions are very old and breeders have developed and stabilised them during
centuries. The real beginning of specialisation of hunting dogs began during
the Middle Ages. The ancestors of our Pointers, Setters and Terriers developed at that time. Some kinds of dogs such as sheep dogs and Greyhounds are
even older in origin.

Scott and Fuller (1965) based their study on this variation in behaviour
between breeds. They selected five breeds for intensive studies: Basenjis,
Beagles, American Cocker Spaniels, Shetland Sheepdogs and Wire-haired Fox
Terriers. Individuals of these five breeds were raised in the same environment and their similarities and differences were measured in sets of tests.
Differences in behavioural development were studied by daily observations
from birth up to 16 weeks of age. Cross-fostering between breeds was used to
analyse whether the maternal environment as well as heredity affected
behaviour. Crosses between breeds and back-crosses were used to find evidence
for the genetic basis of behaviour.

Among the differences found between breeds was that Terriers, Beagles and
Basenjis were consistently more emtoionally reactive than Shelties and
Cockers. These results supported the conclusion that heredity greatly affects
the expression of emotional behaviour and that emotional behaviour is a characteristic of breeds and individuals. Since emotional behaviour is an
important factor influencing success in dog training, these results are of
great importance.

The effect of heredity upon trainability was shown to be very complex. This
was mainly due to the many different behaviour patterns involved and the
interactions between them. In three different forced-training tests (quiet

during weighing, leash training and an obedience test) the Cocker Spaniels were the easiest to train and Basenjis and Beagles the most difficult.

These are just a few examples of the many differences between breeds that were found in the study by Scott and Fuller. It is obvious that there are variations within and between breeds that are inherited.

SELECTIVE BREEDING OF WORKING DOGS

Is it possible to use this knowledge about the genetic background to improve, say, working dogs by selective breeding? For the institutions and training centres that train dogs for services like guiding blind persons, doing police and guard work, it is of great importance to know if it is possible to get a breed or a population within a breed more adapted to the task in question.

One such project has been going on for many years at the Guide Dogs for the Blind, a Training Centre for Guide Dogs in California. The results were published by Pfaffenberger and others (1976).

The reason why this Centre started a breeding programme was that so few of the dogs put in training were considered safe to lead blind persons. The success rate was low. A breeding programme was started to select and raise a breeding stock capable of producing puppies that would be suitable for work as Guide Dogs.

Observations made on the dog's behaviour during early rearing, in a puppy testing programme, at the foster home and during training were considered in the breeding programme. An outstanding change in training success was attained in a relatively short period. The efficiency increased from about 30% to about 60% in five years. The breeding programme was an important part of the background to this development. The breed used was the German Shepherd.

The selection of animals for training and breeding was mainly based upon results from the puppy testing programme. In five of 13 tests there was a significant difference between sire values. The largest sire effect was on a test called Fetch. The between-dam variance was very high for all scores. The between-dam component was on average three times as large as the heritability figures based on sires. This indicates an important effect of the maternal environment - the 'quality' of the dam as a mother.

THE SWEDISH DOG TRAINING CENTRE

At the Swedish Dog Training Centre we were encouraged by the studies of Scott and Fuller (1965), Pfaffenberger and others (1976) and others, and have started a new programme on testing puppies and adult dogs. It is only the puppy testing programme that has been analysed so far.

The Centre is owned by the State. It produces dogs for different kinds of services such as police dogs, guide dogs and different kinds of search dogs. The main breeds used are German Shepherds and Labrador Retrievers. The Labradors are obtained from local breeders while most of the German Shepherds come from the breeding programme at the Centre. The Labradors are mainly trained as Guide Dogs or Search Dogs and the German Shepherds are trained as Police Dogs, Service Dogs in the army or Guide Dogs.

In the breeding programme physical features are also considered. One of them

is selection against hip dysplasia (Hedhammar and others, 1979). The results
from that part of the programme will not be discussed in this paper.

300-400 German Shepherd puppies are born at the Centre every year. At 8 or
10 weeks of age the puppies leave the kennel and are placed in foster homes.
In comparison with some English and American puppy walking programmes for
Guide Dogs, the Centre has a relatively extensive training programme for the
puppies. At 15 months of age the dogs come back to the Centre for testing
and training.

Puppies have passed a certain amount of training before they leave the kennel.
The kennel staff runs a programme starting when the puppies are 4-5 weeks of
age. At 8 weeks the puppies are subjected to a battery of tests. The variance
components and hereditability of test scores have been evaluated. The pred-
ictive values of test scores have not yet been analysed. Thus we cannot yet
relate puppy tests to success in final training.

The puppy testing programme consists of 10 tests and a summary of the results
will be given. Large sire effects were found in five and large dam effects
in nine of the ten tests. As in the study by Pfaffenberger and others (1976)
we found high between-dam variances. This was partly due to the maternal and
litter environment during the eight weeks before testing. In order to analyse
this effect in more detail we have started cross-fostering experiments but
have no clear results so far.

The heritability in the five tests with significant sire effects varied between
0.31 and 0.77. These five tests were: time to first whining after isolation
(0.66), contact with a strange person (0.77), running after and carrying a
small moving object (0.73), activity (0.43), exploration (0.31).

PROBLEMS IN BEHAVIOUR GENETICS

There are some factors that have to be considered which differentiate behav-
ious from other traits such as the morphological ones commonly used by
geneticists. Ehrman and Parsons (1976) in their book on The Genetics of
Behavior have pointed out three main factors.

1.   The difficulty of environmental control. Variations in early experience
      such as maternal effects influence later behaviour.

2.   The difficulty of objective measurement. This factor is of the utmost
      importance. When an element of subjectivity appears it becomes almost
      impossible to assess the relative importance of heredity and environment.
      Objective measurements should be made using instruments such as automatic
      counters and chronometers. The stimuli and the responses in test
      situations should be well defined.

3.   Learning is a factor that influences test results and must be considered
      by the behaviour geneticist. Multiple experience of the same stimulus
      situation might influence the reactions during testing.

In the testing of dogs for working and hunting purposes, these three factors
are not considered as much as they should. This is one of the reasons why
results from hunting competitions show very low heritability, if any.

CONCLUSIONS

The studies by Scott and Fuller, Pfaffenberger and fellow workers and our studies at the Swedish Dog Training Centre have shown that it is possible to make testing programmes for analysis of the heritability of behaviour in dogs. Thus it should be possible to improve breeds or populations within breeds by selective breeding.

REFERENCES

Ehrman, L. and Parsons, P. A. (1976). The Genetics of Behavior. Sinauer Ass. Inc., Sunderland, Mass., U.S.A.

Hedhammar, A., S.-E. Olsson, S.-A. Andersson, L. Persson, L. Petterson, A. Olausson, P.-E. Sundgren (1979). J. Am. vet. med. Ass., 174, 1012-1016.

Pfaffenberger, C. J., J. P. Scott, J. L. Fuller, B. E. Ginsberg, S. W. Bielfelt (1976). Guide Dogs for the Blind: their selection, development and training. Elsevier Sci. Pub. Co., Amsterdam.

Scott, J. P. and J. L. Fuller (1965). Genetics and the Social Behavior of the Dog. Univ. Chicago Press.

Development of Behaviour of the Dog During Maturity

P. L. Borchelt

Animal Medical Center, 501 East 62nd Street, New York, USA

ABSTRACT

As the dog matures from juvenile to adult, its behaviour is likely to change. Sometimes aggression, phobias and separation behaviour problems occur as the dog matures. Maturational changes in these behaviours are discussed and the data presented on the development of possessive, fear, dominance and protective aggression, and mounting, leg-lifting and urine marking.

KEYWORDS

Development; aggression; fears; phobias; separation behaviours; marking; urine marking.

INTRODUCTION

Once dog owners have successfully weathered the inevitable problems and trials of the first 6 months or so, they hope to enjoy many years of close and loving interaction with their pets. But, as the dog develops from juvenile to adult, its behaviour changes. For example, by the end of the juvenile period the permanent teeth are present and 'teething' behaviour wanes. Usually by this time, the dog is also exploring widely and has achieved some degree of independence from the owner and social isolation for several hours or more is tolerated well.

As a dog becomes sexually and behaviourally mature, it reaches full size and its behaviour systems tend to become fully expressed. Sometimes things do not progress as the owner had hoped or planned. A dog may develop aggressive behaviour to strangers, family members or other animals. It may begin to show separation problems when the owners move to a new home or change working hours. It may develop phobias to loud sounds. Some of these behaviours are significantly influenced by biological factors and others influenced less so.

In the following chapter, I will briefly outline some interview data obtained from pet owners during the diagnosis and treatment of behaviour problems of pet dogs living in the human environment. The focus will be on the most

common behaviour problems. These involve aggressive behaviour, fears and
phobias, and separation problems. Data are also presented on the development
of mounting, leg-lifting and urine marking.

AGGRESSION

In young puppies, aggressive behaviour (barking, growling, biting) is usually
limited to the context of possession of food or objects such as bones or toys,
or in the context of dominance relations within a litter. These behaviours
can occur by 5 weeks of age or earlier (Scott and Fuller, 1965). As the dog
matures, however, there are many other contexts in which it may become
aggressive. The incidence of aggressive behaviour in pet dogs is all too high.
Dog bites directed to either human or other animals constitute a major public
health problem. In the United States, over one million people per year report
serious dog bites (Beck and others, 1975; Harris and others, 1974) and it is
likely that there are many times this number of bites which are unreported.
Some dog bites are serious enough to result in human deaths (Winkler, 1977;
Borchelt and others, 1983). Based on observations and interviews with over
250 owners regarding aggressive behaviour of dogs, Borchelt (1983) proposed
a classification scheme for aggressive behaviour of the dog living in the human
environment. In the following sections, the types of aggressive behaviour
problems that typically occur will be described.

Defensive Aggression

Defensive aggression occurs when a dog is in the general situation of defending
itself from a perceived threat or from pain. Defensive aggression can occur
in the context of fear, actual pain or the threat of punishment, and involves
a display of defensive or submissive signals prior to or during the aggression.
Frequently, these signals include flattening of the ears and lowering the tail
or tucking it between the legs. During fear-elicited aggression, the dog often
barks and may alternately approach and withdraw from the eliciting stimulus.
Eliciting stimuli include sounds outside the home, doorbells, knocks at the
door, or the sight of a strange person. A 'strange' person could be someone
who looks different (unusual clothing, walking with a cane, carrying an unusual
package, etc.) or perhaps a child. Fear-elicited aggression may also be
displayed to another animal. A dog exhibiting fear-aggression is likely to
growl or bite only if approached, particularly if approached quickly.

Dominance Aggression

Dominance generally refers to a social relationship between two or more
animals in which one enjoys priority of access to important resources such as
food, shelter, or a mate. Often, there is a hierarchical (but not necessarily
linear) social relationship within a group of animals. The relationship may
be established and maintained by threats and communication signals that
decrease the necessity of injurious fights. While the majority of domestic
dogs living with humans do not exhibit dominance aggression, the problem is
not uncommon. When dominance aggression does occur, it is an extremely variable
and complex behaviour problem. For instance, some dominant pet dogs exhibit
one or more species-typical dominance postures directed to the owner(s). These
postures include 'stand over', direct eye contact or stare, tail and ears held
erect and a tense or rigid posture. The 'stand over' posture may be displayed
in the species-typical topography (Fox, 1971) if the owner, for instance, is
lying on the floor. If the owner is sitting or standing, however, the dog may

attempt to climb in the owner's lap, may paw at or push into the owner, or may block the owner's movements in the home by growling and threatening. Dominant dogs seem to adjust their display of dominance to the owner's behaviour and size.

Other dominant dogs do not exhibit dominance postures, but instead actively or aggressively resist being placed in submissive postures or situations. These dogs may growl or bite if forcibly rolled over onto their backs even though they may readily roll over to be petted. More subtle behaviours of the owner can be interpreted by the dog as attempts to dominate it. For instance, some dogs become aggressive when petted, groomed, picked up, pushed off the couch or the leash is put on or taken off. Frequently a dominant aggressive dog will form a 'dominance hierarchy' in the family. The position in the hierarchy that the dog takes is variable. In some cases, it will display aggression to all members of the family. In other cases, only one or a few family members will be considered 'subordinate' and receive aggressive behaviour. In most cases, however, the dog is extremely friendly to humans outside of the family hierarchy.

Cases of dominance aggression offer an excellent insight into how much the perceptual worlds of humans and canids can differ. Owners of such dogs invariably describe the dog's aggression as 'unprovoked'. In fact, one can identify eliciting stimuli and easily elicit aggression in the vast majority of cases. In the home environment, the owners simply engage in normal human behaviour but are unaware that these behaviours are perceived as dominance signals by the dog.

Possessive Aggression

Possessive aggression occurs when the dog is in possession of some object (e.g. food, bone, toy) and a person or animal approaches and/or attempts to take it away. This behaviour frequently accompanies dominance aggression. In these cases, the dog may actually steal an object and guard it. Not all instances of possessive aggression, however, are accompanied by the other signs of dominance aggression.

Protective Aggression

Many dogs exhibit aggression in the context of 'territorial' behaviour, when a person or animal approaches or enters the property or home. These dogs may respond to sounds outside the home, such as doorbells or knocks at the door. But some dogs also display aggression in circumstances not related to territory. They will respond aggressively to the approach of a stranger (particularly one of unusual appearance) towards the owner, especially to any movement such as a hand shake, back slap, etc. which is perceived as a threat to the owner. They may also incorrectly interpret family behaviour such as hugging or dancing as threats and jump up, paw at, or growl at the 'threatening' person.

Intra-Specific Aggression

Typically, intra-specific aggression involves inter-male and inter-female aggression. It occurs less often between males and females. Intra-specific aggression may occur in the context of dominance postures (stand over, staring), possession of food or objects, or when one or more of the dogs is defensive (ears back, tail down).

Predation

Predation is an appetitive component of feeding. However, some dogs exhibit
the behavioural components of predation, such as visual scanning and stalking,
to small animals or even to people. The eliciting stimuli are usually small
size and/or movement. Catching and killing of 'prey' usually does not occur,
although some dogs regularly kill small animals. Usually, predatory behaviour
directed to people results in nipping rather than multiple bites, but under
special circumstances can involve killing (Borchelt and others, 1983).

Characteristics of Types of Aggression

These types of aggressive behaviour problems do not occur with equal frequency.
Borchelt (1983) found that fear aggression occurred most frequently (23%),
followed by dominance (20%), possessive (17%), protective (17%), and intra-
specific aggression (12%). Punishment-elicited aggression (7%), pain-elicited
aggression (2%) and predation (1%) occurred relatively infrequently. Male
dogs (67.4%) were much more likely to be aggressive than females (32.6%).
Dominance and inter-male aggression occurred in intact males more than castrated
males, as compared to other types of aggression. Specific behaviours exhibited
by the dogs differed among the various types of aggression. Table 1 depicts
the percentage of cases of fear, dominance, possessive and protective aggression
in which specific aggressive behaviours were displayed. Barking, which probably
functions as an 'early warning', is more likely to occur in protective aggression
compared to dominance and possessive aggression. But threats, such as staring,
growling, baring the teeth and snaps (attempted bites) or actual bites, are
more likely to occur in dominance aggression.

Table 1   Percentage of Specific Aggressive Behaviours
           Occurring in Each type of Aggressive Behaviour
           Problem

	n	Bark	Growl	Bare teeth	Snap	Bite	Stare
Fear	86	60.5	53.5	10.5	24.4	33.7	0.0
Dominance	73	27.4	84.9	23.3	30.1	60.3	20.6
Possessive	65	7.7	69.2	12.3	20.0	33.9	0.0
Protective	63	61.9	52.4	3.2	19.1	25.4	1.6

Development of Aggression

Most of the owners were asked about the development of the various aggressive
problems. Figure 1 presents, as a cumulative percentage, the age at which
possessive (n=46), fear (n=63), dominance (n=54) and protective aggression
(n=40) were first exhibited. Several points are noteworthy. First, there
is a wide range over which these problems develop. About 25% of the possessive
aggression problems developed during the first 3 months, but over 10% of the
problems did not occur until between 18-24 months of age. Likewise, about 15%
of the cases of fear aggression developed in the first 3 months, but a few
cases did not occur until the dog was 3 years or older. The same general trend
is seen for dominance and protective aggression. Secondly, possessive and fear
aggression occurred earlier than dominance and protective aggression.
Comparisons at 7-12 months of age revealed that the percentage exhibiting fear
aggression was significantly higher than the percentage exhibiting dominance

aggression (X^2=7.6, p< 0.01) and the percentage for possessive aggression was higher than for protective aggression (X^2=5.4, p< 0.05). The difference in percentage of possessive compared to dominance aggression did not quite reach statistical significance (X^2=3.53, p< 0.07).

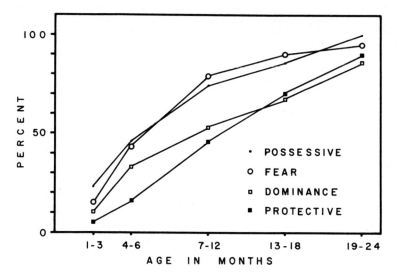

Fig. 1. Cumulative percentage of dogs exhibiting types
of aggressive behaviour problems at different ages

FEARS AND PHOBIAS

Fear is not a unitary concept, but instead involves a wide range of responses. The responses elicited depend on the specific stimulus context. In general fear can include flight or escape responses, expressive signals and physiological concomitants (Archer, 1979). In dogs, escape responses can include running away or attempts to escape such as digging or chewing. Fear expressions include flattening of ears, lowering of the tail, or piloerection. Increases in heart rate, respiration, muscle tremors, urination, defaecation or expulsion of anal gland excretions are among the physiological responses that can occur. The stimuli that elicit fear can generally be divided into those associated with predators, intense physical environmental stimuli, and conspecific threat signals (Russell, 1979). Most of the stimuli that elicit fear behaviour problems in pet dogs are loud noises such as thunder, fire crackers, gun shots, or vehicle noises (engines running, backfires). Sometimes, dogs will generalise fear of thunder to other features of storms such as lightning, rain or wind. In some cases, dogs clearly anticipate the onset of thunderstorms by as much as several hours, perhaps by sensing atmospheric changes or infrasounds. In urban environments, it is not unusual for dogs to become frightened of the movement or sounds of trucks, buses and cars. Fears of animals or people, particularly strangers and children, are common also. Sometimes, dogs become afraid only of unusual stimuli such as popping of chewing gum, clicking sounds, telephones ringing, ironing boards and brooms, sizzling bacon and boiling water, hair dryers and vacuum cleaners.

Development of Fears and Phobias

It is a general phenomenon that fear responses begin to develop early in social animals, simultaneous to, or shortly after, the development of social attachment behaviours. Both maturation and experience play a role in the development of fear (Salzen, 1979). In dogs, individual differences of biological origin are important determinants (Scott and Fuller, 1965; Corson and Corson, 1976) and evidence exists for genetic factors (Humphrey and Warner, 1934; Murphree, 1973; Murphree, Dykman and Peters, 1967). Thus, a fear or phobia could be observed at an early age, in some cases due to constitutional or temperamental factors and in other cases due to lack of experience with the feared stimulus. A phobia could occur in a dog of any age depending on the intensity or novelty of the stimulus, interacting with the dog's previous experience and constitutional characteristics.

Fear of thunderstorms may be influenced by maturation since fewer puppies are presented with these problems than older dogs. However, it is difficult to differentiate the role of maturation from experience in these cases since many dogs are reported to become progressively more frightened with each thunderstorm season. It is also possible that brontophobia in puppies poses less of a problem for the owner than does this problem in older dogs. Fears of traffic and crowds are seen more frequently in younger dogs, probably because these problems immediately interfere with housebreaking and exercising the dog. As reported by Hothersall and Tuber (1979), not all cases of fears and phobias can be attributed to a traumatic conditioning event. But learning usually plays a major role since most fears do generalise to some extent.

                    SEPARATION BEHAVIOUR

The complexity of separation behaviour and its developmental interactions with other behaviour systems have been discussed previously (Borchelt and Voith, 1982; Borchelt, this volume). Assuming that the puppy's separation behaviour has been well managed and that the puppy now tolerates departures of the owner for many hours, there are still numerous circumstances that can lead to a separation problem. Separation problems can occur if the owner changes the schedule of working hours suddenly, or if the owner is home from work for a period of time (due to illness, unemployment, etc.) and then resumes work. Some dogs readily learn to tolerate separations of a few hours (e.g. when the owner is shopping) but exhibit problems when the owner is absent for longer periods. Rarely, some dogs even learn to tolerate departures of quite specific durations, and exhibit separation problems if the owner arrives home late. Frequently, dogs will tolerate daily separations when the owner is at work, but exhibit problems in the evening if the owner again departs.

A common characteristic of separation problems in older dogs is the development of anticipatory anxiety. For instance, the dog may follow the owners around the house as they get ready for work, and whine as they pick up the keys and go to the door. Usually, a long chain of pre-separation stimuli and responses only occurs in older dogs which have had ample opportunity to learn to predict the sequence of departure events.

Early or later experiences involving repeated attachment and separation will also influence the likelihood of separation problems. Older dogs adopted from a shelter or found as strays are likely to attach very strongly to the new owners and then to exhibit separation problems if they are suddenly exposed to the normal schedule of owner departures.

MOUNTING AND MARKING

During diagnostic interviews owners were usually asked about the development
of other behaviours such as mounting, leg-lifting and urine marking. These
behaviours generally occur in males much more frequently than in females.
Figure 2 presents data on the age at which male dogs first exhibited mounting
(n=38), leg-lifting (n=51) and urine marking (n=11). Mounting includes that
displayed either to humans or other dogs, but urine marking includes only
those dogs which urine marked in the home. As with aggressive behaviour,
there was great variation in the age of onset of these behaviours. Mounting
occurred by 3 months of age in some dogs and not until 2 years in others.
Scott and Fuller(1965) noted that incomplete pelvic thrusting and mounting
can occur as early as 3-4 weeks of age. According to owners' reports, some
dogs (not included in this sample) apparently never mount.

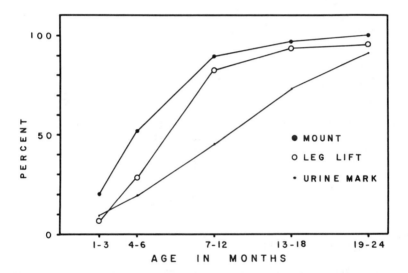

Fig. 2.   Cumulative percentage of dogs exhibiting mounting,
          leg-lifting and urine marking at different ages

Martins and Valle (1948) reported that small and medium-sized fox terriers
in a kennel environment all leg-lifted by 5-8 months, but one Doberman did
not do so until 10 months. Berg (1944) found leg-lifting to first appear
between 19 and 43 weeks in a colony of mixed sized dogs. The data in Fig. 2
indicate leg-lifting to occur anywhere between less than 3 months and 2-3
years or more. This variation may be due to sampling a wide range of breeds
or to differences between home and kennel environments.

Bekoff (1979) observed urine marking (raised leg urination) in free-ranging
dogs to occur much more frequently and at a higher rate in male than female
dogs. Dogs of both sexes marked less frequently in familiar than unfamiliar
areas, a finding consistent with observations of marking in wolves (Peters
and Mech, 1975). In the present sample of pet dogs, urine marking involved
deposition of small amounts of urine, usually on conspicuous objects such as
furniture in various locations in the home.

The function of urine marking is unclear. Scott and Fuller (1965), Scott (1967) and Bekoff (1979) found no evidence that urine marking in dogs was used either to gain or maintain a territory or serve as a boundary marker. The fact that all of the dogs in the present sample urine marked in the home (the area of most familiarity) is interesting. It suggests that the function of urine marking in the home may serve a different function than urine marking as a response to conspecific interactions. However, no data are yet available comparing the rate of urine marking in versus outside the home.

IMPLICATIONS

The relationships among biology, behaviour and environment are dynamic through-out an animal's life. It should not be surprising then that a dog's behaviour may change sometimes dramatically from puppyhood to maturity. Certainly, some dogs are wonderful companions that cause little or no problems throughout their entire life. But other dogs develop behaviour problems as a result of biol-ogical predispositions, maturation, early or later experiences or a complex combination of these factors. A problem can occur in puppyhood, middle age or old age.

A number of practical and theoretical issues are implied by this view. First, attempts to test for 'temperament problems' at a few months of age are only of limited use. These tests may select out the extremes of asocial behaviour (for instance, determine if a puppy is extremely shy of people and not easily desensitised), but cannot be used to accurately determine the potential for problems in most puppies. Developmental correlations for behaviours are notoriously low. Second, behavioural flexibility with respect to acquiring problems implies flexibility in treating them. Usually, dogs of any age can be taught new tricks. Third, the sheer number of behaviour problems exhibited by millions of pet dogs offers an excellent opportunity for field research. All of the important scientific issues in animal behaviour and ethology – function, evolution, control and ontogony – are there in an applied setting.

ACKNOWLEDGEMENTS

I would like to express my gratitude to hundreds of puppy and dog owners who let me (for fair exchange of fees) enter their lives briefly to learn and teach about dog behaviour problems. Their need and desire for information allowed me to satisfy mine also, without financial support from any govern-mental agencies or private foundations. Thanks are also due to William J. Kay, DVM, and Victoria Voith, DVM, PhD, for their encouragement and friendship.

REFERENCES

Archer, J. (1979). Fear in Animals and Man. Van Nostrand Reinhold, New York, pp. 56-85.
Beck, A. M., H. Lorine, and R. Lockwood (1975). Publ. Hlth. Rep., 90, 262-267.
Bekoff, M. (1979). Biol. of Behav., 4, 123-139.
Berg, I. A. (1944). J. exp. Psychol., 34, 343-368.
Borchelt, P. L. (1983). Appl. Anim. Ethol.
Borchelt, P. L., and V. L. Voith (1982). Symp. on Anim. Behav., Vet. Clin. N. Amer. W. J. Saunders, Philadelphia. pp. 625-635.
Borchelt, P. L., R. Lockwood, A. Beck, and V. L. Voith (1983). Publ. Hlth. Rep., 98.

Corson, S. A., and E. Corson (1976). Psychopathology of Human Adaption.
  Plenum, New York. pp. 77-94.
Fox, M. W. (1971). Behaviour of Wolves, Dogs and Related Canids. Harper and
  Row, New York.
Harris, D., P. J. Imperato, and B. Oken (1974). Bull. N. Y. Acad. Med., 50,
  981-1000.
Humphrey, E., and L. Warner (1934). Working Dogs: An attempt to produce a
  strain of German Shepherds which combine working abilities with beauty of
  conformation. Johns Hopkins Press, Baltimore.
Hothersall, D., and D. S. Tuber (1979). Psychopathology in Animals. Academic
  Press, New York. pp. 239-255.
Martins, T., and J. R. Valle (1948). J. Comp. Physiol. Psychol., 41, 301-311.
Murphree, O. D. (1973). Biol. Psychiat., 7, 23-29.
Murphree, O. D., R. A. Dykman, and J. E. Peters (1967). Cond. Reflex, 2, 199-
  205.
Peters, R., and L. D. Mech (1975). Am. Scient., 63, 628-637.
Russell, P. A. (1979). Fear in Animals and Man. Van Nostrand Reinhold, New
  York. pp. 86-124.
Salzen, E. A. (1979). Fear in Animals and Man. Van Nostrand Reinhold, New
  York. pp. 125-163.
Scott, J. P. (1967). Am. Zool., 7, 373-381.
Scott, J. P., and J. L. Fuller (1965). Dog Behavior: The genetic basis.
  University of Chicago Press, Chicago.
Ulrich, R. E. and J. H. Azrin (1962). J. Exp. Anal. Behav., 5, 511-520.
Winkler, W. G. (1977). Publ. Hlth, Rep., 92, 425-429.

MODIFICATION OF
BEHAVIOUR

Communication With the Dog When Training

T. Owren

Stovner Animal Clinic, Stovner Center, Oslo 9, Norway

ABSTRACT

A communication system consisting of the dog handler, the dog, signals (stimuli) and other external influences (noise), is used when training a dog. These sections are discussed. The change of behaviour is more permanent and a new behaviour pattern is established faster when the training is organised in a way where key stimuli that elicit wanted behaviour sequences are introduced many times before a command is conditioned with the stimuli.

KEYWORDS

Structure of the dog's behaviour; communication system; sender; receiver; signals; noise on communication line.

INTRODUCTION

The aim of this paper is briefly to discuss from an ethological point of view the communication system used when training the dog. Practical examples will be given.

Communication in this context can be defined as the methods used by the handler to influence the dog's behaviour patterns so that the tendency to display specific behaviour sequences as a result of a command is greatly enhanced.

To ensure the probability that a signal will elicit certain behaviour sequences, one has to train the animal step by step.

WHY THE VETERINARIAN HAS TO KNOW SOMETHING ABOUT COMMUNICATION AND TRAINING

The purpose of the training can vary from strict obedience training for a family dog or obedience training for competitions, to the more complex training that is necessary for the working dog used by civilians, police or military forces. The communication systems used are the same for all these types of dogs.

To be able to use behaviour modification techniques with success and to
better understand the problems of a client, it is necessary that a small animal
practitioner is familiar with different ways of communicating with the dog.
Often the veterinarian must give advice on simple training methods, and thereby
hopefully later prevent the dog from being a nuisance to the owner, neighbours
or the community (and certainly to the veterinarian).

The veterinarian has a wide biological background that should enable him to
understand the basic principles used when training the dog better than most
dog handlers. However, it is important that theoretical models worked out
scientifically go in hand with the practical work done by experienced handlers.

COMMUNICATION IS A SYSTEM

A communication system consists of:

    (a)   a sender (the dog handler)
    (b)   a receiver (the dog)
    (c)   signals (stimuli)
    (d)   other external influences (noise)

To understand how our signals can elicit certain behaviour patterns and to
learn what they are and when to use them, the structure of the dog's behaviour
repertoire will be briefly discussed.

THE RECEIVER: STRUCTURE OF BEHAVIOUR

Among ethologists it seems to be a trend to organise the behaviour into specific
groups or behaviour systems
different behaviour sequences ('Instinkthandlungen') subdivided into behaviour
steps and fixed action patterns and orientation movements. By organising
behaviour in specific systems, we are able to describe the behaviour more
objectively.

In the animal's natural environment, it is often most practical to describe its
behaviour at the level of 'Instinkthandlungen' (sequences). A certain stimulisummation should reach a fixed threshold value to elicit a behaviour sequence.
These stimuli consist of external signals (plus noise) and internal stimuli
(= motivation).

When the dog is exposed to external stimuli, it will activate a certain
behaviour system ('Funktionskreitz') depending on the motivation level at that
moment, and as a result of these stimuli, display at more or less high intensity
a behaviour sequence (or sequences) grouped under this system.

The sum of internal (motivation) and external stimuli will be analysed in a
motivation control system and compared to the fixed threshold value necessary
to elicit a behaviour system and perhaps a large number of sequences. If the
threshold value of none of the behaviour systems is reached, the animal will
display a neutral behaviour to the stimuli-situation (Fält, 1982).

        THE RECEIVER: HOW TO USE THE STRUCTURE OF BEHAVIOUR IN THE
        COMMUNICATION SYSTEM

If we want the dog to display certain behaviour sequences as a result of a command, we have to :

1. find the stimuli that elicit the sequences;
2. slowly change the motivation level to increase the dog's tendency
    to display the desired sequences and decrease the tendency to perform
    other behaviour patterns or sequences;
3. make a chain of different behaviour sequences to a constructed new
    behaviour pattern;
4. by conditioning teach the dog the connection between the command and
    the stimuli so that later the command will work as the only signal
    to elicit the new pattern of behaviour.

It is debatable whether we can change the various threshold values of an
individual by training or if this can only be done through breeding programmes.

It is important to realise that when training a dog for a specific task, we can
only establish a chain of genetically predisposed behaviour sequences by manipulating the motivation systems (increase and decrease the tendency to display
different behaviour sequences). It is impossible to elicit a behaviour sequence
that·is not genetically preprogrammed.

It is unwise to use force; by doing so we cannot expect to make a permanent
new behaviour pattern. We have to change the level of motivation.

Various dog trainers have proved that this method of training works very well.
To my knowledge Sven Järverud (1980) has best put this system into practical
use: (a) find the stimulus that elicits a wanted behaviour sequence, (b)
construct a new behaviour pattern of these wanted sequences, (c) by conditioning make the dog produce the wanted behaviour pattern by command.

SIGNALS

When communicating with the dog, we have to use signals that can be received
by the animal. They must be of the type that elicit a reaction (preferably
as short or longer chains of desirable behaviour sequences), or the signal
must elicit a behaviour pattern through a learned process of change in different
motivation systems.

Before our signals can be received, we have to establish a channel in which the
signals can be passed. This means that as well as the dog, we have to display
cooperative behaviour and thereby attract the dog's attention.

Signals can be of the following types, classified according to which sense
system is used by the receiver:

1. olfactory signals (chemical);
2. optical signals (visual);
3. audible signals (sound);
4. tactile signals (touch).

When using these signals we have to consider the dog's physical ability to
receive them:

The dog's colour vision and ability to see contrasts seems to be much less than
man's (Price, 1977). By directing the dog with arm movements, we have to be
sure that there is a clear contrast between the arm and the background to enable
the dog to see the movement (see Fält, 1981).

We also have to realise that often a multi-signal system is used when we only intend to use a single stimulus. The dog is put in a state of conflict if signals which elicit opposing behaviour are given.

If we want the dog to approach as a response to an audible signal (a call or whistle), at the same time as we are unconsciously making threatening movements or displaying a dominant body shape by leaning towards and over the dog, we strongly reduce the chance that the dog will approach when called; the dog is in a state of conflict.

We often have to combine a number of stimuli (spatial stimulisummation) or one stimulus repeated several times (temporal stimulisummation) before a behaviour sequence is elicited.

We want the dog to come as a response to an audible signal. At the same time as calling (be sure that the dog can see you), the handler turns away. An optical signal is now added to the call. Since the dog is a pack animal and displays a high tendency to stay with a group, the sight of the handler running away will in most cases elicit a social behaviour pattern (i.e. running after). In the beginning it is important that this behaviour is reinforced every time to make sure that it will be permanent.

An example of a temporal stimulisummation can be seen when watching a dog inviting to play. The same aggression-reducing and play-inviting behaviour (optical, audible and tactile signals) is repeated several times until the other animal makes a positive response.

To be a successful dog handler it is important to master a large selection of the various stimuli used to elicit a wanted behaviour sequence. This can be learned by experience and by watching the interaction of dogs.

It is further important to know at what intensity a stimulus should be used and thereby hinder ambivalent behaviour.

One must also know how a behaviour sequence is conditioned (Voith, 1979); if we have made a clear connection between 'NO' and a punishment, and later consistently pet the dog when repeating the command 'NO' (giving tactile stimuli that are perceived as a strongly positive reinforcement), the effect of this command will very soon become extinct.

NOISE ON THE COMMUNICATION LINE

This can be defined as signals that cannot be controlled by the dog handler. There may not be a sharp distinction between noise and unwanted signals created by a less experienced handler. These hidden errors will many times be the difference between a good and a bad result.

It is important to understand the concept of noise, since these disturbances:

(a) without our being aware of it can actually be the eliciting stimuli;
(b) might be used as an aid in our training;
(c) might have such a high negative influence on our training that the process should temporarily be stopped until the noise has ceased or the sources have been removed.

Quite often people in obedience classes complain about the fact that the dog does well in class, but the result is disappointing when the owner trains on his own; or the dog performs well when an instructor is watching, but completely neglects the owner's command when the instructor is not present. These are examples of how the noise connected with the training environment can be the eliciting stimuli and is necessary to make the dog display a wanted behaviour sequence.

Noise can also be used to our advantage in the training; we can have a dog displaying a certain tendency of flight behaviour when seeing other dogs. By training such types of dog together with other dogs, the handler will achieve maximum attention from the dog and thereby strengthen the communication channel.

On the other hand, dogs displaying high intensity of communicative and cooper-ative behaviour directed towards other dogs, will have great difficulties in receiving signals from a handler when training with other dogs.

THE SENDER

We must be aware that the communication system is a two-way system where the dog will immediately give feedbacks on its reaction to the situation. Our flow of signals must be adjusted according to these reactions. It is therefore important that the sender can see the dog's reactions and understand its response to our signals ('read the dog') (see Fox and Cohen, 1977; Fox, 1965; Fox, 1971).

We must further be capable of perceiving the dog's emotional state at all times in order to avoid conflicts that will lead to ambivalent behaviour or mentally blocking situations where the dog no longer is capable of receiving information (learning).

Before starting a training session, we have to be sure that both the dog and the handler are at the optimal stress level.

ACKNOWLEDGEMENT

The author would like to express gratitude to the good friends Rune Fjellanger, Terje Østlie and Arne Erik Hennum for the many good ideas on how theoretical models can be used in practical work with the dog.

REFERENCES

Fält, L. (1981). Politihunden (in Norwegian), No. 3, 7-10.
Fält, L. (1982). Politihunden (in Norwegian), No. 2, 17-21.
Fox, M. W., and J. A. Cohen (1977). Canid communication. In How Animals Communicate. Indiana University Press, Bloomington.
Fox, M. W. (1965). Canine Behaviour. Charles C. Thomas, Springfield, Illinois.
Fox, M. W. (1971). Behaviour of Wolves, Dogs and Related Canids. Harper and Row, New York.
Järverud, S. and G. af Klintenberg-Järverud (1980). Your Dog (in Swedish), 2nd ed. Studentlitteratur, Lund.
Price, J. H. (1977). The eye and vision. In Dukes' Physiology of Domestic Animals, 9th ed. Cornell University Press, Ithaca.
Voith, V. L. (1979). Behavioral problems. In Canine Medicine and Therapeutics. Blackwell Scientific Publications, London.

Behaviour Problems in the Dog

R. A. Mugford

10 Ottershaw Park, Ottershaw, Chertsey, Surrey, UK

ABSTRACT

Canine behavioural problems commonly presented to the practising veterinarian and behavioural specialist are described, together with alternative approaches to therapy. Aggression in various forms is the most commonly encountered problem in the author's referral practice (69% of cases), other problems being miscellaneous neurotic responses (26%), separation anxiety (e.g. destructiveness, 23%) elimination problems (17%), clinical psychopathologies (13%) and miscellaneous (44%). The roles of veterinarian, psychologist and dog trainer in animal behavioural therapy are discussed.

KEYWORDS

Canine; euthanasia; aggression; neuroses; psychopathology; behaviour-modification.

INTRODUCTION

The pet dog is usually expected to present remarkable qualities of sagacity, adaptability, and friendliness with timely aggression. The demands which people make upon their dogs are rarely constant and it is small wonder that not all are able to fulfil the expectations of their owners. Yet the majority of domestic dogs successfully adapt to the difficult role of companion to humans. However, a minority do not, and they, to varying degrees, present their owners with problem behaviours. There is no absolute definition of what is or is not a problem behaviour. In one setting, loud barking and ferocious aggression at the door can be a desirable attribute but in others a problem.

Veterinarians, psychologists and others professionally involved in the study and treatment of canine behavioural problems rarely encounter extreme pathological disturbances in the dog. Rather, one sees variations of normality that for good or bad reasons are not acceptable to the owner. A general definition of the term behavioural problem can be as follows: deviation in the behaviour of a companion animal from the reasonable expectations of the owner, the owner's family or the wider society. If professional help is sought to resolve a canine behavioural problem, much of the initial discussion is bound to centre upon the owner's concept of reasonableness.

Interest in the application of formal scientific principles to the treatment
of behavioural problems in companion animals is relatively new, and largely
initiated in the USA by Campbell (1975), Tuber, Bothersall and Voith (1974),
and Hart (1980). The relevance of behavioural problems to small animal
veterinary practice is underlined by the results of a survey in Scotland by
Stead (1982), who found that the most common reason for carrying out euthanasia
on otherwise healthy dogs was behavioural in 39% of the non-clinical cases.
Until recently, euthanasia or possibly castration and prescriptions of
sedatives were the main points involvement of veterinarians in the treatment
of behavioural problems in companion animals. Much more effective and
sophisticated therapies are now available from the pooled literatures of
ethology, clinical and comparative psychology, endocrinology and psychopharmacology. These are certainly not just sophisticated variants of traditional
dog training, though obedience training may be incorporated into treatment of,
for instance, dominance-aggression.

The consequences of owning a dog with behavioural problems can be very considerable and one sometimes wonders why people put up with the worst aspects of
their pet's behaviour. For instance, the author has had a case where the dog
destroyed the interiors of seven cars to the value of some £15,000, and another
where the family home had been emptied of virtually all furniture and fabrics
because of the dog's destructive tendencies. Other clients are shunned within
their community because of their dog's anti-social tendencies, they may never
take holidays, or the dog may have become the focus for persistent family
arguments. Rather than put up with such uncompanionable behaviour, some dog
owners reject the pet and allow it to become a stray, thereby causing a public
nuisance. A better alternative is that they seek to modify the pet's behaviour
in a constructive fashion.

The majority of clients referred to the author are psychologically well-balanced
individuals and it is unjust to presume that their dog's problems necessarily
derive from human inadequacies. Rather, one finds that owners seeking professional help are very strongly attached to their pet because the positive
features of the dog's behaviour outweigh the negative (Voith, 1981). The
human/companion animal relationship is in many ways like that between parent
and child. Both parent and dog owner can become committed to a relationship
that they acknowledge is unsatisfactory but can see no way of improving. It
is important that clients owning problem dogs be offered practical help and
not platitudes.

The author would argue that the initial source of help should come from the
owner's veterinarian rather than from a psychologist or other behavioural
specialist. As will be emphasised in later sections of this chapter, the
starting point for most animal behavioural therapy should be a clinical
assessment and differential diagnosis by a veterinarian. He or she may then
refer the client to an appropriately qualified specialist.

          APPROACHES TO TREATMENT

This author has argued elsewhere (Mugford, 1981a) the benefits of seeing pets
with behavioural problems at home and ideally with the whole family particip-
ating in the discussions. One is then able to see the social, financial and
legal consequences of the animal's problem for the client, and hopefully
develop a treatment strategy more relevant to their existing habits. A similar
position is taken by Borchelt (in press) though others such as Washington
(1981), Houpt (1979) and Hallgren (1974) encourage the owner to attend a fixed
facility or clinic. The main argument against home visits is primarily one

of cost if the practice covers a wide geographical area. However, for veterinarians practising in compact urban areas this obstacle does not apply.
Skilful questioning of intelligent owners can obviate the need for home visits
in many cases, and the ideal arrangement is probably to use a clinic for initial
assessment and trials, but home visits for refractory and more complex cases.

At least one hour and more commonly several hours are required to complete a
detailed interview with the client, assess the dog and develop an appropriate
behavioural therapy. The time required to work on a case may seem unduly long
to a veterinarian in successful clinical practice, but it is not excessive by
comparison with behavioural assessment and therapy in human psychiatry. Several
studies in child/parent counselling have shown that the spoken word is a very
inadequate medium for deliverying complex advice to patients: most is forgotten.
A written report which reiterates the main elements of the strategy being
advocated to the owner of a problem dog is invaluable as a practical aide-
memoire to the client, to avoid misunderstanding between client and practitioner
and in a worrisome minority of cases to discourage malicious litigation.

PROBLEMS AND METHODS OF TREATMENT

Space does not allow a complete digest of all the canine behavioural problems
which will be encountered in veterinary practice, but a guide to priorities
for practice and research in this area is suggested by Figure 1. Three hundred
cases referred to the author's practice in 1981 are classified by main
presenting problem behaviour.

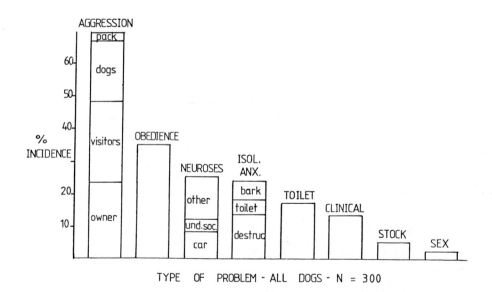

Fig. 1. Percentage frequency of various canine behavioural
         problems: 300 cases referred to the author

AGGRESSION

Of all behavioural problems that are discussed by dog owners with their
veterinarians and behavioural specialists, aggression is the most frequently
cited. It is probably also the most worrisome category of behavioural problem
for the practitioner to deal with because of the legal, medical and other
implications of giving incorrect advice.

The term aggression does not have any sound physiological or behavioural basis:
it is not a unitary scientific concept but rather a convenient bin into which
a large number of often unrelated behavioural phenomena can be assigned. Two
approaches can be taken to classify the types of aggression displayed by the
dog and encountered in practice. One can emphasise the motivational factors
and context within which the aggression occurs (e.g. Moyer, 1968; Borchelt,
in press) or one can simply identify the victim. For purposes of practical
therapy the author prefers the latter, together with some specification of
social and/or physical context: see Table 1.

TABLE 1 A Classification of Canine Aggression

Victim	Context
Owner family	) Domination/rank order) Food/object-centred) Social attachment) Low threshold/random
Visitors strangers	) On territory with owner) Off territory/owner-independent) Fear-elicited) Learned/neurotic
Unfamiliar dogs	) Like-sex/sex specific) Non-sex specific) Learned/neurotic
Familiar dogs	
Other species	) Predatory/food centred) Non-predatory/chase-centred

A host of clinical/medical factors can contribute to the onset of aggressive
behaviour in dogs, together with normal variations in physiological states
such as the bitch's oestrous cycle. Identification and treatment of these
physical and physiological causes must obviously be the clinician's first
priority. For instance, discomfort from anal glands, painful ear, skin and
musculo-skeletal conditions, nutritional deficiencies, neurological disorders,
etc.

One often finds that an aggression problem was apparently initiated by some
distinctive medical or traumatic event, but continued even after complete
recovery to good health. Thus, a behaviour acquired under one set of circumstances (e.g. an irritable, aggressive bitch in pro-oestrous) may generalise
to later changed circumstances (e.g. same bitch, spayed). As an example of
the same effect in the male, one notes that learned antagonism towards
particular classes of dogs (individuals or breeds), or humans (e.g. postmen)
may be acquired as part of a general androgen-dependent territorial behaviour.

Once developed and moulded by the learned outcome of attacks, dislike of say, postmen or German Shepherd Dogs will be quite unaffected by castration or other hormone therapies. In the examples cited above, combined or adjunctive veterinary and behavioural therapies can be specifically tailored to modify both initial motivating factors and subsequent learning contingencies.

The objectives of treating aggressive dog cases are usually to reduce the risk of further bites as rapidly as possible. Logical sequences of drug or behavioural therapies that can be tried, reviewed and modified according to outcome are a luxury that cannot always be indulged in when someone is at immediate risk of being bitten. In such cases one may consider a combination therapy where one simultaneously manages all relevant variables. In other cases, particularly those involving dominance - aggression towards the owner or family, a 'blitzkrieg' approach to treatment may actually increase the short-term risk of attack. Sudden reversal of accustomed traditions between dog and family, especially increased assertiveness by the usually compliant humans may be rejected in favour of a more structured and gentle approach. Whereas it would be irresponsible to advocate short, sharp, shock tactics to owners of aggressive large dogs, it may be sensible if one is dealing with a little dog unable to inflict much bite damage.

Most aggressive behaviour is highly situation- and time-specific, and it is axiomatic that treatment must be located and timed to occur where the dog presents a problem to its owners. Dominant or forced obedience training by third-party dog trainers is an option often chosen by the more affluent owners of aggressive dogs. Numerous studies (see Mugford, 1981a; Borchelt, in press) emphasise that this is often, at best, pointless and more usually worsens matters by contrasting the relative submissiveness of the owner with a dominant stranger. In summary, the first priority for behavioural therapy in aggression cases is to induce change within the dog's and owner's home environment, with a marked emphasis upon controlling short-term hazards.

The majority of aggressive interactions with dogs can be effectively counter-conditioned by reward-centred behavioural techniques. Food and rescheduled friendly social contact with humans are more powerful behaviour-modifiers than punishment. Induced local pain, such as that delivered by pinch-collars, hitting or electric shock collars is more likely to escalate violence in dominant aggressive dogs than suppress it. There is a large experimental literature on pain elicited aggression in a variety of species (see Azrin and Holz, 1966), which is unintentionally reproduced in many current dog training practices (e.g. Loeb and Loeb, 1980).

The behavioural evolution of the wolf has placed greater emphasis upon the presentation of submissive and affiliative gestures than dominant ones, and subtle role-playing is a more developed canid strategy than the notion of dominance heirarchies (Lockwood, 1975). Thus, a technique sometimes favoured by the author in treatment of dominant rank order aggression is to reward systematically and develop submissive routines, so that they compete for the time formerly spent in dominant activities. Analysis of what constitutes dominance vs. submissiveness may in some cases be obvious (e.g. stroking a dog when lying on its back), but others are likely to be novel to most clients (e.g. where the dog initiates petting interactions). In the last example one advises a client to reject the dog for 1-5 minutes, but 1-5 minutes later call it over to be stroked on the owner's terms. The general term for this approach to therapy is response-substitution where one systematically develops positive behaviours incompatible with expression of unwanted sequences (see Thompson and Grabowski, 1977). It can be applied to a host of situations where one wants to suppress rather specific behavioural responses to defined stimuli. If punishment needs to be used, a non-physical, non-interactive approach such as time-out (Nobbe and others, 1980) or intense auditory stimuli such as from anti-mugging alarms would be advocated rather than physical methods. The main problem with the latter is that mere contact between owner and dog can be unintentionally reinforcing of undesired behavioural patterns. Having the dog managed by collar and trailing lead is a useful first step to eliminating these unintentionally rewarding interactions.

Hormonal therapies, especially progestagens in the dominant male and spayed female dog, have an important practical role in short-term treatment of canine aggression (see Voith, present volume). In a good proportion of such cases there is a marked reduction in the dog's motivation to maintain social rank, with consequent reduction in bite risks to the human family. However, clients must exploit the period of progestagen-induced tractability to train long-term changes in social rank. Unfortunately, there is no exogenous hormone-therapy available which mimics or anticipates the full effects of surgical castration. To justify castration, there probably needs to be several consistent indications of concurrent androgen effects (Hopkins and others, 1976). Several studies suggest ovarian suppression of dominant behaviour in dogs (Borchelt, in press) and other species (vom Saal, 1982), so owners should be made aware that spaying aggressive female dogs can be counter-productive.

                    PROBLEMS OF EXCESSIVE ATTACHMENT

The second most common category of behavioural problem about which dog owners are likely to seek professional advice arises from the pet having become excessively dependent upon human company. The reverse situation of the owner making excessive emotional demands upon the pet may be a factor in such cases, but very often the expectation that the owners have of the puppy are quite reasonable. Dogs that are destructive, that howl or bark, that soil the house or that seek to prevent their owners leaving, present some of the classic behavioural consequences of excessive social attachment and subsequent separation anxiety.

Destructive behaviour is often misinterpreted by dog owners and by lay dog trainers as a form of spite and even aggression. This misanalysis seems to be related to the dog presenting a guilty demeanour when the owner returns to find his or her property damaged. Direct corporal punishment therefore seems to be an appropriate remedy, but of course, it is not if disassociated in time from the behavioural act of the dog chewing, scratching or barking. Voith (1979) has outlined a reward-centred approach to accustoming dogs to being left alone and this has proved very effective where the owners have plenty of time at their disposal. In the author's practice, the first approach for treating separation anxiety symptoms is to directly reduce the dependence between dog and people. This is done by rescheduling petting to follow reunions rather than preceed depatures, to allow less time-in-contact in the home, to minimise dominant training and by using bridging stimuli such as tape recordings to provide continuity between the presence and absence of the owner. An 80% success rate was obtained by the author in a 125 case follow-up of canine separation-anxiety problems (unpublished data). Because such dogs are usually both loved and loving, their emotional importance to the client usually motivates conscientious application of behavioural advice.

ELIMINATION PROBLEMS

Urination and defaecation at inappropriate times or places tends to be tolerated in puppies, but by the age of 3-6 months owners expect their dogs to be house-trained. This expectation may not be realisable for a number of reasons: the life style and environment of the owner, mischeduling and content of diet, misdirected punishment, inappropriate early experience and a variety of clinical problems such as malabsorption syndromes.

The author has concluded that most puppies become house-trained in spite of rather than because of the efforts of their owners. The traditional notion that one should rub their noses in it as a punishment for house-soiling is still widely practised by pet owners in the UK despite the obvious irrationality of the technique. The author's starting point for treatment of persistent home-soiling cases is to find a way the owner can commence rewarding elimination in the desired location. If punishment has been used in the past, one may find that the dog is reluctant to urinate or defaecate on a short leash or in front of the owner. One can have the dog on a running retractable lead or release it into a compound. The next stage in treatment is to induce constant habits of food and fluid intake since that critically influences timing of excretion. It may be sensible to advocate feeding in the morning and removal of water by late afternoon, thereby shifting elimination behaviour to the dog's and owner's active daytime period. Exercise of the persistent house-soiling dog may have to be increased to as much as once per hour and a Pavlovian conditioning situation can be devised around the toilet-training timetable. Finally, olfactory factors may be critical in guiding the dog to select particular areas for toileting, both appropriately outdoors or inappropriately indoors. The client should be advised about logical cleaning sequences of soiled carpets, furniture, etc.

LEARNED NEUROSES

The dog is a continuously adaptive organism that tries to monitor and manipulate both physical and social milieu. Old dogs do learn new tricks and at any age they can be remarkably skilful at controlling complex social situations (see Mugford, 1981b). The variety of eccentric behaviours indulged in by dogs never ceases to surprise the author. The majority are amusing and reinforce the owner's desire for a unique pet, but others are a problem. The most commonly encountered context for acquired/neurotic objectionable behaviour in the author's practice is the car. A variety of stereotyped responses in anticipation of release develop as the car is in motion (Mugford, 1981b). A second common neurotic sequence in the dog is directed at the telephone, where the usual motive for eccentric behaviour is to sustain intimate social contact with the owner. However, the practising behavioural specialist will encounter every variant of canine tragi-comedy; dogs that whirl at the end of their walk to prevent leashing, that interrupt intimate contact between owner and spouse or develop irrational fears of commonplace stimuli. The therapies available for modifying acquired neurotic behaviours are sometimes ad hoc and common-sensical, but more often require a sound understanding of learning processes and formal rules of behaviour modification such as those described by Thompson and Grabowski (1977).

BEHAVIOURAL PROBLEMS OF CLINICAL ORIGIN

The interaction of physiological and behavioural states is no longer remarkable in human psychiatry where increasing knowledge of neurochemistry and neuroanatomy has revealed an organic basis for mental illness, previously thought to be of affective or cognitive origin. In the author's practice, some 13% of all behavioural disturbances in dogs could definitely be related to some clinical condition. The list is a long one. For instance, obvious sources of local pain like waxed ears, ectoparasites, or impacted anal glands; non-specific dermatoses and dietary allergies; and more specific conditions such as diabetes, epilepsy, hypoglycaemia and testicular tumours. A detailed analysis of behavioural disorders attributable to physical pathologies is given by Voith (1979), and will not be reiterated by the present author who is not a veterinarian. The importance of these phenomena is that they emphasise the need for veterinary involvement at an early stage in the treatment of canine behavioural problems. This is certainly not an area where the non-academically qualified dog trainer should be permitted to operate without veterinary support or professional accountability. The need for a differential diagnosis is conveniently resolved in the author's practice by having all clients referred by their veterinary surgeon. Thereafter one aims to sustain dialogue between psychologist, general veterinary practitioner and clinical specialists in canine neurology, endocrinology and psychopharmacology.

REFERENCES

Azrin, N. H., and W. C. Holz (1966). Punishment. In W. K. Honig (Ed.) Operant Behavior. Appleton Century-Crofts, New York.

Borchelt, P. L. (in press). Aggressive behavior of dogs kept as companion animals: classification and influence of sex, reproductive status and breed. Appl. Anim. Ethol.

Campbell, W. E. (1975). Behavior Problems in Dogs. American Veterinary Publications Inc., Santa Barbara.

Hallgren, A. (1974). Lyckliga Lydiga Hundar. ICA-forlaget AB, Vasteras, Sweden.

Hart, B. L. (1980). Canine Behavior. Veterinary Practice Publishing Company, Santa Barbara.

Hopkins, S. G., T. A. Schubert, and B. L. Hart (1976). Castration of adult male dogs. Effects on roaming, aggression, urine marking and mounting. J. Am. vet. med. Ass., 168, 1108-1110.

Houpt, K. A. (1979). Aggression in dogs. The Compendium on Continuing Education for the Small Animal Practitioner, 1, 123-128.

Lockwood, R. (1975). Dominance in Wolves: useful construct or bad habit. In E. Klinghammer (Ed.) The Behavior and Ecology of Wolves. Garland STPM Press, New York.

Loeb, J. and P. Loeb (1980). Super-Training Your Dog. Prentice-Hall Inc., New Jersey.

Moyer, K. (1968). Kinds of aggression and their physiological basis. Communications Behav. Biol., 2, 65-87.

Mugford, R. A. (1981a). Problem dogs and problem owners. The behaviour specialist as an adjunct to veterinary practice. In B. Fogle (Ed.) Interrelations Between People and Pets. Charles C. Thomas, Springfield, Illinois.

Mugford, R. A. (1981b). The social skills of dogs as an indicator of animal awareness. In D. G. M. Wood-Gush, M. Dawkins, and R. Ewbank (Eds.) Self-Awareness in Domesticated Animals. UFAW, Hertfordshire, England. •

Nobbe, O. E., B. R. Niebuhr, M. Levinson, and J. E. Tiller (1980). Use of time-out as punishment for aggressive behavior. In B. Hart (Ed.) Canine Behaviour. Veterinary Practice Publishing Company, Santa Barbara.

Stead, A. C. (1982). Euthanasia in the dog and cat. J. small Anim. Pract., 23, 37-43.

Thompson, T., and J. Grabowski (1977). Behavior Modification of the Mentally Retarded. Oxford University Press, New York.

Tuber, D. S., O. N. Hothersall, and V. L. Voith (1974). Animal clinical psychology. A modest proposal. Am. Psychol., 29, 762-766.

Voith, V. L. (1979). Behavioural problems. In E. A. Chandler, and J. M. Evans (Eds.) Canine Medicine and Therapeutics. Blackwell Scientific Publications, Oxford.

Voith, V. L. (1981). Attachment between people and their pets. Behaviour problems of pets that arise from the relationship between pets and people. In B. Fogle (Ed.) Interrelations Between People and Pets. Charles C. Thomas, Springfield, Illinois.

Washington, C. (1981). The first year of an animal behavior clinic in a veterinary school: problems and outcome. In B. Fogle (Ed.) Interrelations Between People and Pets. Charles C. Thomas, Springfield, Illinois.

vom Saal, F. (1982). Prediction of adult aggressiveness by intra-uterine positioning in male and female house mice. In R. Blanchard, and C. Blanchard (Eds.) Proceedings of the Society for Research on Aggression Conference. Lexington Press.

Cat Behaviour Problems

V. L. Voith

Center for the Interaction of Animals and Society, Clinical Studies,
School of Veterinary Medicine, University of Pennsylvania, 3800
Spruce Street, Philadelphia, PA, USA

ABSTRACT

In the U.S., cats comprise 30% of the cases seen by animal behaviourists.
The most common complaint concerns elimination, either spraying, urinating
or defaecating in the house. These behaviours can often be corrected by
manipulating the environment to discourage use of inappropriate areas and
encourage use of the litterbox. Progestins may be effective in suppressing
spraying behaviour. The second most common complaint is aggression towards
other cats. Intermale aggression is likely to stop if the cat is castrated
or treated with progestins. If the underlying cause is fear, desensitisation
and counterconditioning techniques are usually successful in ameliorating the
aggression. Territorial or 'dispersing' aggression has a poor probability of
being suppressed, although extensive exposure sometimes works. Aggressive
behaviour directed toward people is usually a manifestation of play and can
easily be treated using a combination of redirection of the play to another
object and a mild, but effective and consistently administered punishment,
such as a loud noise or water.

KEYWORDS

Cat behaviour problems; spraying; urination; defaecation; aggression; play.

ELIMINATION BEHAVIOUR PROBLEMS

Elimination behaviour problems can involve marking, urination or defaecation.
Marking behaviours are usually in the form of spraying, but it is also believed
that some cats urine mark using the squatting posture. To classify urinating
in a squatting posture as marking, the behaviour should be performed in a
territorial, sexual, or agonistic context. There is no reported evidence that
domestic cats defaecate in the house as a form of marking. Urinating in a
squatting posture and defaecating in the house outside of the litterbox is
usually not a form of marking behaviour. For whatever reason, most of these
cats simply prefer to urinate and defaecate in a place other than where the
litterbox is or prefer to use a scratching substrate other than the litter
material provided.

Urine Marking

Urine marking by cats is usually performed by spraying (Fig. 1). Spraying is performed in a standing posture. The urine is squirted backwards in a horizontal stream onto a vertical object. The cat's tail is held straight up in the air and may quiver. The cat's back feet may step alternately. Occasionally a cat may scratch the floor or wall before or after spraying but scratching usually does not accompany spraying.

To determine whether a cat is urine marking, the clinician should obtain an accurate behavioural description of the cat engaging in this behaviour or obtain a description of where the urine is found. Many owners may use the term spraying but do not really know what it means. They may erroneously believe that spraying is anytime a cat urinates outside the litterbox. It is important to differentiate accurately whether the cat is spraying or squatting to urinate in order to maximise the probability of correctly treating the problem.

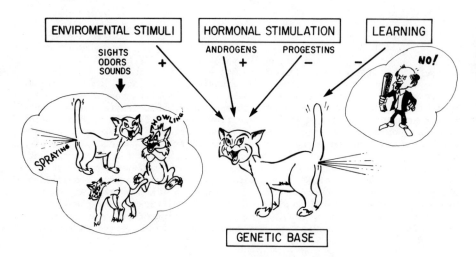

SPRAYING BY MALE CATS

Fig. 1.   Internal and external stimuli play a role in spraying.
In V. L. Voith, June 1979, *Calif. Vet.*, by permission.

Intact males spray more often than intact females or neutered males and females. Castration has been reported to be effective in suppressing spraying behaviour in 20 of 23 (87%) of male cats presented for spraying regardless of the age of the cat or duration of the problem (Hart and Barrett, 1973). Some females only spray when in oestrus; consequently neutering these cats should resolve the spraying problem.

If a cat is spraying only in a few locations, the behaviour may stop if the significance of the locations is changed by converting them to feeding or play areas. This might be accomplished by placing containers of food or hanging toys or strips of aluminium foil in these locations. Sometimes spraying can be stopped by making the areas aversive so that the cats avoid these locations. This might be accomplished by placing mothballs or a noxious odoriferous substance in these areas.

Reducing the numbers of cats in the household or reducing the accessibility to the sight, sounds or odours of outside cats might reduce spraying behaviour. Jemmett and Skerritt (1979) have shown that a linear relationship exists between the number of cats in a household and the probability of spraying behaviour. Their survey of 150 households indicated that spraying occurred in 25% of the single cat households increasing to 100% of households with ten or more cats. Numerous clients have remarked that their cats have begun spraying when and outdoor cat began visiting and spraying on or near the house of the resident cat. When the roaming cats ceased coming over, the resident cat stopped spraying. I recently had a case in which the owner noticed that when her cat saw an outdoor cat, it would become very agitated. Then her cat would leave the window and immediately go to a specific location in the living room and spray. Whenever the owner covered the windows or drew the drapes the incidence of spraying decreased in the house. One of Dr. Borchelt's cases in New York involved a cat which began spraying on the firewood in the house. It was discovered that outdoor cats were spraying on the woodpile. When the wood was brought into the house, the resident cat would smell the urine of the marauding toms and consequently spray. Covering up the woodpile with plastic in order to prevent visiting cats from spraying on it helped resolve this problem. Clearly, external stimuli can play a significant role in spraying behaviours.

Synthetic progestins are frequently used to reduce or stop spraying behaviour by male cats and neutered females. These drugs are not used for behavioural problems in intact females because of potential overian-uterine pathologies. Suggested dosages vary but the general consensus is to use as low a dose as possible and for as short a time as possible. Megestrol acetate is frequently dosed at 5 mg/cat/day per os for 7 to 10 days followed by 2.5 to 5 mg weekly. Periodically, the medication should eb discontinued to determine if the cat is still motivated to spray. Not infrequently the environmental stimuli that triggered the cat to begin spraying are no longer present or the cat habituates to these stimuli. Consequently it is no longer necessary to use drugs to suppress the spraying behaviour. Repository medroxyprogesterone acetate is also used to suppress spraying behaviour. The usual dosage is 100 mg/cat administered subcutaneously or intramuscularly as needed. There are potential side-effects with the use of progestins and these are described elsewhere in this volume (p   ).

Two neurosurgical techniques have been employed to reduce spraying behaviour when all conventional therapeutic procedures have failed. Medical preoptic-anterior hypothalamic lesions reduced spraying in all of six male cats but none of three female cats (Hart and Voith, 1978). However, previously unreported side-effects of hyperphagia and a 'startled reaction' during sleep preclude the advisability of the use of this technique as a clinical procedure. Bilateral olfactory tractotomies have been reported to reduce or stop spraying behaviour in six of eleven male cats and one female cat who had not responded to conventional therapies (Hart, 1981). Except for an occasional transient anorexia, the owners did not report any undesirable side-effects following the use of this procedure. The cats are anosmic and it is likely that it is the lack of smell (the reduction of olfactory external stimuli) that is the cause of success of this procedure. In view of the recent report of regeneration of olfactory nerves from the nasal mucosa to the brain following olfactory bulbectomies in mice (Wright and Harding, 1982), it will be interesting to follow the long-term effectiveness of olfactory tractotomies for spraying behaviour of cats.

Urine marking in a squatting posture can be treated with the same techniques as spraying behaviour. The difficulty is determining that the cat is marking.

Urinating and/or Defaecating Outside the Litter Box

The species-typical behavioural sequence involved in eliminative behaviour of cats is scratching in a suitable substrate, making a depression, eliminating in the depression, and then covering up the urine and/or faeces. Usually the most suitable substrate for such behaviour is the litter material provided by the owner. Kittens, 4-5 weeks old, will readily use such material (previously unused by other cats) and without ever having seen another cat eliminate in such materials. The first response of a tiny kitten being put into litter material is to taste it. After repeated tasting attempts, the kittens begin stratching, squatting, and then eliminating in the material. There appears to be an innate tendency or predisposition to scratching and eliminating in litter-like material. Young kittens readily learn the location of such materials and subsequently travel to them to eliminate.

Theories concerning the factors that may initiate and/or maintain urinating and/or defaecating behaviours outside of the litter box have been addressed in detail in a recent article (Borchelt and Voith, 1981). Factors involved in eliminative behaviour outside the litter box may be location preferences, substrate scratching preferences, the avoidance of aversive odours or the attraction of other odours, avoidance of the location of the litter box, fear responses, and/or anxiety. Treating such problems involves implementing two principles: (1) increasing the attractiveness of the appropriate area, and (2) decreasing the attractiveness of eliminating in inappropriate areas.

Increasing the attractiveness of where the cat should eliminate. Firstly, the desirability of the litter material and the location of the litter box should be examined. Is the box cleaned frequently enough? Is the litter material aversive to the cat, e.g. some cats seem to avoid litter with chlorophyll or perfume pellets. Some cats avoid the use of litter boxes with lids, perhaps because of the odour that is trapped within the system or the cats may not prefer to be in an enclosure. Some cats develop an aversion to the litter box or litter box area if it is near noisy machinery or if the cat is caught there for medication purposes or by children for play, or if the cat is placed in the litter box immediately after being punished. Sometimes the cat stops using the litter box simply because it is afraid to cross the open spaces between where it usually stays and where the litter box is located. If it can be identified that the cat is afraid of a particular individual or animal in the household, this fear can be desensitised and counterconditioned. Then the cat is likely to again resume using the litter box. Until the time when the cat is accustomed to the frightening object, a litter box should be kept where the cat has easy access to it. Occasionally a cat is prevented from using a litter box because of another cat. Providing a number of litter boxes in different locations is often a good idea in a multi-cat household.

Some cats seem to simply dislike commercial cat litter. Such cats rarely cover their faeces, usually shake their paws when they leave the litter box, and even balance on the edge of the litter box rather than touch their feet to the litter material. If it appears that the cat does not enjoy touching or digging in the litter material provided, it behoves the clinician and owner to test the desirability of other loose scratching materials such as sand, earth, shredded materials, sawdust, or laboratory animal bedding. Cats that do not dig in loose substrates often have a history of being raised on smooth surfaces, such as in cages, without litter material available.

The initiating cause may differ from the continuing cause for not using the litter box. For example, a cat may have stopped using the litter box because it wasn't cleaned regularly. However, now despite the fact that the owner cleans it carefully, the cat continues to eliminate outside the box. When the possible initiating cause has been corrected and the cat persists in the inappropriate behaviour, the cat is usually maintaining the behaviour because it has developed a preference for a new scratching material, e.g. carpets, rugs, tile surfaces, etc. or the cat has developed a new location preference for eliminative behaviours.

Decreasing the attractiveness of the inappropriate area. In conjunction with increasing the attractiveness of where the owner wishes the cat to eliminate, it is usually necessary to decrease the attractiveness of where the cat prefers to eliminate.

If the cat is eliminating in only one or two locations, changing the significance of that location to a feeding of play area may cause the cat to resume using the litter box. Sometimes these areas can be made aversive by placing a noxious odour or substance in these locations.

Some cats eliminate in several areas outside of the litter box and indicate a scratching preference for certain substrates. If the cat can be prevented from scratching on such materials, the cat may not complete the eliminative behaviour sequence. For example, if the cat prefers carpeted areas, these areas can be covered with plastic or aluminium foil. Although the cat has access to these areas and may walk on the covering materials, it usually does not like to scratch on such surfaces and subsequently returns to the litter box for elimination. If the cat resumes the use of the litter box and has been reliably using it for several months, the covering material (plastic or aluminium foil) can be gradually removed until the room again resumes its normal appearance. If the cat indicates it prefers to scratch on smooth surfaces such as bathtubs, tile, linoleum, wooden floors, these surfaces may be covered with newspaper (which often does not provide the same tactile feedback as the other smooth surfaces) or loose carpets or rugs. Bathtubs and sinks can be filled with a small amount of water for a temporary time. Since a cat with a preference for a smooth scratching surface is not likely to resume using the litter material, it is helpful to provide these cats with an empty litter box when their preferred smooth scratching areas have been blocked off. When the cat has resumed using the empty litter box for several weeks, an appropriate litter material for both owner and cat can be gradually introduced.

If placing food, toys, noxious substances, and/or substituting a non-preferred scratching material, does not prevent the cat from eliminating in the inappropriate areas, the cat is demonstrating a very strong location preference for its eliminative behaviour patterns. When this occurs, the litter box should be placed in the area the cat is eliminating. Precisely on the spot the cat is eliminating if possible. The litter box should be made as attractive as possible, utilising all the appropriate stimuli that may induce the cat to use the litter box. When the cat resumes using the litter box, the litter box can very gradually be moved back to the location the owner wishes it to remain. It is very important that the box be removed very slowly, often no more than an inch a day.

Most cats demonstrate a combined location and scratching preference and this must be taken into consideration when treating problems. For example, if a cat is eliminating in several locations along the perimeter of a carpeted room, the entire perimeter of the room should be covered with a non-preferred

scratching substrate such as plastic. Generally the cat resumes using the
litter box. If, instead, the cat shifts to the centre of the room, the entire
room should be covered with plastic and carpeted material might be attached
to the litter box to encourage the cat to scratch it and therefore use the
litter box. If the cat eliminates on the plastic, the litter box should be
placed where the cat eliminated.

It has been suggested that treating eliminative behaviour problems in cats is
like playing a chess game with the cat. First, the clinician makes a move
and then the cat makes a move; and then the clinician makes a move and the
cat makes a move, until one of the players wins.

Additional comments. Of course, the areas where the cat is eliminating should
be well cleaned. Products such as 'Feline Odour Neutraliser' chemically
inactivate or neutralise the odour of cat urine. If these products can
penetrate the surface to each the soiled areas, they usually do a good job in
eliminating odours. If such speciality products are not available, diluting
the urine with water and then using a commercial cleaning compound or vinegar
usually masks the urine odour. Cleaning agents with ammonia should probably
be avoided as the diluted ammonia odour may attract the cat to the area.

Punishment by itself rarely corrects elimination problems even when appropriately
applied. Punishment can, however, teach the cat to be afraid of the owner.
Bringing the cat back to the area after it has eliminated and punishing it is
not an effective way of treating the problem. The cat does not pair the
punishment with the act of eliminating. Immediately placing the cat after it
has been punished into the litter box may actually contribute to the problem.
In this case, the punishment is temporally paired more closely to the litter
box than the act of eliminating in the inappropriate area. Catching a cat in
the act of urinating and then punishing it is not contraindicated and may help.
However, many cats simply learn to avoid eliminating in the presence of the
owner.

FIGHTING AMONG CATS

A uniformly accepted definition of aggression has not been agreed upon.
Moyer (1968) provides a fairly good working definition of aggression as a
behaviour which leads to, or appears to an observer to lead to, the damage
of some goal entity. The term aggression usually also includes associated
behaviours such as snarls, hisses, stares, etc.

In the wild or feral state, most aggressive behaviours of animals have an
adaptive function. Aggression is a means of obtaining a resource or defending
oneself. Although aggression may be a normal behaviour, it is generally very
undesirable when it occurs in household pets.

It is difficult to develop a classification system for aggressive behaviours.
Systems can be devised based on specific stimuli that elicit aggression,
general environmental situations that predispose an animal to aggression and
physiological states that influence aggressive behaviour. Most clinicians
try to take all of these variables into consideration when they attempt to
classify aggressive behaviours (Borchelt and Voith, 1982). If the motivational
state and external stimuli can be identified, the probability of treating the
aggressive problem is enhanced. Admittedly, developing a motivational aggressive
classification schema for animals is a deductive process and subject to
subjective interpretation.

Intermale Aggression

Leyhausen (1979) describes ritualistic aggressive behaviours that occur
between male cats that are independent of territorial or other types of
aggressive behaviour. Although these patterns involve ritualised sequences,
severe injuries can result. It is likely that intermale aggression is what
is affected by castration. Hart and Barrett (1973) reported that 88% (29 of
33) male cats greatly reduced or ceased fighting following castration. Since
progestins tend to suppress the same types of behaviour that androgens
facilitate, progestin therapy is likely to reduce intermale aggressive
behaviour.

Territorial Aggression

Leyhausen describes territorial aggression as involving direct and rapid runs
by the territorial cat and rapid delivery of blows with the paws. Such cats
may engage in 'boxing' behaviours. This type of behaviour sequence is very
different from ritualised intermale aggressive behaviour. Territorial
aggression does not seem to be sex related; males as well as females engage
in territorial aggression.

In household cats, territorial aggression may occur when a new cat is introduced into a house, a cat is reintroduced after an absence, or when one or
both resident cats (that may have lived peaceably together for years) reach
behavioural maturity.

The aggression between newly introduced or reintroduced cats may abate if the
cats are repeatedly exposed to each other without allowing them to engage in
aggression. This can be accomplished by rotating the cats among the rooms
where they are kept. This allows the cats to experience the odours of the
other cat. The cats may also be allowed to see each other - albeit at a
distance or between a crack in a door. Gradually the cats are brought closer
together or more fully exposed to each other. Sometimes the cats can be fed
at progressively closer distances. Eventually, the cats may be allowed to
move freely near each other but on leads so that they are not able to reach
each other. Eventually the cats are allowed to be completely free in the same
environment. All of the above stages of introduction should occur gradually
while the cats are in non-aggressive states. It has been my clinical
impression that progestin therapy is not usually effective in suppressing
territorial aggressive behaviour in cats.

Cats that gradually begin fighting are not as easily treated as newly introduced or reintroduced cats. Such situations frequently occur when one or both
cats in the household reach 2-3 years of age. Generally, one cat is the
aggressor. This cat not only initiates fights when the cats accidentally meet
each other but also seeks out the other cat to harrass it. The non-aggressive
cat may actively meet all challenges or try to avoid fights by running and/or
hiding. Such aggressive behaviours usually begin slowly, occurring periodically
but gradually increasing in frequency and intensity. When owners present such
a case, they are generally worried that the aggressive cat is abnormal and
perhaps 'pathologically' aggressive. They are also concerned whether the cat
will begin attacking them or other people. Rarely are cats with such a history
suffering from a pathophysiological disorder. The type of aggressive behaviour
that is occurring is usually a normal behaviour - a dispersing mechanism. Cats
in feral situations usually have their own territories and once they reach
adulthood, live relatively solitary lives. Most domestic household cats,
which are in a different environmental milieu than feral cats, do not appear

to be highly motivated to maintain exclusive territories. However, those
that are so motivated are not abnormal. These cats are unlikely to be
aggressive to people and can be delightful pets as long as they are the only
cat in the household. One can try the exposure techniques described above.
However, often the only solution to territorial aggressiveness is to maintain
the cats in such a way that they simply never meet or find one of the cats in
a new home.

Fear Induced Aggressive Behaviour

Fear induced or defensive aggressive behaviour between cats usually has a
sudden onset. The facial and body postures of both cats are indicative of
fear or defence. Such cats do not seek each other out to fight but become
aggressive when they happen upon each other. Not infrequently these cats
have got along well for years. Mutually induced fear or defensive aggressive
behaviour has a high likelihood of being successfully treated.

Although the initiating incident or aetiology of this problem cannot always be
determined, typical case histories involve a sudden traumatic incident
involving both cats. For example, a book shelf falls or a very sudden frightening noise occurs. One or both cats react with a defensive aggressive
posture. The other cat perceives the threat as being directed towards itself,
and consequently reacts similarly. Both cats then react aggressively to each
other. This situation does not resolve but each time the cats see each other,
they react aggressively. Surprisingly, a typical history involves one cat
getting in the way of the aggressive attack of the other cat towards a third
cat. For example, Cat A is sitting at the window. Cat B, further away from
the window, sees an outdoor cat and rushes in an aggressive manner towards
the window. Cat A turns and sees the approaching, threatening cat and
perceives the threat to be directed at it. Cat A then reacts aggressively.
Cat B then acts aggressive to Cat A and a fight ensues. Thereafter, each
time they see each other, a defensive aggressive posture is assumed and
fighting ensues. Sometimes the return of a cat who has been away or an introduction of a new cat elicits a defensive aggressive posture, not a territorial
aggressive stance, from the resident cat. The cat being introduced then reacts
to the aggressive behaviour of the resident cat and a mutually aggressive
situation erupts. Sometimes this type of vicious cycle stems from a redirected
aggressive encounter. Cat A sees a cat outdoors and becomes agitated and
aggressive. Cat A redirects its aggression to a nearby Cat B. B defends
itself and conversely A becomes more aggressive and/or frightened of B. And
the aggressive cycle begins.

Since this type of aggression is primarily fear induced or defensive, it is
amenable to exposure, desensitisation, or counterconditioning techniques.
Repeated exposures in situations that do not allow aggression, similar to
those described for territorial aggressive behaviour, eventually allow the
cats to interact again with each other. A more regimented therapy would
involve desensitisation and counterconditioning. Unconditioned stimuli, such
as eating, play, or grooming behaviour, can be used in the counterconditioning
procedures. For example, the cats are brought closer and closer together as
they are fed. Sometimes the cats can be encouraged to play with each other
beneath the door or beneath cracks in doors and gradually allowed to interact
more and more. Serendipitously, it was discovered that self- or mutual
grooming can suppress fear induced aggression (Borchelt, pers. comm.). An
owner who was having no success in reintroducing her cats to each other using
food or play behaviours, happened to bathe each cat. When she placed them
down, she put them in the same room. They became so involved in grooming

themselves, and then eventually each other, they did not fight. The cats
again experienced each other in a non-aggressive state and consequently
their former amicable relationship was restored.

The treatment of any fearful behaviour is accomplished by somehow allowing
the frightened individual to experience the fearful stimulus (in this case
the other cat) <u>without being afraid or aggressive</u>. Techniques employed to
accomplish this are various methods of exposure (habituation, desensitisation,
or flooding) and/or counterconditioning.

AGGRESSIVE BEHAVIOUR TOWARDS PEOPLE

Occasionally a cat is presented to a behavioural therapist for aggression
towards people. Sometimes the aetiology is fear. In such cases, the cat is
usually being reached for, or picked up by a stranger and the cat exhibits a
typically fearful response. Exposure, desensitisation, and/or counterconditioning are highly successful in treating such behaviour. Although it
is rare that a person is attacked as a consequence of territorial aggression,
I have had a few cases where an unafraid cat is very unfriendly towards
visitors. Such a cat will growl at visitors, even though the cat is not
being approached. One cat that was presented to me actually had chased a
repairman out of the house! As with intraspecific territorial aggression,
exposure techniques might work in resolving such cases, but the prognosis is
guarded. These cats are generally very dangerous.

Sometimes cats redirect aggressive behaviour to an owner. Such situations
usually involve a cat that is threatening another cat. When the owner intervenes in the situation, she/he is bitten. Even if the owner intervenes after
an aggressive encounter, the owner may be bitten. Owners should not approach
or interact with a cat that has recently been aggressive until the cat
indicates by switching to another behavioural system, such as eating or
playing, that it is out of the 'aggressive' mood. Sometimes just the smell
of the aggressive antagonist is enough to elicit a redirected aggressive
behaviour. I have had a few cases where owners have been bitten by one of
their cats if they have immediately previously handled another cat that was
known to fight with the other cat. When these owners washed their arms and
hands after handling one cat, they could safely pick up the other cat. The
easiest, most rational, and safest approach to deal with redirected aggressive
behaviour is to avoid situations that might lead to an encounter.

The aetiology of most aggressive behaviours of cats towards people is excessive
play behaviour. Play is a reciprocal interaction involving constant communication which regulates the intensity of play between the participants. If one
partner is unable to or does not communicate that play is too rough, the other
partner will continue to escalate the intensity of the play. Play behaviour
in young carnivores, such as the cat, typically involves components of
predatory and aggressive behaviour and when one of the participants is a
young or elderly human being, severe injuries can be incurred.

The typical history of the too playful cat is a relatively young cat, often
one or two years of age, who is very active and is not regularly played with
in other circumstances. Such a cat may only attack specific members of the
family, often its 'favourite person'. The attacks may occur in rather specific
circumstances such as when the owner steps out of the bathtub or shower, goes
up and down the steps or begins making the bed at night. The cat may engage
in all sorts of components of aggressive behaviour involving 'halloween'
postures, stalking, chasing, grabbing and biting the owner's legs, etc.

Usually the play is somewhat inhibited but unless the owner communicates that the play is too rough, wounds can result.

Treatment of play induced aggressive behaviour is highly successful. Therapy involves redirecting the play to an appropriate target and punishing the cat when it plays too roughly. An appropriate play target may be another cat, mobile toys, etc. Sometimes an owner can divert an attack by immediately producing a mobile target for the cat to redirect its play. The owner can carry toys that can be thrown and retrieved quickly to immediately redirect an attack to the toy. Owners should also initiate play so that they can immediately direct the play in an appropriate channel. The owners might also carry around a mild punisher, such as a spray bottle of water or a loud noisemaker, to immediately discourage the cat whenever it begins to attack them. If a punisher is used, it should be available to the owner at all times. That means the owner should carry it with him/her constantly in order that it might be administered immediately and every time an attack occurs. Intermittent punishment is not an effective way to treat any behaviour problem. It is important that punishment not be the only technique the owner employs. It is imperative that the owners provide the cat with appropriate activity outlets. Most cats will outgrow this behaviour, particularly if the play can be directed to a suitable object.

REFERENCES

Borchelt, P. L. and V. L. Voith (1981). The Compendium on Continuing Education, 3, 730-738.
Borchelt, P. L. and V. L. Voith (1982). In Voith and Borchelt (eds.), North American Veterinary Clinics: Small Animal Practice, 12: Symposium on Animal Behaviour. W. B. Saunders, Philadelphia.
Hart, B. L. (1981). J. Am. vet. med. Ass., 179, 231-234.
Hart, B. L., and R. E. Barrett (1973). J. Am. vet. med. Ass., 163, 290-294.
Hart, B. L. and V. L. Voith (1978). Brain Research, 145, 405-409.
Jemmett, J. E. and G. Skerritt (1979). Poster display at the AVMA Ann. Meeting, Seattle.
Leyhausen, P. (1979). Cat Behaviour. STPM Press, New York.
Moyer, K. E. (1968). Commun. Behav. Biol., Part A, (2), 65.
Wright, J. W. and J. W. Harding (1982). Science, 126, 322-323.

Possible Pharmacological Approaches to Treating Behavioural Problems in Animals

V. L. Voith

Center for the Interaction of Animals and Society, University of
Pennsylvania,3800 Spruce Street, Philadelphia, PA, USA

ABSTRACT

There is a variety of drugs that might be effective as a primary or ancillary
treatment of behavioural problems in animals. Progestins are often effective
in reducing typically masculine behaviours by dogs and cats such as marking,
roaming, intermale fighting, and mounting or 'humping', and in reducing
dominance aggression manifested by dogs towards owners. Drugs with anti-
anxiety effects are meprobamate, benzodiazipines, sedative anti-histamines,
amitriptyline, phenothiazines, barbiturates and the progestins. It should be
remembered that animals can easily be aroused while under the influence of
phenothiazines, and that this class of drugs facilitates seizure activity.
Phenothiazines and butyrophenones, which are dopamine antagonists, are likely
to facilitate lactation and maternal behaviours during pseudocyesis.
Amphetamines have been demonstrated to inhibit hyperkinetic behaviour in dogs.

Clinicians should thoroughly familiarise themselves with potential side-
effects of drugs used to influence behaviours and always inform the owners of
these side-effects and whether or not the drug is approved for use in animals.
The use of psychotropic drugs should be weighed against the probability of
side effects, other therapeutic techniques and the probability of euthanasia.

KEYWORDS

Psychotropic drugs; progestins; amitripyline; phenothiazines; benzodiazipines;
amphetamines.

INTRODUCTION

Traditionally, veterinarians have used drugs that affect the central nervous
system as a means of restraining or suppressing normal behavioural patterns
of animals. Drugs have been used to facilitate handling of animals for
diagnostic purposes, to restrain frightened animals, to reduce the likelihood
that an animal will respond to a learned aversive stimulus (for example, a
veterinarian approaching with a needle and syringe), and to decrease the
stress of transportation. Drugs utilised for such purposes are usually

general and selective central nervous system depressants such as hypnotic,
sedative, and tranquilizing drugs, e.g. the barbiturates, benzodiazepines,
and phenothiazines. Drugs, particularly hormones such as antiandrogens and
progestins, are frequently used to suppress undesirable normal behaviours of
cats and dogs such as intermale fighting, marking and mounting behaviours,
and dominance aggression directed towards owners. With the exception of the
diagnosis and treatment of hyperkinesis and narcolepsy, central nervous
system stimulants are rarely used therapeutically in veterinary medicine.
However, the use of stimulants (and depressants for that matter) have been
used to accentuate or modulate the behaviour of animals, including man, in
sporting events since the conception of competition (Tobin, 1981).

In 1977, Lapras presented a paper at the World Congress of Small Animal
Veterinary Medicine in Amsterdam that encouraged the use of modern 'psychotrope therapy' in dogs (Lapras, 1977). Over a period of three years, he had
treated 138 animals with imipramine (1-2 mg/kg/day per os), trimeprimine
(2-4 mg/kg/day per os), and medifoxamine (3-6 mg/kg/day per os). Although
he did not objectively describe the behaviours for which he treated the dogs,
the subjective descriptions were indicative of essentially neurotic, anxious
or depressed behaviours. The 'syndromes' Lapras treated were listed as
'depressive reactive states, troubles of affective behaviour, psychopathic
anomalies, psychogenic anorexia, obsessional and maniacal syndromes, phobia-
fear, psychomotor trouble (irritability-excitability), syndrome of anguish,
enuresis, and psycho-affective epilepsy'. He believed the drugs helped
relieve these symptoms and noted few intolerances other than that of
occasional sleepiness which occurred with imipramine and trimeprimine. He
implied that there was a potential usefulness and value in the use of psychotropic drugs in the treatment of behavioural problems in animals.

Numerous drugs have been developed as ancillary or primary treatment of
behavioural disorders in people. Many of these drugs might be beneficial in
the treatment of animal problems, although the drugs are not marketed for
the use of behavioural therapy in animals. There is little information
available as to what drugs might be used in animal behaviour therapy. There
are several reasons for this paucity of information. Behavioural disorders
in animals are only beginning to be identified and accurately diagnosed, and
as with the other medical disorders or problems, the diagnosis dictates the
treatment. Secondly, there is little readily available information
concerning possible therapeutic dosage levels, toxicities or side effects.
Not much can be said with conviction about the use of psychotropic drugs
until objective differential diagnostic methods, systematic use of dosages,
and a large number of treated cases are obtained. And then double blind
placebo/treatments should be utilised to determine the true effectiveness of
the drug therapy. For the time being, much of what is discussed concerning
psychotropic therapy of animals must be interpreted cautiously. Clinical
animal behaviour is very much an infant science, case loads are still
relatively small and a uniform diagnostic system has not yet been agreed upon.
When it comes to discussing the clinical application of psychotropic drugs,
veterinarians frequently expand upon and maximise the educational benefit of
a case load of one. Despite these warnings and shortcomings, I believe a
competent and careful clinician can benefit clients by trying psychotropic
drugs for specific behavioural problems in animals. To limit the choice of
drugs to the few tranquilizers and hormones marketed for use in animals
potentially reduces the possibility of successful treatment of several
serious behavioural problems in animals. It should be remembered that psychotropic drug effects can vary greatly between species. Extrapolation should
be done cautiously.

Whenever I suggest a drug that is not marketed for animals, I always advise
the client that the drug is not approved for use in animals. I explain that
it has been used in people for a similar behavioural problem but, technically,
it should be considered an experimental drug in animals. I familiarise the
owners with the potential side-effects that are known to occur in people or
in laboratory animals. I also caution the owner to watch for any strange or
different behaviours while their pet is on drug therapy. When I prescribe a
drug that might be used when an owner is gone, I first have the owners give
the drug to the pet when they will be home for 12 hours. I ask them to watch
for any side effects.

I will now review some drugs that might be useful in the treatment of behavioural disorders in animals and share with you my clinical impression of the
effectiveness of some of these drugs. Bear in mind, however, that this
information is relatively subjective and is based on small case loads. The
list of therapeutic agents, their usages, and their dosages, is incomplete
and lends itself to improvement.

Goodman and Gilman (1980) group drugs that act on the central nervous system
(CNS) into three major categories:

1.   General (non-specific) CNS depressants such as anaesthetic gases and
      vapours, aliphatic alcohols, and some hypnotic sedatives. These drugs
      share the characteristics of being able to depress excitable tissues at
      all levels of the CNS by stabilising neuronal membranes, decreasing the
      amount of transmitter released by nerve impulses, or depression of post-
      synaptic responsiveness and ion movement.

2.   General (non-specific) CNS stimulants. These drugs produce stimulation
      by blocking inhibitors or by directly inducing neuronal excitement
      (increasing transmitter release, prolonging transmitter release,
      labilisation of post-synaptic members or decreasing synaptic recovery
      time).

3.   Drugs that selectively modify CNS function. Agents in this group can
      either depress or stimulate activity. Sometimes the very same drug can
      produce both effects simultaneously in different systems of the brain.
      It is in this mixed bag group of drugs that are found most of the agents
      used for treating behavioural disorders in people and potentially in
      animals. Many drugs in this group can be classified in more than one
      way and have more than one action.

      The drugs in this third group tend to be classified as (1) anti-
      convulsants; (2) antiparkinsonism drugs; (3) analgesics; (4) analgesic-
      antipyretics; (5) certain stimulants; (6) neuroleptics (antidepressants,
      antimanic, and antipsychotic agents); (7) hypnotics; (8) sedatives;
      (9) tranquilizers.

            HYPNOTICS AND SEDATIVES

Hypnotics and sedatives produce drowsiness and promote sleep. They can also
calm anxious and disturbed patients. They decrease activity level, modulate
or moderate excitement and calm the recipient. These drugs often have widespread depressant effects on the CNS and therefore sometimes are also used
as antiepileptic agents, muscle relaxants, anti-anxiety drugs, and anaesthetics.
Barbiturates, chloral derivatives such as chloral hydrate, and meprobamate
fall within this category. Meprobamate promotes muscle relaxation, has anti-

anxiety, anti-convulsive properties and has been reported to decrease aggressive behaviour in animals. Benzodiazepines are also in this group although they are not a general CNS depressant.

ANTI-ANXIETY SEDATIVES

This category includes meprobamate, benzodiazepines, sedative antihistamines, and barbiturates. The most commonly used drugs for anti-anxiety in people are the benzodiazepines, diazepam (Valium [R]), chlordiazepoxide (Librium [R]). The success of benzodiazepines in people would suggest that they are a likely candidate for treatment of anxieties in dogs and cats. Potential usefulness is made more attractive by statements in pharmacology books that animals decrease their aggressiveness and become tamer when treated with these drugs. Mice and rats reportedly decrease defensive aggressive behaviour; however, offensive aggression remains the same or may be elevated. 'Taming effects' and reduced aggressiveness have been reported in several species of wild animals (Booth, 1982).

It should be remembered that benzodiazepines are not a general depressant and they can actually cause excitement in certain systems of the brain. In general, the effects of benzodiazepines are sedation, hypnosis, decreased anxiety, muscle relaxation, and anti-convulsive activity. However, several owners have reported to me that their dogs have become restless, agitated or aggressive following the use of Valium [R] and Librium [R]. Lapras also noted that diazepam was 'capable of increasing excitability and worrying the animal'. However, the only drug I have found that decreases the fear response to thunderstorms is diazapam, at a dose of approximately 1 mg/lb per os. A 45 pound female German Shepherd Dog was so severely afraid of storms that the owner had to tie the dog up and sit with her during storms to prevent the dog from destroying the house or injuring herself. The dog's fears had generalised to other noises at non-thunderstorm times such as the slamming of a car door, etc. The dog was becoming a constantly nervous animal and the owner was considering euthanasia. Phenothiazines and amitriptyline had had no effect on the dog's behaviour during storms. If chlorpromazine (Thorazine [R]) did prevent the dog from destroying the house, it only did so because the dog became ataxic and was physically unable to move. The dog remained frightened although it could not control its motor functions. One mg per lb. of Valium [R] administered orally prior to the onset of the storm reduced the dog's fear. Rather than attempting to run, shake, tremble, and destroy items, the dog merely crawled behind the living room couch and remained there in a relatively unanxious state during the storm.

For dogs, I generally dose Valium [R] at $\frac{1}{2}$-1 mg/lb per os and Librium [R] at 1-3 mg/lb per os. I treat cats with 1-2 mg of Valium [R] per cat, orally.

ANTIPSYCHOTIC, NEUROLEPTIC AND TRANQUILIZING AGENTS

The term neuroleptic is applied to drugs that suppress spontaneous movement and complex behaviours without affecting spinal reflex and unconditioned nociceptive-avoidance behaviours. These drugs generally decrease interest in the environment, arousal, and emotional states. But animals can be easily aroused from these states.

The phenothiazine drugs are predominantly used for their sedative effects and to treat severe psychiatric illnesses in people. In animals, the pheno-thiazine derivatives (e.g. promazine and acepromazine) are generally termed tranquilizers and are used to treat anxiety. Despite the fact that the animal appears depressed, it can easily be aroused (as most veterinarians have experienced). Phenothiazines reportedly depressed learned behaviours but not unconditioned responses. For example, animals that have learned to press a bar to avoid a shock will stop pressing the bar under the influence of the drug but if the animal is shocked it will respond to the pain. The dog that has learned to be afraid of an approaching veterinarian with a needle and syringe may not demonstrate that fear under the influence of the phenothia-zines, but when it is injected and experiences pain, which can elicit an unconditioned response, the animal may bite. Periodic bouts of excitement are not uncommon with the use of phenothiazines, and a recent article in the AVMA journal indicated sudden aggressiveness following the use of acepromazine maleate in dogs (Wächter, 1982).

It should also be remembered that the phenothiazines potentiate seizure activity and are contraindicated in epileptic animals. Phenothiazines and butyrophenones are dopamine antagonists and probably should not be used in animals manifesting pseudocysesis because PIF (Prolactin Inhibiting Factor) is thought to be dopamine.

MOOD STABILISING AND ANTIDEPRESSANT DRUGS

These drugs include the tricyclic antidepressants, monamine oxidase inhibitors and lithium carbonate. Amitriptyline hydrochloride is the only drug in this group that I have used. In addition to being an anti-depressant, amitriptyline also has anti-anxiety effects.

I have frequently used amitriptyline for separation anxiety, with and without behaviour modification therapy. If a separation anxiety response is mild, drug therapy alone will often suppress the problem behaviour. After the dog experiences being alone without being anxious, the drug is slowly withdrawn over 2-4 weeks. Thereafter, the dog usually retains its non-frightened behaviour in the absence of the drug therapy. In very severe separation anxiety problems (dogs that cannot be left alone for even a few minutes without engaging in serious disruptive behaviours), I generally use drug therapy in combination with behavioural modification procedures. Although the literature indicates that the anti-depressant effects of amitriptyline may not be apparent for 2 to 3 weeks in people, owners generally report an anti-anxiety effect within a few hours. I generally treat separation anxiety dogs with 1-2 mg/lb per os for 2 weeks, then progressively decrease the medication over several weeks.

Occasionally, I have used amitriptyline in cats to treat displacement activities, such as excessive grooming and hair pulling. In cases where I identified a potential stressor that could not be removed and the cat's behaviour seemed to be correlated with the presence of the stressor, I have found that 5-10 mg of amitriptyline per os per cat divided b.i.d. reduced these self-mutilating behaviours.

I have also used amitriptyline and imipramine at a dose of 1 mg per lb. in dogs to treat enuresis.

Clinicians should familiarise themselves with the potential side-effects of the tricyclides, such as amitriptyline. Whenever prescribing a drug marketed for people and not animals, one should consult a current human drug therapy book, such as the Physician's Desk Reference, before dispensing the drug to animals. Potential side effects of amitriptyline in people are anti-cholinergic

responses, such as blurred vision, a dry mouth, constipation, and urinary
retention. Cardiac arrhythmias, tachycardia, orthostatic hypotension, a
general weakness, muscle tremors, and occasionally manic episodes may also
result.

CNS STIMULANTS-ANALEPTICS

The use of most CNS stimulants is irrelevant in the treatment of behaviour
disorders although the drugs have been periodically tried to enhance the
performance of sporting animals. Methylphenidate and amphatamines have been
used for therapeutic purposes in animals.

While conducting neurophysiology experiments at the Ohio State University,
the Corsons discovered naturally occurring hyperkinetic dogs (Corson and
others, 1976). These dogs were described as being overactive, having a short
attention span, were difficult to teach, tended not to respond to tranquilizers
that usually suppressed activity, and the dog resisted restraint, often
damaging several hundreds of dollars worth of equipment. Approximately 50%
of the dogs that exhibited such behaviours, responded to amphatamines or
methylphenidate. The therapeutic dose varied among individuals. Corsons
reported methylphenidate (2-4 mg/kg per os) reduced hyperactivity but was not
as effective as the amphetamines. The hyperkinetic behaviour was reduced by
the oral administration of 0.2-1.3 mg/kg of dextroamphetamine or 1.0-4.0 mg/kg
of levoemphetamine per os (Corson and others, 1976; Corson and others, 1980).
Dextroamphetamine was four times as potent in suppressing the hyperactivity.

If I were to treat a dog for hyperkinesis with amphetamines, I would hospitalise
the animal to determine the therapeutic dose for that individual. First, I
would obtain an activity baseline by some objective behavioural measure, and
then begin with the lowest dose recorded to be effective, and evaluate the
animal's behaviour and physiological responses 1-2 hours post administration
of the medication. If there was neither adverse nor beneficial response to
the medication, I would wait 24 hours and treat the dog again. I would
increase the dose at 24 hour intervals in increments of 0.2 mg/kg of dextroamphetamine or 0.5 mg/kg of levoamphetamine. It is important to increase the
dosage slowly because hyperkinetic dogs can be overdosed with amphetamines
resulting in even more activity. I would slowly increase the dose until the
dog either decreased its activity level or increased it. The latter response
indicating the dog might not be hyperkinetic or that I missed the 'therapeutic
window' of the drug.

Amphetamine overdose in dogs results in an increase in activity level, elevated
heart and respiratory rate, increased oxygen consumption. The animal may
become anorectic, exhibit stereotypic behaviours (nonsensical repetitive
movements such as running in circles), hyperthermia, and convulsions.
Amphetamine poisoning has been reported to be treatable with 0.1-1.0 mg/kg of
acetylpromazine maleate intramuscularly, immersion in cold water, and if
necessary, barbiturate anaesthetic (Stowe and others, 1976).

The Corsons also noted that amphetamine would reduce the aggressive behaviour
of some hyperkinetic dogs. Interestingly, the dextro- and levo-isomers were
equally potent at 0.2-1.3 mg/kg per os in suppressing aggressive behaviour.
One dog, Jackson, was able to be socially rehabilitated under the influences
of the drug and maintained its non-aggressive state in subsequent non-drug
therapy states.

Amphetamine is also used in the diagnosis and treatment of narcolepsy in dogs.

This syndrome is adequately covered in numerous neurological texts on companion animals.

PROGESTINS

The progestins are effective in treating typically masculine behaviours in animals and as anti-anxiety agents. I have found the progestins effective in suppressing intermale aggression among dogs and cats, urine marking in male dogs and spraying by male and female cats, mounting behaviour by male dogs, roaming behaviours by male dogs, aggression towards people by cats, and dominance related aggression of dogs towards people. It has been my clinical impression that progestins do not suppress territorial aggression among cats or territorial or protective aggression by dogs, or fear-induced aggressive behaviours exhibited by cats or dogs towards people. I have found the progestins effective in reducing the anxiety of separation and in suppressing responses to exciting external stimuli such as noises or visual stimuli.

In dogs, I generally use 1-2 mg/kg per os of megoestrol acetate for 2 weeks and then progressively reduce the dose at two week intervals. I rarely use the drug longer than two months. When I use injectable progestins, I use medroxyprogesterone, a repository drug, at a dose of 10 mg/kg for dogs. I generally treat cats with 0.25-0.5 mg/kg of megoestrol acetate or 10-20 mg/kg of medroxyprogesterone. I prefer to use the orally administered progestins rather than the repository injectables in case side effects develop.

There are potential side effects with the use of progestins. Lethargy and increased appetite are a common complaint and mammary gland hyperplasia occasionally occurs. Adenocarcinomas have been reported to occur during prolonged administration of medroxyprogesterone acetate (repository) in cats (Hernandez and others, 1975). Numerous pathologies have been reported as a consequence of naturally occurring progesterone and the administration of synthetic progestins in dogs (Eigenmann, 1981; Eigenmann and Haagen, 1981; Eigenmann and Eigenmann, 1981; Eigenmann and Rijnberk, 1981). Medroxyprogesterone and naturally elevated progesterone levels, such as occurs after oestrus, can result in hyperglycaemia, elevated insulin levels, elevated growth hormone levels, acromegaly, glucose intolerance/diabetes mellitus, polyphagia, polyuria and polydipsia unaccompanied by hyperglycaemia, lowered packed-cell volume, reduced exercise tolerance, thickening of the gall bladder epithelium with possible sequela of jaundice, development of mammary gland nodules, and the intact female chronic hyperplastic endometrium-pyometra complex. Prolonged use of progestins should not be taken lightly. The use of progestins should be weighed against the possibility of side effects, other therapeutic techniques and the probability of immediate euthanasia.

REFERENCES

Booth, N. H. (1982). In N. H. Booth and L. E. McDonald (Eds.) Veterinary Pharmacology and Therapeutics. The Iowa State University Press, Ames, Iowa. pp. 321-345.
Corson, S. A., E. O.'L. Corson, L. E. Arnold and W. Knapp (1976). In G. Sergan and A. Kind (Eds.) Animal Models in Human Psychobiology. Plenum Press, New York.
Corson, S. A., E. O.'L. Corson, R. E. Becker, B. E. Ginsberg, A. Trattner, R. L. Connor, L. A. Lucas, J. Panksepp, and J. P. Scott (1980). Pav. J. Biol. Sci., 15, 5-11.

Eigenmann, J. E. (1981). J. Am. anim. Hosp. Ass., 17, 805–812.
Eigenmann, J. E., and R. K. Eigenmann (1981). Acta Endocr., 98, 603–608.
Eigenmann, J. E., and A. Rijnberk (1981). Acta Endocr., 98, 599–602.
Eigenmann, J. E., and A. J. Venker, van Haagen (1981). J. Am. anim. Hosp. Ass., 17, 813–822.
Goodman, A. G., L. S. Goodman, and A. Gilman (1980). Goodman and Gilman's The Pharmacological Basis of Therapeutics. Macmillan Publishing Co. Inc., New York.
Hernandez, F. J., B. B. Fernandez, M. Chertack, and P.A. Gage (1975). Feline Practice, 5, 45–48.
Lapras, M. (1977). Proceedings 6th World Congress, World Small Animal Veterinary Association. Post Academisch Obderwijs Publikatie, No. 8. pp. 129–130.
Stowe, C. M., R. E. Werdin, D. M. Barnes, J. Higbee, J. Miller, L. W. Knoll, R. M. Dayton, and D. C. Sittig (1976). J. Am. vet. med. Ass., 168, 504–506.
Tobin, T. (1981). Drugs and the Performance Horse. Charles C. Thomas, Springfield, Illinois.
Wächter, R. A. (1982). J. Am. vet. med. Ass., 180, 73–74.

INDEX

Abdominal disease 76
Accidental trauma 91
Accommodation 39
Acepromazine 230
Activation 141-42, 144
Activity patterns 7, 177-78
Affection 150
Aggression 142, 143, 145, 148, 154,
    172, 173, 178-79, 190, 207, 208,
    210-12, 217, 230
  characteristics of types of 192
  classification 222
  defensive 190
  definition 222
  development of 192
  dominance 190
  intermale 223
  possession 191
  territorial 223
  towards people 225-26
Aging effects 8, 119
Agonistic behaviour 173, 179
Alaskan Huskies 89
Alaskan malamutes 108
Aldosterone 113
Alimentary system
  disorders of 97
  sensitisation 99
Alimentary tract 56, 66
Aliphatic alcohols 229
All meat syndrome 74
Allergies, food induced. See Food
    allergies
Alopecia 109
Amino acids 65, 120, 121, 124
Aminosulphonic acid 36
Amitriptyline 227, 230, 231

Amphetamines 232
Amygdala complex 114
Anaesthetic gases 229
Angiotensin II 113
Animal companions. See Companion
    animals
Animal training. See Training
Antidepressants 170, 231-32
Anti-nutritional factors 37
Antipsychotic agents 230
Anxiety 231
Arachidonic acid 36
Arginine 123, 124
Artificial rearing 27-30
  complete 28
  environmental requirements 28
  indications for 27-28
Ascites formation 113
Attachment 148, 151, 152, 153, 170,
    171, 194, 212
Avidin 37
Azotemia 122

Barbiturates 227, 228
Barking 135, 207
Basic recipe 47
Behaviour 131-36
  affective and instrumental 145
  naturally occurring 142
  neural substrate of 142
  neurophysiology of 139-46
  normal vs. abnormal 134-35
Behaviour development 165-74, 189-
    97
Behaviour differences between breeds
    184-85

Behaviour genetics 165, 186
Behaviour literature 165
Behaviour modification techniques 202
Behaviour pattern 203
Behaviour phenomena 132
Behaviour problems
  cat 148-49, 175-81, 217-26
  definition 207
  dog 148-49, 166-67, 190, 207-15
  of clinical origin 213-14
Behaviour sequences 202, 203, 204
Behaviour structure 202
Behaviour studies 132
Behaviour systems 165, 166, 167, 189
Behaviour therapy 209
Behaviour traits 148
Benzodiazepines 227-30
Bilateral olfactory tractotomy 219
Bitches
  litterweight in 14
  major element requirements 15-17
  milk 14, 106, 107
  mineral metabolism and require-
    ments 13-24
  trace element requirements 18-19
Biting 172, 173
Black box behaviourism 132
Bladder control 170
Bland diet 49
Blood pressure 126
Body temperature 26
Bone characteristics 82
Bone meal 59
Bones, ash, Ca and P content 21
Boredom 9
Brain 139, 140, 141, 145
Breeding programme 185
Breeding requirements 51-52
Bromocriptine 94
Butyrophenones 227

Calcium carbonate 125
Calcium excretion 17
Calcium homeostasis 17
Calcium intake 82
Calcium levels 20, 86-88
Calcium retention 17
Calcium-rich diet 125
Calorie coverage 159
Canine parvovirus infection 31
Carbohydrate 36, 37, 46, 47, 62
  93, 95, 117
Cardiac disease 112-15
Cardiac failure 112, 114
Cardiac insufficiency 112-14
Carrageenan 73, 75, 77
Castration 218

Cat behaviour problems. See Behav-
  iour problems
Cat food 37, 159, 161
Cat litters 39
Cat owners 150, 154-56, 158, 162
Cat populations 4, 158, 159
Caterwauling 179
Cellulose 73, 75, 77
Central male position 180
Central nervous system 140, 141,
  227, 229
Cervical spondylopathy 85
Chewing 170, 193
Chlordiazepoxide 230
Clostridium perfringens 65
Coat condition 39
Colonic disease 76
Colostrum 38, 39
Colour vision 203
Communication 131, 184, 201-5
Companion animals 131, 132, 134,
  148, 151, 208
Conditioned reflex 132
Conditioning 203, 204
Conformation range 7
Connective tissue 64, 65
Constipation 60
Copper 18
  content in liver 23
  levels in milk 19
  retention in suckling pups 22
Coronoid process 84
Corticosterone response 145
Counterconditioning 217
Cramps 93
Crate training 168, 172
Creatinine 122, 124
Creep-feeding 52
Cutaneous manifestations 103
Cysteamine 94

Daily intake requirement 52, 53
Defaecation frequency 73-74
Defense, use of term 143
Deficiency disease 112
Degenerative diseases 8
Deimatic behaviour 143
Den dwelling 171
Depression 170
Dermatology 106
Dermatoses 103-10
  practical considerations 109
  zinc-responsive 108-9
Desalination 114
Desensitisation 169, 217
Destructive behaviour 212
Diabetes mellitus 76, 112, 115-17

Diagnosis 228
Diarrhoea 61, 170
Diarrhoea-dehydration-stress-syndrome (DDSS) 93-94
Diazepam 230
Diet 43, 44, 47, 85, 95, 101, 116
Dietary fibre. See Fibre
Digestibility 55-69, 95
  apparent 56, 59, 61, 63, 67, 75
  importance of 55
  quantitative studies on 8
  true 56
Digestion trials 57
Digestive disturbances 66
Digging 170, 193
Disease control 38
Disinfectants 39
Distemper vaccination 31
Diuresis 114
Dog behaviour inheritance 183-87
Dog behaviour problems. See Behaviour problems
Dog food 159
Dog owners 150, 152, 156, 158, 162
Dog populations 4, 158, 159
Domestic cat 175
Domestication 147, 148, 175
Drive 141-42
Drug therapy 227-34
Dry matter diet 45

Egg white 65
Elimination behaviour 167-70
Elimination diet 49
Elimination problems 213, 217-22
Emotional behaviour 145, 184
Emotional state 205
Endochondral ossification 81
Energy content 116
Energy deficiency 104
Energy density 45, 46, 95
Energy intake 116
Energy requirement 44, 82, 116, 117
Enjoyment of food 8-9
Enostosis 85
Entorhinal-hippocampal loop 144
Environmental requirements for artificial rearing 28
Epileptic animals 231
Ethology 132, 133, 135, 142
Excitement urination 170, 171
Exertional rhabdomyolysis 93

False pregnancy 94
Fat content 45, 46, 95
Fat deficiency 104

Fat digestion 58-62
Fat excretion 56, 57, 59, 61, 62
Fat intake 57, 58, 61
Fat requirements 36
Fatty acids 59, 60, 107
Fear 142, 143, 148, 169, 193-94, 217, 224-25
Feedability 47, 93
Feedback 141
Feeding advice 161
Feeding behaviour 133
Feeding habits 159-61
Feeding process 87
Feeding routines 43
Feeding utensils 39
Feline calicivirus 39
Feline infectious enteritis 39
Feline odour neutraliser 222
Feline panleucopaenia 39
Feline rhinotracheitis 39
Feline viruses 39
Female cats 176, 180
Feral 177
Fibre 71-77
  adsorbing property of 74
  beneficial effects of 73, 116, 117
  components of 72
  definition of 72, 77
  dietetic effects 76
  digestability 73, 75
  functional action 71
  role of 77
  terminology 72
Fighting 91, 133, 179, 222-25
Fixed action patterns 140
Flooding techniques 169
Food allergies 97-101
  case history 98
  clinical features 98-99
  diagnosis 98
Food consumption 82, 87
Food energy 47
Food types 160
Food usage 160
Foot injuries 90-91
Free ranging cats 176
Functional disorders 112

Gastro-intestinal tract 71
Generalised pruritis 99
Genetic prewiring and learning 139
Genetic variance 139
Geriatric diets 49, 121
Glomerular filtration rate 123
Glucocorticoids 108
Glucose 76, 116

Gonads 119
Greyhounds 94
Growling 172, 173
Growth rate 39, 82
Growth requirements 52-53, 106
Guide Dogs for the Blind 185

Habituation 142, 144
Haematocrit in suckling pups 23
Haemoglobin in suckling pups 23
Health factors 7, 8
Heart rate 26
Heat stress 92
Hepatitis vaccination 31
Heritability 183-87
High-fat diets 61
Hip dysplasia 85
Histidine 124
Home ranges 178
Home visits 208-9
Hormonal therapies 212
Hormones 228
Housetraining 167-69, 213
Human/animal relationships 147-56,
    208
Human contact 170
Humidity effects 92
Husbandry 38-40, 43
Hygiene measures 39
Hyperactivity 172
Hyperglycaemia 233
Hyperkinesis 232
Hypersensitivity 97
Hypertrophic osteodystrophy 83
Hypervitaminoses A and D 104
Hypnotics 229
Hyposensitisation 101
Hypothermia 38

Imipramine 228, 231
Immunoglobins 38
Immunosuppression 108
Inheritance of dog behaviour 183-87
Instrumental behaviour 145
Insulin 76
Interactions among ingredients 45
Intervening variables 142
Intoxication 112
Intra-specific aggression 191
Investigatory behaviour 169
Iron levels
    in milk 19
    in newborn and adult dogs 18
    retention in suckling pups 22

Keratin 65, 66
Kidney diet 121, 122
Kidney disease 119-27
Kidney function 119-27
Kidneys, aging effects 119
Kittens
    feeding and care of 35-40
    nutrition requirements 35
    survival and growth comparison 40
Kwashiorkor 104

Lactation 13, 36, 51, 106, 109, 227
Lameness 91, 93
Learned neuroses 213
Learning 140, 144
Least-cost diet 45
Least-cost supplement 47
Leg-lifting 195
Librium R 230
Linoleic acid 107
Litter box 39, 217, 220-22
Litterweight in bitches 14
Liver, copper content of 23
Low-chloride diet 126
Low-fat diet 49
Low-fibre diet 71
Low-phosphorus diet 125
Low-protein diet 120, 125
Low-purine diet 50
Low-salt diet 125
Low-sodium diet 114

Maintenance requirements 44
Malassimilation 104
Male cats 177, 179
Malnutrition 108
Management decisions 167
Management trechniques 168
Manganese levels 18
    in milk 19
Marasmus 104
Marking 179-80, 195, 217, 218
Maturational changes 189
Maximum growth 6
Meat digestibility 62
Meaty recipe 48, 52
Medifoxamine 228
Megoestrol acetate 233
Mental health 7
Mental illness 214
Meprobamate 227
Metabolic acidosis 124
Metabolic diseases 76, 112
Metabolic disorders 115
Metabolism, quantitative studies on
    8

Metacarpal lameness and fractures 91-92
Metanephros 119
Metaphyseal osteopathy 83
Methylphenidate 232
Milk, trace elements in 19
Milk composition 85
Milk diets 47
Milk production 14, 52
Milk substitute composition 28-29, 36
Mineral deficiencies 104
Mineral metabolism 13-24
Mineral requirements 13-24, 36, 45
    base figures for calculating 14-15
Minerals retention in suckling pups 21
Minnesota study 123
Mood stabilising drugs 231-32
Mortality statistics 31-32
Motivation 141-42, 202, 203
Mounting 195
Mouthing 172

Narcolepsy 232
Neonatal diseases 27, 38
Neonatal period 25, 26
Nephrectomy 122, 123
Neural substrate 142
Neuroethology 143
Neuroleptic agents 230
Neurophysiology of behaviour 139-46
Neuropsychology 143
    in instrumental behaviour 144-45
Neurosurgical techniques 219
Neutering 218
Niacin 36
Nitrogen balance 121
Noise concept 204
Noise effects 204-5
Normal growth 6
Nutrient excretion 74
Nutrient intake 44
Nutrient levels 105-6
Nutrient requirements 85, 105
Nutrition
    and disease relationship 112
    objectives for companion animals 6-9
    overview 3-10
Nutrition requirements 7
    of kittens 35
Nutritional adequacy 87
Nutritional deficiencies 103
Nutritional problems 89-96
Nutritional secondary hyperpara-
    thyroidism 82
Nutritional standards 45-47
Nutritional therapy 106

Obedience training 154, 169, 201, 204, 208
Obesity 76, 116
Oestrus 94, 117, 180, 218
Olfactory tractotomy 219
Optimal regimens 43-53
Osteochondritis dissecans 84
Osteochondrosis 84
Osteodystrophia fibrosa 82
Over-feeding 52, 112
Over-nutrition 7
Oversupplementation 37
Owner's attitude 9

Palatability 9
Pancreatitis 61
Panosteitis 85
Paper training 167-69
Parakeratosis 108
Parasites 39, 97
Parenteral administration 106, 107
Parturition 52
Pathological disturbances 207
Pennsylvania Animal Behaviour Clinic 122-23, 148
Peripheral male positions 180
Pet animals 207
Pet food industry 162
Pet foods 44, 50-51
Pet-human bonds 134
Pet-owner relationship 134
Pet owners 133-34, 189
Pet populations 157-59
Pet talk 152, 154
Pharmacological treatment 227-34
Phenothiazines 227, 228, 230, 231
Phobias 148, 169, 189, 193-94
Phosphorus levels 20, 86-88
Photon absorptiometry 92
Physical features 183-85
Physical health 7
Physiological values for neonate puppies 26
Pigmental changes 108
Plant proteins 66, 67
Play 172, 204, 225-26
Predation 192
Predator/prey relationships 147
Pregnancy 13, 36, 51, 52
Problem solving 144
Progestagens 212
Progesterone 94, 233
Progestins 217, 219, 227, 233
Prolactin 94
Promazine 230
Proprietary foods 120
Protective aggression 191

Protein content 45, 46, 95
Protein deficiency 104
Protein digestibility 62-68
Protein excretion 57, 67, 68
Protein intake 64
Protein levels 86
Protein requirements 36
Protein restrictions 123-24
Pruritis 99
Pseudopregnancy 94
Psychology 135, 142
  nomenclature 143
Psychotrope therapy 228
Psychotropic drugs 227, 228
Punishment 212, 213, 222
Punishment techniques 168-70, 172,
  173
Puppies, care and feeding in post-
  natal and weaning period 25-33
Puppy behaviour development 165-74
Puppy testing programme 186
Pyelonephritis 122

Queens' milk 36
Questionnaires 152, 154

Racing diet 95
Racing sled dogs 89-96
Radio-tracing techniques 133
Recommend daily intakes 43
Rectal bleeding 94
Red blood cell indices 95
Red blood cells in suckling pups 23
Reducing recipe 48
Reflexes 139
Renal failure 123-25
Renal function 120, 122
Renal insufficiency 124
Reproductive efficiency 148
Reproductive performance 8, 9
Respiratory disease 38
Respiratory rate 26
Respiratory tract sensitisation 99
Retained cartilage 84
Retinoids 107
Rice 47
Rickets 82
Rickets-like conditions 83
Roaming 148

Salt restriction 114
Scandinavian pet environment 157-62
Sedatives 227, 229, 230
Selective breeding of working dogs
  185

Self-regulating networks 141-42
Sensitisation 142, 144, 169
Separation 170, 171, 194
Separation anxiety 148, 212, 231
Septo-hippocampal loop 144
Sexual behaviour 180
Side-effects 227, 229, 233
Signals 202-4
Skeletal characteristics 82
Skeletal diseases 81-88
  related to nutrition 82-85
Skin changes 99, 100
Skin disorders 103
Skin tests 100
Skinner box 132
Sleeping area 38
Social behaviour 165, 175-81
Social organisation 176-77
Social structure 145
Socialisation 26, 30-31, 165
Sodium content 114, 115, 125
Sodium levels 114
Sodium restriction 114
Space management 167
Sports anaemia 95
Spraying 135, 217-19
S-R pathway 141
Stearic acid 60
Stimulants 232
Stress effects 46, 47, 93, 121
Submissive behaviour 169
Submissive urination 168, 169
Suckling pups
  haematocrit in 23
  haemoglobin in 23
  mineral metabolism in 13-24
  mineral retention in 21
  red cells in 23
  trace element requirements 22
  weight gains in 15
Supplementation 30, 47, 49, 87,
  107, 109
Swedish Dog Training Centre 185
Symbiotic relationship 147
Syndrome I 108
Syndrome II 108

Taurine 36
Temperament problems 196
Test meal investigations 100
Testosterone 94, 145
Thermoregulation 38
Thiaminase 37
Toe dislocation 91
Toxic substances 74
Toys 38
Trace elements 108

Trace elements (contd.)
  metabolism and requirements of
    18-19
  suckling pups 22
  supply recommendations to bitches
    19
Tractability 148
Trainability 184
Training 144, 201-5, 132, 144,
    201-5
  see also Obedience training
Tranquilizers 228, 230
Transit time 73-74
Transition period 25, 30
Treatment approahces 208, 227-34
Tricalcium phosphate 82
Tricyclides 231
Triglycerides 49
Trimeprimine 228
Tripalmatic acid 60
Tristearin 60
Tube feeding 29
Tug-of-war game 172
Tying-up 93

Under-feeding 52, 112
Urbanisation 159
Uremics 120-21, 123-26
Urine marking. See Marking
Urticaria 99, 101

Vaccination 31, 38, 39
Valium R 230
Veterinarian visits 161
Video 133
Vitamin A 86-88, 104
Vitamin B complex 104
Vitamin C 87, 104
Vitamin D 82, 86-88
Vitamin E 104, 106
Vitamins 36, 37, 104, 107
Vocalisation 170-72

Water requirements 38
Weaning 36, 52
Weight gain 26
  in suckling pigs 15
Wheat bran 48
Whelping 25, 26
Wobbler-syndrome 85
Working dogs 185, 201
Worming 31

Zinc levels
  in milk 19
  in newborn and adult dogs 18
Zinc retention in suckling pups
    22
Zinc-responsive dermatoses 108-9
Zinc supplementation 109